STRIKING BEAUTY

STRIKING BEAUTY

A Philosophical Look at the
Asian Martial Arts

BARRY ALLEN

Columbia University Press   *New York*

Columbia University Press
Publishers Since 1893
New York   Chichester, West Sussex
cup.columbia.edu

Library of Congress Cataloging-in-Publication Data

Allen, Barry, 1957–
Striking beauty : a philosophical look at the Asian martial arts / Barry Allen.
pages cm
Includes bibliographical references and index.
ISBN 978-0-231-17272-1 (cloth : alk. paper)
ISBN 978-0-231-53934-0 (e-book)
1. Human body (Philosophy)   2. Mind and body.   3. Martial arts—Philosophy.   I. Title.
B105.B64A45 2015
796.815'501—dc23
2014049265

Columbia University Press books are printed on permanent and durable acid-free paper.
This book is printed on paper with recycled content.
Printed in the United States of America
c 10 9 8 7 6 5 4 3 2 1

COVER IMAGE: Superstock.com
COVER DESIGN: Evan Gaffney

FOR GRAND MASTER DON CHA

Once one has traveled through the gates of the sages, it is hard
to take anything else as a teaching.
MENCIUS

CONTENTS

PREFACE

When the martial is matched with the spiritual and it is experienced
in the body and mind, this then is the practice of martial arts.
"YANG FAMILY FORTY CHAPTERS"

When my hapkido teacher, Grand Master Don Cha, watches one of us perform a technique, he often says, "Good!" if it was OK, because he likes to be positive. A more competent performance may earn a praiseful "Excellent!" But we know we are doing well when he exclaims, "*Beautiful!*"

Even though we are training in techniques of extraordinary violence, there is no violence in our training, as we amiably practice with each other in the *dojang*. But *what* we are training in, what it is *for*, is violence. Where is the beauty in something so vested in violence? The question remains unanswerable until we understand something about beauty and something about violence. We also need to know something about the Asian martial arts themselves to understand their paradoxical relationship with beauty and violence.

What I mean by "Asian martial arts" is the originally Chinese, then East Asian, and now global traditions of usually unarmed personal combat. This is the martial arts of the kung fu movies, China's contribution to world cinema. It is also the martial arts one finds taught in practice halls in nearly every major city of the world. One can train in Shōtōkan karate in Nairobi and wing chun in Stockholm. Probably millions of people, speaking all the languages of the world, have had some training in these martial arts traditions.[1]

The unexampled popularity of Asian combat arts might prompt philosophers to look into the practice and its values and assumptions, but in fact, few have. That is one reason for my writing this book. Another concerns the situation of philosophy in what might be called the post-Western period. Nearly all the martial arts I discuss date back to China. Over the centuries, practitioners and connoisseurs of these arts developed philosophical interpretations in written teachings that draw on the main currents of traditional Chinese thought, making the Asian martial arts a milieu for comparative philosophy. Accordingly, we can look at Chinese philosophy through the perspective of the martial arts and compare what we find in Western traditions. Working out this comparative argument explains my chapters and their topics.[2]

Chapter 1 places the Asian martial arts in the context of China's philosophical traditions. Texts by martial arts masters draw from Daoism, Buddhism (especially Chan or, in Japanese, Zen), and the military art of war philosophy. Confucianism, long China's official philosophy, has a more conflicted relation to the martial arts, and we shall have to ask why.

Chapter 2 shifts to Western traditions, beginning with Greek athletics and a polemic that the first philosophers raised against it. These philosophers invented the idea of "mind" and "body" as exclusive, independent realities and located human excellence on the mental side of our dissevered nature, leaving philosophy with no motivation or resources to think about corporeal arts or their knowledge. Asian martial arts philosophy predictably evades a dichotomy of mind and body. One cannot fight the body and ignore the mind because as Sunzi's *Art of War* says, to fight the mind is the very *dao* of combat. Dualism is not Western antiquity's only legacy to philosophy, however. The same Greek traditions also invented materialism, the first philosophy of the body. Not before Darwin, however, was materialism finally able to discredit idealism and begin to evolve new lines of corporeal philosophy, with possible new ideas for the appreciation of martial arts thought and practice.

Chapter 3 takes up the question about beauty and violence from the aesthetic end. We pass from comparative philosophy to comparative aesthetics, comparing the martial arts with sport and dance. Martial arts practice is like sport but is not sport and is dancelike but is not dance. Unfolding differences among these practices brings the aesthetic distinction of the martial arts into view. We see where the aesthetic qualities of these arts come from and why they have them.

Chapter 4 takes up the other end of the question: the relation between the martial arts and violence. Despite their athletic beauty, ritual etiquette, and ethical seriousness, these arts are combat arts, designed and trained for competent violence. Violence is a complex subject filled with many controversies. By describing some of them, we will be able to see where the practice of martial arts fits in the economy of violence.

This book does not have just one audience, unless it is simply the curious. It is a work of academic philosophy, albeit in an interdisciplinary mode. Sometimes I address questions of aesthetics, especially sport and performance aesthetics and somaesthetics. These arguments may interest those who work in the philosophy of art, of sports, and of the body. Readers unfamiliar with Chinese philosophy will find a curious angle into the subject, while others with expertise in Chinese philosophy may be interested to see its connections with the martial arts made thematic and discussed, as they seldom are. I hope I also have something to say to practitioners of the Asian martial arts, who may be interested in a philosophical appreciation of their practice.

I do not assume personal experience with the Asian martial arts, though I also do not explain them for someone who knows nothing about them. Accordingly, I assume some degree of familiarity on the reader's part. Merely having seen a few martial arts movies would be adequate, although the ideal reader would have a fair level of training (a few years). Some notion of what the Asian martial arts look like and some of their lore is enough, however, provided the reader also is interested in discovering what philosophy can say about this material. It is possible that this book speaks more to philosophers curious about the martial arts than to martial arts practitioners seeking a philosophy of their practice. My purpose is not to explain a "philosophy of the martial arts." Instead, I study selected features of Asian martial arts practice and traditions from a comparative philosophical perspective, identifying qualities that seem to me to sustain fruitful questions of the sort that I regard as philosophical rather than historical, technical, or religious.

I should be clear about three other things. There are more martial arts, Asian and otherwise, than I discuss in this book. I write most about the arts in which I have personally trained—kung fu, wushu, taijiquan, wing chun, karate, and hapkido—four Chinese, one Japanese, and one Korean art. I have trained in Korean hapkido the longest and still train for several hours each week. Another point concerns competition, both *kata* (forms) competition, and fighting tournaments, which have played no part in my training experience. I have trained in *kata*, sparring, and grappling, but I have never entered a competition and never will. In my first martial arts studio, where I trained in kung fu for three years, entering competition was expressly forbidden, but in my karate *dōjō*, it was encouraged. In the hapkido *dojang*, no one cares, though no one does it. Accordingly, martial arts practitioners to whom competition is important may find that I neglect their experience. Finally, I have never used martial arts training in a violent encounter. The one time I was confronted by a knife-wielding would-be assailant (actually there were four of them, but only one knife) occurred some years before I began training in martial arts, and I was able to resolve the situation without violence. Nothing that I have learned about self-defense from training in martial arts makes me wish I had done anything differently, except perhaps to have been better at evading the confrontation in the first place.

ACKNOWLEDGMENTS

I thank the martial arts teachers whose patience I have tried, in Canada, Shanghai, and Hong Kong, and fellow students who generously taught me how little I know, especially the training brothers at Hwa Won Yue hapkido under Grand Master Cha.

I am indebted to Weng Haizhen 翁海貞 for her unfailingly generous assistance with the Chinese language, though I must take responsibility for any errors that may have crept in despite her vigilance.

Parts from some of my chapters first appeared in earlier publications. A portion of chapter 1 appeared in "Daoism and the Chinese Martial Arts," *Dao* 13, no. 2 (2014): 251–66, and part of chapter 3 appeared as "Games of Sport, Works of Art, and the Striking Beauty of Asian Martial Arts," *Journal of the Philosophy of Sport* 40, no. 2 (2013): 241–54. I thank the editors and publishers for kindly allowing me to use this material.

STRIKING BEAUTY

THE *DAO* OF ASIAN MARTIAL ARTS

Themes from Chinese Philosophy

The *dao* does not contend but is good at victory; does
not speak but is good at responding.
DAODEJING

What the world knows as the Asian martial arts began in China. China is not the only civilization to have spiritualized combat arts; there are other, no less ancient, examples in India and Mesopotamia. Yet the Chinese, drawing on the resources of a mature civilization, merged their arts of armed and unarmed combat with Buddhist meditation and Daoist inner alchemy, two of the most dynamic currents of their postclassical culture. Creatively synthesizing combative arts with these prestigious teachings reinvented their practice as a way of self-cultivation. Indeed, scholars increasingly recognize that "without reliable research and informed commentary on the martial arts, our knowledge of Chinese society and culture in general is uneven and incomplete."[1]

The idea that the Chinese martial arts conveyed to nearly all the (later) fighting arts of East Asia (karate, jujitsu, hapkido, taekwondo, and so on) is the dual cultivation of the spiritual and the martial, each through the other, each perfected in the other, with the proof of the perfection consisting in a kind of effortless mastery of violence. The result is very different from Greek or Indian combat sports, and in fact, these martial arts are not sports at all, as the emphasis lies not on competition but on self-cultivation. The training is not so acrobatic that it must be reserved to the young; instead, it is approached as a lifelong practice that ties self-cultivation to continuous somatic development.

The prominence of ideas from Zen and Daoism in the martial arts literature is obvious. Confucianism, long China's orthodox system of thought, has had a less conspicuous interaction with the martial arts. Although Confucians did practice archery, they carefully separated power and skill. The prize went to one who could hit the target without penetrating the hide. In other words, the mind that aims the arrow is superior to the martial power that pierces the target. The mind has a virtue of its own and does not require force to be effective.[2]

Chinese martial arts thought refuses this opposition of mind and body (or ritual body and martial body). Martial arts practice is both a way of self-cultivation (as is Confucian ritual) and an effective fighting art. The "Yang Family Forty Chapters," a taiji classic, states,

> When the martial is matched with the spiritual and it is experienced in the body and mind, this then is the practice of martial arts. . . . Our ancestors who were masters of the spiritual and the martial taught the arts of self-cultivation through physical culture, but not through the martial arts. . . . I have applied this to the martial arts, but it must not be viewed as a superficial technique. It must remain on the level of physical culture, self-cultivation, the dual development of body and mind, and the realm of sagehood and immortality. . . . My teachings should be transmitted as a martial art for self-cultivation.[3]

In this chapter, we look at points of interaction between Asian martial arts and sources in Chinese philosophy. I follow up on the allusions that martial masters use in writing about their art and discuss passages of Chinese philosophy that will resonate for modern readers with martial arts experience.[4]

SHAOLIN TEMPLE AND THE LEGEND OF BODHIDHARMA

The usual Chinese word for what we refer to as martial arts is *wushu*: *wu*, "martial," plus *shu*, "arts" or "techniques." The term dates from the sixth century. Another expression is *wuyi*, "martial arts," used from the third to the seventeenth century. No one category of the Asian martial arts practiced today adequately describes past practice in China, and it would be a mistake to insist on a single term for all of Chinese history for what *we* call "martial arts," though *wushu* seems to come close.[5]

According to legend, these arts were introduced by Bodhidharma, a Buddhist monk who traveled from India to China in the fifth century and also was the founder and first patriarch of Chan Buddhism. Supposedly he carried a teaching from Buddhism's homeland that had passed unwritten from mind to mind in an unbroken lineage from Gautama Buddha himself. After arriving in China, Bodhidharma found his way to Shaolin Temple. Dissatisfied with the Buddhist regimen he found there, he retired to a nearby cave, where he spent several years in meditation. Then he came down the mountain and began to teach the monks of the temple. The teaching is called Chan (in Japanese, Zen), from the Sanskrit *dhyāna*, meaning "meditation." Finding the monks unfit for the demanding meditation he wanted to teach, Bodhidharma, born into India's warrior class, instituted martial arts training to get them in shape. The same Indian teacher who was the founder of Chan (Zen) Buddhism was thus also the father of the Chinese martial arts.

Bodhidharma seems to have been a historical individual and not entirely legendary. He was a native of south India, a Brahmin, a Mahayana Buddhist, and meditation instructor who arrived in south China in around 479 and moved north to the Loyang (Shaolin) area, where he died around 530. More than that is hard to know from the evidence, which may be thin because Bodhidharma was not as extraordinary in life as later legend made him out to be. His story is almost entirely a fabrication, with some parts added as recently as the twentieth century. Scholars cannot find any mention of Chan anywhere until the eighth century, two centuries after Bodhidharma's arrival in China, and when Chan does appear, it is not at Shaolin but at the so-called East Mountain School, which was unaware of its descent from Bodhidharma. Eventually, an East Mountain master settled at Shaolin Temple, which became a center for Chan practice. It is apparently at this time, centuries after Bodhidharma, that his name and Shaolin Temple became associated with Chan Buddhism, though still without a martial arts connection.[6]

Buddhism and martial arts should be oil and water. Buddhist law forbids weapons and fighting for monks. Moreover, *ahimsa*, "nonviolence," is one of the most important precepts in all Buddhist traditions. Self-defense is expressly forbidden to Theravada clergy, as is any association with the military or involvement in combat. Violations of *ahimsa* are supposed to lead to excommunication from the *sangha* (a Buddhist monastic order) and rebirth as an animal or hungry ghost in hell. Designated violations of nonviolence include actual killing, counseling others to kill, or merely entertaining thoughts of killing. Monks are not permitted to carry weapons or even things that could be used as weapons, although every monk carries with him a knife and often a staff. Despite these legalities, China has a long history of military monks. As Buddhism took hold in their country, the Chinese increasingly questioned the necessity of obedience to monastic rules imported from India. A scholar of the subject concluded that the frequency of martial violence among Chinese Buddhist monks was inversely proportional to the actual political and military strength of the state. When the state was unable to handle bandits, rebellion, or enemy invasion, the *sangha* resorted to self-help.[7]

Administrative records document Shaolin monks being prosecuted for rebellion during the Northern Wei dynasty (386–534). By the early Tang (seventh century), evidence of Shaolin military monks abounds (see box). Their first fame was for staff fighting, not hand combat, which did not become a Shaolin specialty until the sixteenth century. Staff fighting draws on a Buddhist heritage, while hand fighting was based on Daoist *daoyin* self-cultivation methods. The *Treatise on Military Affairs* (ca. 1560) says that "the Buddha is an expert magician, master of many techniques, [and] Shaolin hand combat in the entire world is hardly equaled." The *Exposition of the Original Shaolin Staff Method* (1610) calls their fighting technique "unsurpassed Buddhist wisdom" and observes that Shaolin monks consider martial training as a way to "reach the other shore," a Buddhist expression for enlightenment. The author describes his own mastery of Shaolin martial art as a Zen "sudden enlightenment." But there apparently is no reference connecting Bodhidharma to the martial arts of Shaolin Temple before the twentieth century. The connection is first made in a popular novel,

Travels of Lao Ts'an (ca. 1907), which was quickly confirmed in the *Illustrated Explanation of Shaolin Boxing Methods* and again in *Secrets of Shaolin Boxing*, both written by unknown authors around 1911.[8]

A passage in a sermon attributed to Bodhidharma explains perfect knowledge as "being always aware and nowhere obstructed." In the Heart Sutra, a canonical Chan text, these obstructions are called "attainments" and are to be avoided: "Because there is no attainment in the mind of the Bodhisattva who dwells in *prajna paramita* [perfect wisdom,] there are no obstacles and therefore no fear or delusion." This idea of obstruction secures the affinity between Chan/Zen and the Asian martial arts. Takuan Sōhō, a Japanese Zen master (1573–1645), addressed his "Mysterious Record of Immovable Wisdom" to a martial master. He identified ignorance, which both arises from and feeds

THE DYNASTIES OF CHINA	
Xia	205–1766 B.C.E.
Shang	1766–1045
Zhou	1045–256
Spring and Autumn Period	722–481
Warring States Period	403–221
Qin	221–206
Han	202 B.C.E.–220 C.E.
Six Dynasties	222–589
Sui	589–618
Tang	618–907
Five Dynasties and Ten Kingdoms	907–960
Song	960–1279
Yuan (Mongol)	1279–1368
Ming	1368–1644
Qing (Manchu)	1644–1912

delusion, as the chief obstacle to enlightenment. In Zen, delusion does not mean a faulty appearance mistaken for reality; to be deluded is to have a mind that stops. Every stopping point is a delusion, a deceptively glittering jewel in a veil that the evil Maya casts over emptiness. This idea of stopping and its danger makes brothers of the Zen meditationist and the practitioner of martial arts, for whom nothing is as fatal as stopping, or what martial arts practitioners know as a "freeze." As Takuan stated, "In Buddhism, we abhor this stopping and remaining with one thing or another. We call this stopping *affliction*. It is like a ball riding a swift-moving current: we respect the mind that flows on like this and does not stop for an instant in any place."[9]

Be like water, even in your mind, especially in your mind: "In not remaining in one place, the Right Mind is like water." The sagacious

Zen master appreciates the deceptive value of speed in the martial arts. The belief that speed is important is an insidious liability. "When the mind stops, it will be grasped by the opponent. On the other hand, if the mind contemplates being fast and goes into quick action, it will be captured by its own contemplation." Speed is moving rapidly from one stop to another. More important to the martial arts is that one's movements are one musical beat, one temporal measure, with a single interpenetrating duration. For that, one must stop stopping: "While hands, feet, and body may move, the mind does not stop any place at all, and one does not know where it is."[10]

A mind that has stopped stopping is a mind in ceaseless flow. Such a mind is unmovable precisely because it never stops. Moving implies stopping, moving from one stop to another. What never stops is thus unmovable, and the enlightened never stop. The consummate expression of martial efficacy turns out to be what the Zen meditationist attains by a different path. Martial masters confirm the complementarity. "There are many things in martial arts that accord with Buddhism and correspond to Zen," declared a samurai author. "In particular, there is repudiation of attachment and avoidance of lingering on anything. This is the most urgent point. Not lingering is considered quintessential. . . . If your mind stops and stays somewhere, you will be defeated in martial arts."[11]

THE ART OF WAR

I understand the word "art" in "martial art" as Greek *techne* or, in Latin, *ars*. *Techne* refers to a corpus of knowledge that endows voluntary human action with a predictable outcome. This *techne* knowledge makes the world more amenable to our needs and desires and can be communicated to others. Archery, navigation, dance, carpentry—all are *techne* in that sense, and so are the Chinese martial arts. What is artlike about them is the principled knowledge expressed in a system of techniques and a philosophy of the body.

I apply the same explanation to the Chinese "art of war." The famous *Sunzi bingfa*, or *Master Sun's Military Methods*, commonly known as *The Art of War* (or simply as the *Sunzi*), is the greatest work of China's military philosophy and also the oldest we know of, perhaps even the first. It begot a tradition of military philosophy that came to include works attributed to Jiang Ziya (Jiang Taigong), legendary strategist of the dynastic Zhou conquest, and by historically attested post-classical figures like Zhuge Liang, China's most storied strategist, and the Tang emperor Taizong (598–649).[12]

The great discovery of the art of war is simply that there can be an *art* (a *dao* and a *techne*) of war: "Victory is something that you can craft and bring into being." War is therefore not condemned to brutality; it becomes instead a problem of art and knowledge. The *art* of war is victory achieved in an artful, even sagacious, way. The challenge (to art and knowledge) is not merely to triumph or cover oneself in glory, but to win the most with the least exposure, doing very little, ideally nothing at all. "To prove victorious in every battle is not the best possible outcome," says Sunzi. "The best possible outcome is to subdue the enemy's troops *without* fighting (*bu zhang*)." The victory of one who is good at war does not depend on divine favor, great courage, or superior force. A strategic commander wins because, having knowledge of the strategic situation, he positions himself where he is sure to win, prevailing over someone who has already lost. Knowing how to arrange that outcome is the art, the *techne*, the cunning technical sagacity of strategy. Since the decisive actions are inconspicuous and nearly invisible, there is nothing glorious in the victories. They look easy, despite being a case of "easy once you see it." If you do not see it and it traps you, you are defeated. It is not a fluke. It is a work of art, *techne*, superlatively effective knowledge.[13]

Sunzi's "no-fighting" principle is sometimes taken to mean that the best victories are bloodless, an interpretation that, however traditional, is probably the wishful thinking of the literati who kept the historical records. Elsewhere in the military classics it is evident that "no fighting" does not mean no fighting *at all*. It means not having to fight a lot, for a long time, with hard losses. The stratagems that make "no fighting" possible are seldom decisive. They merely expose the enemy's weakness, which is then attacked in a more or less orthodox way. Stratagem to Sunzi is not a bloodless alternative to violence but a way to enhance its effectiveness, so that a little can be made to go a long way. All the military classics insist that the commander must strike the right balance of orthodox and unorthodox deployments. Unorthodox misdirection sets up the violence of an orthodox strike that follows the opening that the stratagem creates.

Sunzi and this whole tradition place a high value on deception (*gui*), which is not merely one weapon in war's armory; Sunzi calls deception the very "*dao* of warfare," an extraordinary remark that this concise text repeats twice. No Western military thinker—from Julius Caesar to Machiavelli and Clausewitz—esteems deception. While Western methods of war have evolved toward greater applications of people and technology, Chinese operations "invariably have a strong psychological aspect even today," says a military specialist. Deception is invaluable to the disadvantaged party, which is the perspective from which this tradition tends to formulate strategic problems. Perhaps the greatest military victory in China was the Zhou conquest of the Shang (1122 B.C.E.). The forces were almost cosmically asymmetrical, as the Shang army may have been larger than the entire population of the Zhou territory. Yet the Zhou's much smaller force defeated the Shang, killed their wicked king, and established the great dynasty of classical antiquity. Chinese military philosophers never forgot this, and their ideas about strategy tend to be worked out from the perspective of a disadvantaged party that does not want war but is forced to respond to aggression. The texts favor scenarios of seemingly impossible odds, such as this, from the *Wuzi*, one of China's seven military classics:

> Marquis Wu asked: "Their forces are extremely numerous, martial, and courageous. Behind them are ravines and dangerous passes; on their right, mountains; on the left a river. They have deep moats and high ramparts and are defending their positions with strong crossbowmen. Their withdrawal is like a mountain moving, their advance like a tempest. As their foodstocks are also plentiful, it will be difficult to defend against them for very long. What should be done?" Wuzi replied: "A great problem indeed! This is not a problem of the strength of chariots and cavalry but of having the plans of a sage."[14]

As the *dao* of warfare, deception means more than clever ruses and deceit; it means fighting the mind. If you use deception to manipulate where an adversary *thinks* his advantage lies, he will wear himself out lunging at shadows. His strength becomes an unknown vulnerability, just as your former vulnerability becomes a source of strength. A strategic commander attacks minds before attacking soldiers. As Sunzi's *Art of War* states, "In military operations, it is best to attack the enemy's strategy. Next best is to attack the enemy's alliances. Next best is to attack the enemy's troops. Worst of all is to lay siege to the enemy's cities." The principle finds favor with martial arts masters both ancient and modern. "Amateurs fight bodies," explains Rory Miller, a jujitsu master and jail guard. "They study bodies, they break down bodies and they train to counter techniques. Professionals fight minds. . . . The thing that gives you a chance against weapons and multiple attackers or any situation of extreme disadvantage is to fight the mind." It is, as Sunzi said, the *dao* of combat.[15]

Next after deception, Sunzi and his tradition praise the quality of flexibility, using terms not so different from the (much later) Zen image of movement like water, an image that Daoists and, later, Chan/Zen learned from the military philosophy. Flexibility comes from a kind of emptiness, a fluidity of form that never stops or excludes transformation. In a seminal metaphor, the *Sunzi* compares these "empty" forms to the movement of water: "The strategic potential of an army has no fixed course or expression; just as water has no fixed disposition or form." To be able to flow like water is the ultimate martial art: "Those who are able to achieve victory by changing and transforming in response to the dispositions of their enemies are called 'spirit-like.' . . . Subtle! So subtle! They are without form. Spirit-like! So spirit-like! They make no sound. And so, the enemy's fate lies in their hands."[16]

The epitome of strategic flexibility is the art of *quan bian*, "weighing changes," which a military classics commentary explains as "weighing changes in the interactive relationship with the enemy." Strategies originate in what the opponent offers, not in a predetermined plan. The art of war is an art of response, even if it is a provoked response. The adversary makes the first move, and the strategy captures him. According to Yu Qian, a minister of war during the Ming dynasty (1368–1644), "The methods of employing the military instrument are hard to perceive, just like yin and yang; and hard to comprehend, just like ghosts and spirits. Thus one should stress responding to change at any particular moment. It is difficult to seek [victory] on the basis of a fixed [plan]."[17]

Martial artists use the same terms to explain their approach to unarmed combat: "Untrained people fight the force, not the emptiness." They set themselves against the other's strength, which they think they have to destroy. In order to discern and adapt to the emptiness, one must be empty oneself. As a contemporary martial arts practitioner observes, "In the martial arts, freedom of movement—physical but also spiritual freedom—is facilitated by a quality of detachment. It is a surrendering of control over 'this thing here,' an abandoning also of the illusion of control and a willingness to 'invest in less' that results in mastery." Miyamoto Musashi, Japan's greatest samurai, writes in his *Book of Five Rings*: "Without any confusion in mind, without slacking off at any time, polishing the mind and attention, sharpening the eye that observes and the eye that sees, one should know real emptiness as the state where there is no obscurity and the clouds of confusion have cleared away."[18]

There is no strength without correlated vulnerability and no attack that is not also an opening for counterattack. If an opponent is full, solid, and committed somewhere, the martial strategist will seize the inevitable emptiness, which makes his response both highly effective and seemingly effortless. In Sunzi's words, "Take advantage of the enemy's lack of preparation, approach by unexpected routes, and attack places left unguarded." This art of war praises the combination of overwhelming force and precise timing:

> The swiftness of a rushing torrent can float boulders; this is a matter of the water's strategic potential. The swiftness of a diving hawk can break the back of its prey; this is a matter of the hawk's precise timing. And so, those good at waging war unleash overwhelming strategic potential and employ precise timing. Strategic potential is like a drawn crossbow. Timing is like pulling the trigger.[19]

Overwhelming force does not mean having more men or arms but being irresistible where the enemy is unknowingly weak. Victory is not a matter of strength, not between armies, and not in unarmed combat, either. It is a problem of knowledge. A scholar of Chinese military philosophy explains the concept of strategic potential (*shi*) as "a calculus of differentials in configuration, momentum, timing, terrain, morale, equipment, logistics, and so on, that constitute the propensity of circumstances, and that can be calibrated and adjusted to produce welcome outcomes." A taiji classic makes a somewhat garbled paraphrase of the *Sunzi*: "Know yourself and know others: in one hundred battles you will win one hundred times." Then it observes, "Practicing the [taiji] form every day is the *gongfu* of knowing yourself. . . . Push hands (*tui shou*) is the *gongfu* of knowing others."[20]

Those points that martial artists tend to emphasize from the Chinese art of war are to not waste energy fighting the opponent's strength; to be flexible and adaptable, alert to inevitable evolution; to develop an unconventional technique for surprise; and to combine overwhelming force with precise timing. Deception and fighting the mind become indispensable when the warring parties are asymmetrical and the weaker one is forced to respond to a stronger antagonist. In this scenario, the problem is to reverse the strategic situation. The insight of *The Art of War* is that to do so reliably you have to use deception and fight the mind. At this point, a difference emerges between an art-of-war strategy and the unarmed solo martial arts. The practice of martial arts does not typically use a dramatically asymmetrical scenario as a training assumption. The usual training scenario is an immediate need to respond to a usually solo assault. Training scenarios with multiple attackers are relatively advanced. An asymmetry of force becomes prominent in this training only in the multiple-attacker scenario, especially with weapons in play. In this specific sort of scenario, it is then that it becomes crucial to fight the mind. But this scenario of overwhelming odds is not the usual one in martial arts training.[21]

The *dao* of Asian martial arts, it seems to me, lies not in deception but in achieving an "effortless" response to incoming violence. What is artful in the martial arts is a response to violence that is at once maximally effective and minimally exposing. A martial arts technique is always a response to something, whether an actual attack or the intention to attack. To direct violence to another irresponsibly, that is, not in response to the other's violence, is not martial arts, or at least not in the Asian tradition of most contemporary practice. The power, the virtue, the *dao* of these martial arts is the "effortless" neutralization of another's violence. By "effortless," I mean an expressive ease of movement, sinuous and flowing, that seems not to throw obstacle against obstacle but to redirect incoming energy in an unexpected way that undermines the violent purpose for which it was launched. The response to violence that these arts teach is not to avoid it, as a pacifist would, or to turn the other cheek, as a Christian would, or to return a greater violence and destroy the opponent, as Rambo would. Instead, the most masterful response reveals the futility of the assault by means of neutralization. The more obviously violent martial arts techniques are mere expedients for those still on the road to mastership.

In the art-of-war scenario, a conventionally stronger army confronts a disadvantaged party. The strategic commander artfully reverses the asymmetry and achieves an "effortless" victory. The word "effortless" refers to a technical concept, *wuwei*, meaning "not doing" or "non-action," which I discuss later. In a typical martial arts training scenario, the opponent *thinks* he has an advantage and attacks. But the would-be victim is not as disadvantaged as the assailant believes, and he responds with surprising effectiveness. Deception is indispensable to reverse a strategic asymmetry, but skill in martial arts means that the strategic situation never becomes asymmetrical in that disadvantageous way.

A canny commander knows how to reverse a strategic situation and make victory seem easy. The martial arts master is never in that asymmetrical situation. What makes the martial arts response effective is not psychology but corporeal *techne*, drawing on a sophisticated understanding of the body that makes martial arts techniques both elegant and highly effective. The martial arts master looks disadvantaged only to people who know nothing about the body's capacities and vulnerabilities. Martial arts techniques work because most violent people have conventional assumptions about how others will respond to their violence. Because these conventions do exist, such violence is often successful. But a neutralizing response (you may get hurt, but the violence will not be successful) is possible and can be learned.

A response to personal violence unfolds in a different space and time than does the movement of troops over a battlefield. In chapter 3, we look at some of these differences. They make martial arts less strategic than responsive or interactive—I might almost say dialogical—because as a reply to another's violence, this response is closer to a speech act than a military strategy, delivering an unexpected answer to an uninvited aggression. It is not like reasonable speech. It is not offered to sustain a conversation but to stop one from happening, one that is also not reasonable and begins with violence. If the ethics of discourse defines the form of a reasonable reply to another's speech, the martial arts teach a conversation-stopping response to unsolicited violence.

DAOISM AND THE MARTIAL ARTS

Daoist ideas and terminology are commonplaces of the literature that martial arts practitioners write for themselves. To study the interaction of this tradition with the martial arts, therefore, it is useful to know more about its ideas. The two foundational works are the *Daodejing*, also known as the *Laozi* after its legendary sage author; and a work named after its only partly legendary author, *Zhuangzi*, or *Master Zhuang*. Modern scholars find it impossible to agree on which one came first, so it seems simplest to think of them as approximately contemporary, from around the mid-fourth century B.C.E., China's Warring States period. The *Daodejing* shows no awareness of Zhuangzi or the *Zhuangzi*. The latter is a work of thirty-three chapters, each a short treatise of characteristic style, energy, and philosophical invention. Modern scholars consider only the first seven chapters, the so-called Inner Chapters, to be the work of the eponymous fourth-century author, Zhuang Zhou. The remainder, more than two-thirds of the received text, emerged from unknown hands some years after the master. Some of the hands involved in some of the probably later treatises had heard of a sage Laozi, or Lao Dan, but whether they knew him as the author of the *Daodejing*, or merely as another sage, is inconclusive.[22]

A Mind Like Dead Ashes

The second chapter of the *Zhuangzi* opens with an allusion to what became a distinctive Daoist form of meditation: "Ziqi of the Southern Wall was reclining against a low table on the ground, releasing his breath into Heaven above, all in a scatter, as if loosed from a partner." Someone observing Ziqi comments, "What has happened here? Can the body really be made like dried wood, the mind like dead ashes?" A mind like dead ashes? Yes, Ziqi explains. "What has happened here is simply that I have lost *me*" (Z 9).[23]

This scene alludes to a meditation practice that later tradition knew as "sitting in oblivion" (*zuowang*), an expression that first appears (elsewhere) in the *Zhuangzi*. Another account of similar breathing is found in the early postclassical, Daoist-leaning *Huainanzi*, or *Master of Huainan*:

> The method of the sages can be observed, but how they established their methods cannot be plumbed. . . . Wang Qiao and Chisong exhaled and inhaled, spitting out the old and internalizing the new. They cast off form and abandoned wisdom; they embraced simplicity and returned to genuineness; in roaming with the mysterious and subtle above, they penetrated to the clouds and heaven.

Wang Qiao was one of China's foremost reputed *fangshi* (shaman), with a reputation for shape-shifting, instantaneous travel, and alchemy, concocting the elixir of immortality; indeed, the advanced goal of these breathing exercises is to become an immortal (*xian*).[24]

That does not mean a soul that never dies. In Daoism, immortality is less concerned with death and what happens after it than with life. Longevity—that is, not dying before your time—is the highest form of health. In the words of the *Zhuangzi*, "You get something when it's time. You lose it when it's passed. If you are content with the time and abide by the passing, there's no room for sorrow or joy. This is what the ancients called 'loosening the bonds'" (K 238). Daoist "immortality" implies liberation from the bonds of gravity, being able to change places instantly, to vanish and reappear again, to be as light and elusive as a bird. Daoist adepts were (and still are) described as "bird-men" or "masters of wings" (*yushi*). Such people do not die; they just keep on transforming. The enlightenment they pursue is the culmination of a corporeal discipline and somatic refinement carried out best in seclusion on a mountain. Self and death become matters of indifference to one who can vanish into the becoming of the world like a fish in a stream.[25]

Chapter 6 of the *Zhuangzi* describes such a sage, there called a genuine person (*zhenren*). What is genuine about these people is their knowledge (*zhenzhi*). For them, to consciously reason to a conclusion is never more than an expedient, "arising only when the situation made it unavoidable" (Z 42). Genuine knowledge cannot be reduced to a speech or formula. The knowledge is not discursive but rather is enacted and corporeal, the knowledge of a meditatively rehabilitated body. The adept acquires intensified power to see through beings to their becoming. Instead of representing objects to a subject, genuine knowledge folds the body into the aborning environment, penetrating and neutralizing obstacles to a spontaneous response. The knowledge makes one unstoppable, unopposable, immovable, not from muscular mass, which may be negligible, but because one is minimally invested in actuality. When one has few hostages to fortune, one offers the fewest targets for obstruction—by anything, whatever happens. These adepts are never at a loss, never without an effective response to change. Their life becomes indistinguishable from the original becoming (*dao*) of an entire environment. Thus do they vanish into things.

This depiction of the genuine person becomes a model for a later literature of the Chinese martial arts. Amid an extravagant discourse on such persons, Zhuangzi praises their ability to breathe from the heels. Genuine people "breathe from their heels, while the mass of men breathe from their throats" (Z 40). A later chapter says that "the incipient impulse of all that flourishes" comes from the heels (Z 52). This curious image recurs in the *Huainanzi*, where Huzi, having been informed by a shaman that his physiognomy portended short life, "remained indifferent to the idea and the reality of it and allowed the dynamism [of the breath] to rise up from his heels."[26] To breathe from the heels is to breathe all the way down to the heels, or all the way up from the heels, and not to let the breathing stop short in the throat, as most people do. Establishing this corporeal circuit from the heels upward opens a channel for the influx of terrestrial *qi*.

Such breathing and circulating of *qi* belongs to the context of the *daoyin*, "guided stretching" exercises. These are gentler than calisthenics and involve more than mere stretching, such as training in breathing. Yoga is a distant comparison, as is taiji, a much later development. *Daoyin* exercises are illustrated on Han tombs where an important early *Daodejing* also was found. Note, however, that the character for and the pronunciation of *dao* in *daoyin* are different from those for the *dao* of Daoism. Nevertheless, this *daoyin* is explicitly named in the *Zhuangzi*, when the author describes the huffing and puffing "of the practitioners of the *daoyin* exercises" (K 265). A second allusion may also be in the remark "I level out the impulses of the breath" (Z 97).

According to a scholar of classical Daoism, "There is concrete evidence that the author of the Inner Chapters of the *Zhuangzi* was aware of—and likely followed—such inner cultivation practices." Heel breathing (*zhongxi*), as distinguished from throat breathing (*houxi*), is part of what Daoists call embryonic respiration (*taixi*) and harmonizing the breath (*tiaoxi*). The soles of the feet emerge as critical junctures for the flow of *qi* through the body. Primordial *qi* divides and multiplies, dispersing into myriad flows, each with its own quality and intensity. A basic division of these flows is between the *qi* flowing through the heavens (*tianqi*) and the *qi* flowing through the earth (*diqi*). The heel-breathing exercise opens one to this terrestrial *qi*, the subtle breath of the earth, which enters from the feet at the *yongquan* (bubbling well) acupuncture point, in the center of the foot.[27]

If Zhuang Zhou belonged to a circle practicing *daoyin*, sitting in oblivion, or other proto-Daoist breathing and meditation techniques, there assuredly was no martial arts practice involved. We have to wait some two thousand years for this connection to be made, or at least to be documented. The *Change Muscle Classic* (1624), attributed to Bodhidharma, is the earliest work to associate *daoyin* and the martial arts. Nevertheless, we can appreciate why martial artists would want to be able to sink their breath all the way down to their heels, where the flow of terrestrial *qi* enters the body. One becomes an earth, unmovable as a mountain, fluid as a stream.[28]

Robert W. Smith described performing taiji's pushing-hands exercise (*tui shou*) with Master Zheng Manqing. (I should mention that this and all authentic taiji exercises are cunningly disguised martial arts techniques.) Zheng told him,

> As you touch the opponent in your attempt to elicit resistance, inhale to the sole of your foot with your mind. Then as you exhale all your power comes from the sole, rather than the hands. . . . The ability to transmit *qi* from the sole of one's foot up through the fingers takes decades."

In his 1947 treatise on taijiquan, Zheng explained, "The point of force is in the foot. . . . Although we use the hands to make contact, the motivating force originates in the feet. This is wonderful and without equal!" A taiji classic attributed to the legendary founder Zheng Sanfeng states, "The motion should be rooted in the feet, released through the legs, controlled by the waist, and manifested through the fingers." Of course, if your ankle buckles or your feet slip, nothing else you do will matter. It is impossible for combative techniques to achieve maximum intensity when the footing is not secure. As Chang Naizhou, the "scholar-boxer" author of the eighteenth-century martial arts treatise *Peiyang zhongqi* (*Nourishing Central Energy*), noted, "If foot-tips, heels, outer edges, insteps, [or] the ankles' extension or arching, inside and outside, once have any uncoordination, then body-energy does not enter!"[29]

The practice of heel breathing and *daoyin* to which *Zhuangzi* alludes may be related in another way to Chinese martial arts. A perennial claim in the origin myths of these arts is that they were invented in imitation of animals and their ways of fighting. Zhang Sanfeng was supposedly inspired to invent taiji by observing a snake defend itself from attack by a bird. Wing chun is attributed to Ng Mui, a Shaolin nun, and her observation of a confrontation between a snake and a crane. These accounts are assuredly fanciful, but why are they so insistent a theme in Chinese martial arts?

The explanation may lie in an idea dating back to the Shang dynasty of the second millennium B.C.E., that the universe is under the control of spirits (*shen*) and people can acquire their power through ritual imitation of animal movement. Animal skins and shells were used to make drums and other ceremonial instruments, and shamans decked in ritual hides and feathers mimicked animal movements in a magical effort to obtain their power. According to legend, the trigrams of the *bagua*, the foundation of the *Yijing* (*Classic of Changes*), also forge a link between human beings and the daimonic efficacy of animals. The sage Fu Xi observed the patterns of birds and beasts and accordingly made the eight trigrams to concentrate and epitomize their numinous power, including their violence. The ancient sage-kings were said to have used animals in their armies and to have invented weapons in imitation of animals' natural weapons. The Yellow Emperor, the most ancient of the ancient sages and the ancestor of all Chinese people, created the first army by organizing and instructing animals, whom he then turned into human beings armed with weapons derived from animal prototypes.[30]

The protean potential to acquire spiritlike powers through the imitation of animals was at first reserved for shamans. Beginning in the Warring States period (479–221 B.C.E.), however, new arts of self-cultivation imported these ritual movements into *daoyin* practice, producing manuals promising to convey this daimonic potency (and the good health that is its most conspicuous expression) to anyone who diligently practiced the techniques these works describe. We have an example in the *Stretching Book* (*Yinshu*), a long-lost work recovered in 1973 and thought to date from the second century B.C.E. The work enjoins readers to

> perform the Eight Principles stretching, blow out and breathe in the vital essence and *qi* of Heaven and Earth, extend your abdomen and straighten your waist, forcefully extend your arms and legs, push down your heels and curve your toes . . . thus you will be able to avoid disease.

The *Stretching Book* associates these *daoyin* exercises with Peng Zu, "Ancestor Peng," China's legendary figure of longevity:

> When those who follow the *dao* [of Ancestor Peng] are joyful then they quickly exhale, and when they are angry they increasingly puff out, all in order to harmonize [their emotions]. Inhaling the vital essence and *qi* of Heaven and Earth . . . they are able to be without disease."[31]

These exercises are given animal names like "tiger twists" and "bear strides." The *Guiding and Stretching Diagram (Daoyin tu)*, a silk painting in the Mawangdui corpus illustrating and naming *daoyin* poses, includes "dragon mounting" and "gibbon shouting." The *Zhuangzi* alludes to these, too, writing of "Peng Zu's ripe-old-agers," who "huff and puff, exhale and inhale, blow out the old and draw in the new, do the 'bear-hang' and the 'bird stretch,' interested only in a long life" (G 265), mentioning two exercises from the *Stretching Book*: "Bird stretch is good for the shoulder joints; bear stretch is good for the lower back." Hua Tuo, a physician of the Latter Han dynasty (25–220), recommends *daoyin* animal forms to expel the bad air in the system and promote free circulation of the blood:

> The used doorstop never rots, so [too] for the body. That is why the ancients practiced the bear's neck, the fowl's twist, swaying the body, and moving the joints to prevent old age. . . . The frolics of the five animals (*wu qin zhi xi*), which are the tiger, deer, bear, monkey, and bird . . . remove disease, strengthen the legs, and ensure health.[32]

The opening to martial arts came when these *daoyin* animal movements were incorporated into fencing routines, starting in the first century C.E., and then into unarmed martial arts techniques from the Ming dynasty, if not earlier. The crisis-ridden time of the transition from the Ming to the Qing dynasty (1644–1911) is also when the whole idea of martial arts "systems" (*tixi*) and "styles" (*pai*) with distinct names arose. Sometimes these names refer to a supposed founder, such as Hung Gar; or a key principle, for example, Xingyi; a reputed place of origin, like Emei Boxing; or a supposed animal model, such as White Crane or Monkey Fist. Each system has a myth of origin with a founder and lineage of transmission, a set of techniques and practice forms (*quan tao*), and a central principle or concept, such as the bagua principle of circular motion or wing chun's centerline principle. It seems likely, then, that the enduring myth of animal origins in Chinese martial arts recalls the ancient idea of people acquiring daimonic powers by imitating animal movements, an idea transmitted to the martial arts tradition through the incorporation of *daoyin* exercises, with their animal names, into the armed and unarmed techniques of the earliest systems of Chinese martial arts.[33]

ANOTHER PASSAGE in the *Zhuangzi* that speaks to martial arts practitioners relates a conversation between Lord Wenhui and his cook, who is at work butchering an ox. The cook has a way of butchering that is beyond technique. He does not use his eyes, only his spirit, and has not had to sharpen his knife in nineteen years. He follows the natural patterns and finds the space between bones and ligaments to be ample and easily negotiated. Meat falls off his knife like clods of earth from a spade. This cook becomes an image of martial arts mastery. He responds to the ox as the martial master does to an opponent. He does not use his eyes but his *qi*. What seems quick to others is to him slow and clumsy. There is so much time, and the adversary's moves are so obvious, that an effortless evasion evolves into a devastating response. As a Qing-dynasty martial arts author writes:

> The book says: "strike in the big hollows, guide the knife through the big openings." Why does it say so? Because when Cook Ding cut up oxen "he no longer saw the whole ox." I say it is the same with hand combat. Why? Because I am looking for my opponent's soft points, acupuncture points, and those forbidden to strike as I engrave them in my mind's eye. For this reason, the moment I lift my hand, I am able to target my opponent's empty points, and strike at his acupuncture points, "no longer seeing the whole person."[34]

In a preface (1784) to the *Hand Combat Classic*, another martial arts author looks to Zhuangzi for an image of his art:

The subtlety of the method's application depends entirely on internal strength. It cannot be exhausted by words. Like an old hunchback who catches cicadas. . . . When one's resolution is not distracted, when his spirit is concentrated, he will begin to acquire the agility of "mind conceiving, hands responding." At this point there is sure to be no straining of muscles nor exposure of bones.[35]

The reference to cicadas alludes to a passage in the *Zhuangzi* in which a hunchback explains his knack:

I settle my body like a rooted tree stump, I hold my arm like the branch of a withered tree; out of all the vastness of heaven and earth, the multitude of the myriad things, it is only of the wings of a cicada that I am aware. I don't let my gaze wander or waiver, I would not take all the myriad things in exchange for the wings of a cicada. How could I help but succeed? (G 138)

The words are no less a description of the martial artist clearing his spine, emptying his mind, calmly awaiting the other's departure, leaving last but arriving first.

A series of textual echoes show the *Zhuangzi* interacting with both the art-of-war tradition and later martial arts thought. Earlier I mentioned the strategic principle of empty and full. There is no strength without correlated vulnerability, therefore no attack that is not also an opening. If one's opponent is full, solid, and committed somewhere, then strategy advises one to target the inevitable emptiness, thereby making the response both highly effective and seemingly effortless. According to Sunzi, "One skilled in warfare sees the enemy's strength, and from this is able to appreciate the enemy's weakness." The key to combat success is knowing how to make the indirect route direct: "What is difficult about the clash of arms is to make the indirect route the most direct and turn misfortune to your advantage." Difficult but crucial: "Those who begin by understanding the strategy of how to make the indirect route the most direct shall be victorious." We have this example: "Take a circuitous route to reach the enemy, tempt him with advantages (*you zhi yi li*). Though I set out after him, I reach my destination before him (*hou ren fa, xian ren zhi*)."[36]

The presumably later author of the thirtieth chapter of *Zhuangzi*, "A Discourse on Swords," echoes this language when he describes individual weapons combat: "The master swordsman . . . lays himself wide open, tempts you to take advantage (*kai zhi yi li*), is behind in making his move, is ahead in striking home (*hou zhi yi fa, xian zhi yi zhi*)" (G 245). Some two thousand years later, Chang Naizhou, an eighteenth-century martial master, made this idea a principle of his teaching:

> When the opponent's strike is just about to land on our body, we take advantage of this to make our move. This leaves the opponent no opportunity to retreat or to block. There is no more marvelous principle. . . . This is the principle of "strike second but land first."

The sixteenth-century *Sword Classic* also alludes to this principle— "Entice his old force to pass by while new force is not yet shot out, and ride it"—and Chang Naizhou explains the strategy in terms of his alchemical energetics:

> Borrowing active energy is borrowing a man's energy in action to hit him. Generally, when his dynamic shoots out, already nearing my body, before contact, I then take this moment to shoot my dynamic. He desires to retreat but cannot, desires to deflect but is too late. Thenceforth there are no untoward possibilities. If slightly too soon, then he can still retreat back. If slightly too late, then I have already suffered loss. This is what is meant by: "Be last to shoot, first to reach" [*hou fa xian zhi*].[37]

Japanese masters, absorbing Chinese martial arts with their Zen, know this principle too. For instance, in his *Family Traditions on the Art of War*, the samurai Yagyū Munenori advised: "Gain victory by inducing your opponent to take the initiative. . . . Control [your own] mind and keep it impassive while using physical aggressiveness to get the opponent to make the first move, and thus you gain victory." This is called "being a step ahead of the one who takes the initiative," in other words, leaving last and arriving first. That is also the strategic meaning of Gichin Funakoshi's famous statement that there is no first strike in karate. Rather, it is the art of a second strike that is the first to land:

> There is no first strike in karate—this is what I deem to be the essence of *karate-do*. In other words, respond to your opponent once he moves, without initiating the action. He who is able to read circumstances in his mind before they transpire, to see the playing out of opposing forces yet to begin, as if with eyes behind one's head, is capable of knowing the path to certain victory.[38]

Strategists everywhere discover this principle, which modern military theory calls the "power of the defensive." According to the military historian B. H. Liddell Hart, "All skillful commanders [seek] to profit from the power of the defensive, even when on the offensive." Entice the opponent to strike a target, thinking you are vulnerable there; then while he is tied up in that, seize the opportunity he supplies by unintentionally collaborating in your strategy. The pugilist Jem Mace summed up his experience in the ring: "Let 'em come to ye, and they'll beat theirselves." Kid McCoy, another boxer, advised, "Draw your man into attack—and get him so that he has both his hands out of business and you have one hand free."[39]

THE CHINESE found more in archery, their premier battlefield art, than an efficient means of killing. Its practice has a spiritual element that goes beyond battlefield violence without sacrificing a martial power that is effective in a way that no ritual can be. Earlier I explained that Confucians made archery part of their self-cultivation practice. The *Liezi*, another Daoist classic, shows the Daoists' different approach to the same material. Liezi was a magician whom we meet in the *Zhuangzi*, where we learn that he can ride the wind and no longer relies on his feet. But Zhuangzi criticizes him for still relying on something, namely, the wind. Thus Liezi remains an apprentice, with more work to do, more of "himself" to forget. In the (probably later) *Liezi*, we find this same Faustian figure wanting to demonstrate to a friend his skill in archery:

He drew his bow and placed a cup of water on his left forearm. Then he notched an arrow and let it fly. Before the first arrow hit the target, he had let off the second and the third. When he saw that all three arrows hit the center of the target, Liezi was quite pleased with himself. So steady was his hand and so focused was his concentration that the water in the cup did not spill.

The friend is unimpressed. He says to Liezi:

"What you showed me was merely the skill of eye and hand, and not the state of mind of the true archer. Let's go up to the mountains and stand on the edge of a cliff. If you can shoot accurately under those conditions, then I shall be convinced of your mastery in archery."

The two went into the mountains, and when they reached the top of a peak, Liezi's friend walked toward the edge of a cliff that dropped a thousand feet below. Standing with his back to the drop and a foot half over the ledge, he invited Liezi to join him. At the thought of standing with his back to the abyss, Liezi fell on his face and broke into a cold sweat. His friend commented:

"The master archer can fire an arrow under any condition. Whether he sees the clear sky or faces the yawning abyss, he can still shoot with the same state of mind. He is not affected by conditions of life and death, for nothing can move the stillness of his mind. Look at yourself now. You are so scared that you can't stand up or look straight. How can you even begin to demonstrate the art of archery?"[40]

THE DAO AND ITS POWER

Tradition attributes the *Daodejing* to the sage Laozi, and history does record a man named Lao Dan, a Zhou court librarian with a reputation for learning. According to legend, when he was very old, Lao Dan decided to ride his ox toward the West until he died. At China's western border, he had to cross a mountain pass supervised by an official, who implored the sage to leave a record of his wisdom. On the spot, Lao Dan dashed off the *Daodejing*, a short work of some five thousand characters, then disappeared into the West. He may have reached India before dying, where he may have enjoyed a second fame as the Buddha. He reappeared centuries later in visions that inspired a new spiritual movement, the Daoist religion still practiced in China and throughout Asia and the world.[41]

The earliest attested reference connecting Laozi to this book occurs in the Confucian *Xunzi* (ca. 250 B.C.E.). The Confucians have a legend about an encounter between Laozi and the young Confucius who, knowing Laozi's reputation for learning, sought out the elder. After an interview in which the old master dazzled the callow literatus, Confucius announced, "I have seen the dragon!" Angus Graham, a sinologist at the London School of Oriental Studies, showed that this story of a meeting with Confucius is older than all the other stories about Lao Dan, including his supposed authorship of the *Daodejing*. In other words, the legend of the sage Laozi was invented by the Confucians independently of the *Daodejing* that he was supposed to have written. Graham thinks that when the *Daodejing* emerged in its current form from the hands of unknown redactors, it was attributed to this sage in order to claim the authority of "the man who talked down to Confucius."[42]

A story by Kanō Jigorō (1869–1938), the Japanese founder of judo, conveys the *Daodejing*'s evocative power for the philosophy of Asian martial arts. He recounts the origin of jujitsu, the Japanese battlefield martial art from which Kanō derived judo. A man named Chingempin left China after the fall of the Ming dynasty and traveled to Japan, where he lived in a Buddhist temple in Tokyo with three *ronin* (masterless samurai). Together they devised a fighting art that became jujitsu when it spread throughout the country. Kanō lists five principles of this fighting art, each a virtual paraphrase of lines from the *Daodejing* (which he does not mention, even denying any Chinese influence on jujitsu). Here are Kanō's principles followed by relevant lines from the Chinese classic:

1. Do not resist an opponent, but gain victory by pliancy.

The supple and weak overcome the hard and the strong. (DDJ 36)

The most supple things in the world ride roughshod over the most rigid. (DDJ 43)

2. Do not aim at frequent victory.

Those who are good at military action achieve their goal and then stop. (DDJ 30)

A military victory is not a thing of beauty. (DDJ 31)

3. Do not be led into bickering. Keep the mind empty and calm.

Sages put themselves last and yet come first; treat themselves as unimportant and yet are preserved. Is it not because they have no thought of themselves that they are able to perfect themselves? (DDJ 7)

Only by avoiding contention can one avoid blame. (DDJ 8)

To be haughty when wealth and honor come your way is to bring disaster upon yourself. To withdraw when the work is done is the *dao* of Heaven. (DDJ 9)

4. Do not be disturbed by things.

Attain extreme emptiness (*xü*); preserve stillness (*jing*) whole. (DDJ 16)

The still (*jing*) rules over the agitated. (DDJ 26)

Clarity and stillness set everything right. (DDJ 45)

5. Do not be agitated in any emergency, but remain tranquil.

[Be] still and inactive, revealing no sign. (DDJ 20)

Those good at fighting are never warlike. Those good at attack are never enraged. (DDJ 68)

"The violent and overbearing will not die a natural death." I shall take this [saying] as the father of all my teachings. (DDJ 42)[43]

Kanō tells another story that attributes the origin of jujitsu to a physician named Akiyama, who went to China to study medicine. He returned having learned a fighting art that he tried to teach others, but all his students were unsatisfied and deserted him. Akiyama then retreated to Tenjin Shrine in Tsukushi and worshipped there for a hundred days, after which time a new fighting art was finally revealed to him. During a snowstorm he observed a willow tree whose branches were covered in snow. Unlike the pine tree, which stood erect and broke during the storm, the willow yielded to the weight of the snow on its branches but did not break under it. He realized that martial arts must be practiced in the same way. So he named his school Yōshin-ryū, the Spirit of Willow school. The principle is not quite the revelation the story implies, though. The *Daodejing* already knows that "the stiff and strong are the disciples of death, the supple and weak are the disciples of life. That is why a weapon that is too strong will not prove victorious, a tree that is too strong will break" (DDJ 76).

TO UNFOLD the resonant sonority of this work for the philosophy of the martial arts, I next survey six themes from the *Daodejing*: (1) references to the art of war philosophy; (2) references to meditation practice, breathing, circulating the *qi*, and arts of the body; (3) passages on emptiness and non-action; (4) passages on the power of non-contention; (5) passages on discerning and responding to the minute and subtle; and (6) passages on the theme of hard and soft.

1. The unknown ancient redactors of the *Daodejing* obviously were familiar with the military art-of-war philosophy and associated their thought with it. In one place, the text alludes to Sunzi's idea of the pinnacle of strategic excellence to overcome the enemy without fighting: "The *dao* of heaven/nature (*tian*) is winning the war without going to battle" (DDJ 73). A second allusion is more explicit:

> Military strategists have a saying, "I never dare to play host but prefer to play guest. I never dare to advance an inch but retreat a foot." This is called a formation without form, rolling up one's sleeve but having no arm [or throwing a punch without raising a hand], forcing the issue but lacking an enemy. (DDJ 69)

Again: "Follow what is strange and perverse in deploying your troops; follow no activity and gain the world" (DDJ 57).

The first passage alludes to the strategy of leaving last and arriving first, the second to what the military philosophy calls "unconventional strategy," which Sunzi praises: "In general, in battle one engages with the orthodox and gains victory through the unorthodox. Thus one who excels at sending forth the unorthodox is as inexhaustible as Heaven." "Unorthodox" translates the Chinese word *qi*, which also describes the marvelous, strange, and extraordinary. Military usage emphasizes the unexpected and uncanny, which makes unorthodox strategy fathomless and inexhaustible. "The changes of the unorthodox and the orthodox can never be completely exhausted. The unorthodox and orthodox mutually produce each other, just like an endless cycle. Who can exhaust them?"[44]

2. Many passages of the *Daodejing* seem to refer to meditation practice, breathing, circulating the *qi*, and arts of the body; for instance, "Concentrating your *qi* and attaining the utmost suppleness, can you be a child?" (DDJ 10). Another meaning of the words *lao zi* is "old child." An obliging tradition says that Lao Dan was born with an old man's features. The tradition is appropriate because the tendency of sagehood in this work is toward something childlike: "Those who are steeped in virtue [*de*, power] are like newborn children. . . . They can wail all day without growing hoarse. This is because they are perfectly balanced" (DDJ 55). In this work, the child is not an image of innocence but of vital power, unstoppable *qi*. The adept strives to regain that condition, to become once again that empty, that uncommitted, that unstoppable; and what the *Daodejing* calls "concentrating the *qi*" is the way to do it.

Qi is a word for any gaseous substance—steam, clouds, smoke, the air, or breath. In fact, it is the modern Chinese word for "weather." *Qi* has two basic characteristics. The first is to come in gradations of subtlety, like ice gradually turning into steam. The second is to be dynamic, not static, constantly moving and changing, like water flowing down or steam rising up. *Qi* is material, provided that matter is understood dynamically as interchangeable with energy and never at rest. It has a spatial extension and is in constant transformation independent of awareness. As the original material of all things, it penetrates everywhere and makes all things flow. What we call a "thing" is a more or less momentary stability, nothing substantial or "for itself." *Qi* fills the body more dramatically than do Descartes's animal spirits. Cartesian animal spirits, being matter (however volatile), are inert and move solely by impulse. In contrast, *qi* is energetic, vibratory, and incapable of being still. (What we perceive as stillness is synchronous change.) *Qi* has always been associated with the dynamics of yin-yang alternation, as the stuff of which they are phases or the material of their continuum. This *qi* may be upright (*zheng*), flowing freely and creating balanced states, regular weather, health, absence of disasters, and peaceful coexistence. Likewise, the *qi* can be wayward (*xie*), meaning disorderly, turbulent, and dysfunctionally depleted and depleting. Chinese martial arts literature has a specific meaning of the word *qi* for body energetics. The optimal flow of the *qi* through the moving body comes with correct skeletal alignment and a coordinated use of the muscular system, thereby generating maximum force with minimum expenditure.[45]

Daoist *qi* cultivation is a variation of the Confucian practice of self-cultivation (*xiu shen*). The Confucian practice laboriously works their table of values deep into the body. Daoist self-cultivation is a no less corporeal cultivation, but adjusted to different values: "Those who revere their bodies as if they were the entire world can be given custody of the world. Those who care for their bodies as if they were the entire world can be entrusted with the world" (DDJ 20). Daoists eventually develop the programs of physical cultivation that I mentioned, such as the *daoyin* techniques of breathing, stretching, and meditation, both seated and moving. The point of the routines is to collect and intensify the *qi* so that it ceases to dissipate in futile resistance to change. Longevity does not mean retaining a fixed shape (forever young). Instead, it is the ideal of good health, retaining vital energy despite the body's changes. We get only so much *qi* in life. The more carefully we use it, the more we will save, and the longer we will last. The proto-Daoist *Stretching Book* says:

> People live their lives following their dispositions and do not know how to cherish their *qi*. For this reason they contract many diseases and are quick to die. The reason why people's [bodies] tend to deteriorate and why their yin [sexual potency] tends to prematurely wane is due to their inability to control their *qi*. Being able to effectively control their *qi* and honor their yin, they will benefit their bodies.[46]

An idea prominent in later Daoism already seems entertained in the *Daodejing*, that the adept make themselves a hermetic body without openings:

> Stop up the openings;
> Close the gates;
> To the end of one's life one will remain unperturbed. (DDJ 52)

> Stop up the openings;
> Close the gates;
> Blunt the sharpness;
> Untangle the tangles;
> Soften the glare;
> Merge with the dust.
> This is known as enigmatic unity. (DDJ 56)

I think we might guess at another allusion in these lines to *daoyin* breathing exercises. It is possible that such practices were trained among the communities that wrote and circulated what eventually became the *Daodejing*. The *Inward Training* (*Nieye*), a proto-Daoist text of the fourth century B.C.E., also refers to breath and posture discipline:

> Be not joyous, be not angry,
> just let a balanced and aligned breathing fill your chest.
> When your body is not aligned,
> the inner power will not come.

. . .

Align your body, assist the inner power,
then it will gradually come on its own.
When you enlarge your mind and let go of it,
When you relax your *qi* and expand it,
When your body is calm and unmoving,
And you can maintain oneness and discard the myriad disturbances—
Then you will see profit and not be enticed by it,
You will see harm and not be frightened by it.
Relaxed and unwound, yet acutely sensitive,
In solitude you delight in your own person.
This is called revolving the *qi.*
Your thoughts and deeds seem heavenly.[47]

A modern Chinese editor comments,

Inward training means inner achievement. It refers to the practice (*gongfu*) by which one cultivates and nourishes the inner mind and preserves vital essence and vital energy. . . . While the author of this text points out the importance of proper drinking, eating, and physical movement, the most basic and emphatic point of this practice lies completely within the inner mind. Therefore it is called *Inward Training.*

At their origin these techniques for health and spiritual enhancement have no connection to the martial arts. But we shall see that the theory and practice of "internal" martial arts is a development of this Daoist inner training.[48]

3. Schools of Chinese martial arts teach techniques that are "soft" in that they do not require force or strength, unlike Western boxing or wrestling, in which strength and body mass make a big difference. In contrast, with practice, both genders can perform Asian martial arts techniques well, because they rely on the subtle art of their innovators and long-practiced skills rather than force. To explain the effectiveness engendered by art, martial authors refer to non-action and emptiness, both prominent themes in the *Daodejing*. Like a martial arts master, Laozi's sage is good at accomplishing a lot while seeming to do very

little. Both know how to wait—wait for others to move, wait for the moment when the slightest action suffices to nudge development in a preferred way. In the words of the *Daodejing*, such people reside in non-action: "Comprehending all within the four directions, can you reside in non-action?" (DDJ 10). Like this sage, the martial master is blank and uncommitted, "still and inactive, revealing no sign" (DDJ 20).

Let me mention a few more lines referring to non-action, to confirm how thematic the idea is in this work:

Those of highest virtue practice non-action. (DDJ 38)

Sages . . . perfect through non-action. (DDJ 47)

Gaining the world is accomplished by following no activity (*wushi*). As soon as one actively tries, one will fall short of gaining the world. (DDJ 48)

Act, but through non-action (*wei wuwei*). (DDJ 63)

"Non-action" translates *wuwei*, which literally means "no action" or "not doing." In philosophical contexts, though, it describes action that does so little so easily as to *seem* (for example, to an opponent) to be nothing at all. To have this quality, action must flow spontaneously, without deliberation, calculation, or indecision.[49]

Wuwei is not simple non-activity. It is knowing how to do without help, artfully refraining from action, art appearing artless. The action is effortless—not merely efficient—in that it produces its effect by means of an inconspicuous expenditure artfully chosen to maximize the difference between effectiveness and intervention, with "doing nothing" and "nothing left undone" the ideal limiting case. *Wuwei* is an intensive quality, the intensity of an event, and always a matter of degree. Such action is intentional in that it is an optimal response to a situation, leaving nothing to complain of, no requisite unmet. That does not happen accidentally and confirms the inaction as intentional, indeed artful, even sagacious. The idea is not that *nothing* be done (an always virtual limiting case) but that nothing *seem to be* done, which is relative to perspective and not always easy, even though art can make it look that way. *Wuwei* effectiveness always has its *wei*, its doing; invisibility or emptiness is relative to the other's knowledge.

The *Daodejing* makes a connection between *wuwei* effectiveness and the condition it calls *xü*, tenuous or empty, probably following the *Sunzi* chapter "Xü shi" (Empty and Full). The oldest meaning of *xü* is "a big hill" and, by extension, anything vast and expansive, which connotes a kind of emptiness. It is the emptiness of the sky, clouds, steam, a virtual vapor that can coagulate into many forms, an emptiness that is not *non-being* but non-formed, uncommitted, not full, or fully present, instead chaotic, stirring with tendency. All the images of *wuwei* in this work are figures of efficacious emptiness, like the potent void at the center of a wheel, the hollow of a jar, or the space between walls. *Wuwei* effectiveness requires that we cultivate this emptiness, empty ourselves of desire, forget about words. Then the response to circumstances can be spontaneous, natural, so of itself (*ziran*), and, in that sense, *wuwei*. The art of the *dao* is one of exquisite minima, doing the most with the least: "Looked for but not seen, its name is 'minute.' Listened for but not heard, its name is 'rarified.' Grabbed for but not gotten, its name is 'subtle'" (DDJ 14).[50]

The expression *wuwei* is less common in the *Zhuangzi* than in the *Daodejing*, though it does occur with the sense of effortless effectiveness; for example, in chapter 6: "*Dao* has feeling and is trustworthy, effortlessly effective (*wuwei*) without leaving traces behind" (G 86, modified). The commentary tradition does not hesitate to read this idea into the work; for instance, in the classical commentary by Guo Xiang: "Even if you are responding to ten thousand situations, you will be as if vanishing into them, unaware of any affairs requiring effort." For a later commentator, "The great functional effectiveness of non-deliberate action—the whole meaning of the entire book [*Zhuangzi*] is contained in this one phrase."[51]

Effortless effectiveness also is attractive to theorists of the Asian martial arts. In the words of a taiji classic, "Being able to attract to emptiness, you can use four ounces to deflect a thousand pounds." The Korean hapkido that I train in is epitomized in three principles: harmony (Chinese: *he*, Korean: *hwa*), circularity (*yuan*, *won*), and flow (*yuan, yu*). The difficult art of *hwa* harmony teaches calm in the face of immanent violence, composure rooted in knowing there is no force of assault that cannot be neutralized. The key is to avoid a clash, never to meet incoming force with comparable directness. The most effective response neutralizes violence by harmonizing with its energy. One becomes "empty" in the sense that one's body offers no obstacle to the force launched against it, and one's response seems effortless because it requires no energy beyond what is supplied by the opponent.[52]

4. "The Way of the sage is to act but not contend" (DDJ 81). "Because they do not contend, no one in the world can contend with them" (DDJ 22). These passages on the virtue of non-contention (*bu zheng*) recall the Chinese art of war. In war, the best general wins without combat (*bu zhan*). In the martial arts, the best fighter never has a fight. Not because he is a Leviathan, unendurably more violent than all others. He simply cannot be engaged. You cannot hit him, cannot hold him, cannot stop him with violence, so it never comes to a fight. Describing his performing taiji pushing hands with Zheng Manqing, Robert W. Smith said that trying to hold him was like trying to hold water. Imagine trying to grab a handful of water. How can you fight water? The so-called internal martial arts resonate with this ethos of non-contention: "By learning the skill," Smith observes "there is no need to use it." To avoid contention without sacrifice, especially without submitting to another's violence, is a more artful and ethically nuanced accomplishment than either pacifism or competition.[53]

5. Discerning the minute and subtle. "To really see the little things is called enlightenment" (DDJ 52). To really see the little things is to see the big things they betoken and to see them well before they become obvious. Such seeing penetrates to the virtual depth of the world, to the subtle incipience, the smallest beginnings of change. The proof of such insight is the effectiveness of the action it enhances. In the Chinese martial arts tradition, this kind of sagacious penetration is called "interpreting energy" (*dong jing*). "The ability to measure the opponent is impossible without being able to interpret energy":

> If you are unable to interpret energy, how can you understand the opponent's incoming energy and thus use your own energy to draw

it in? This marvel must be grasped intuitively and cannot be explained in words. Only when it is known in the mind can the body know it; but knowing with the body is superior to knowing with the mind.[54]

I understand interpreting energy as interpreting becoming, interpreting incipience, perceiving what is tending and virtual in another's body, apprehending what is becoming before there is a being, an actuality, or an act. Interpreting energy is the experimental dimension of taiji practice. The "Yang Family Forty Chapters" explains it as a way to "extend our knowledge and investigate the world." Referring to taiji pushing hands, the author says, "If you want to gain the ability to break and reconnect, you must be able to observe the hidden and disclose the subtle." This idea of sage-knowledge, apprehending what is merely tending and not yet actual, recurs in a seventeenth-century samurai work I mentioned earlier, Munenori's *Family Traditions on the Art of War*. The author enjoins the swordsman to "strike when the mind is presented in the [opponent's] hands but has not yet moved." Becoming good at perceiving that tenuous incipience is half the art, the first half. The samurai author calls such perception "the first sword": "[The expression] 'the first sword' is a code word for seeing incipient movement on the part of opponents . . . seeing what opponents are trying to do is the first sword in the ultimate sense."[55]

To use this sword well is to achieve what the author calls the vanguard of the moment. "The vanguard of the moment is before the opponent has begun to make a move. . . . To accurately see an opponent's energy, feeling, and mood, and to act accordingly in their presence, is called the vanguard of the moment." To apprehend the incipient attack before the aggressor actually moves has been called "the ultimate goal of martial arts training." It is difficult to learn and has risks that go beyond losing a fight. When the first sword's preemptive initiative destroys an attack before it is fully in play, it may look to witnesses like a first strike, despite its being a defensive movement. Try explaining that to the police.[56]

6. Hard and soft. "The supple and weak overcome the hard and the strong" (DDJ 36). "What is brittle is easy to shatter" (DDJ 64). "The stiff and strong are the disciples of death; the supple and weak are the disciples of life. That is why a weapon that is too strong will

not prove victorious; a tree that is too strong will break" (DDJ 76). As we saw with judo founder Kanō Jigorō, Asian martial arts practitioners tend to like these passages, in which they see a principle of their art. What makes the soft both soft and effective is emptiness and disciplined non-action: "The most supple things in the world ride roughshod over the most rigid. That which is empty can enter in, even where there is no space. That is how I know the advantages of non-action!" (DDJ 43). The efficacy of non-action is the paradoxical efficacy of emptiness, water being the best example. Water is empty of form, its form depending on what contains it. It benefits without contention, overcomes by softness, is infinitely flexible, and effortlessly accommodates any obstacle. It seems weak, soft, and yielding, yet no one can confront it. Try to confront it and it changes course, moves elsewhere, never stops flowing. "In all the world, nothing is more supple and weak than water; yet nothing can surpass it for attacking what is stiff and strong" (DDJ 78).

This theme of hard and soft is the precursor of the distinction between "internal" and "external" martial arts. The distinction was not documented until the Qing dynasty in the seventeenth century, which is very late compared with the time of classical Daoism some two thousand years earlier. Mediating events so removed in time is the history of what eventually became known as "Inner Alchemy." The story of this alchemy begins when practitioners of the proto-Daoist inner cultivation techniques (such as *daoyin*) crossed paths with the *fangshi*, or masters of formulas, shamanistic magicians and concocters of elixirs of immortality. Ancient rulers patronized these *fangshi*, who became prominent in the courts of the First Emperor and the Han emperor Wudi. It was under their protection, and sometimes under their very eyes, that the earliest Chinese alchemy was practiced.[57]

A hybrid scion of mingling between *fangshi* alchemy and Daoist inner cultivation is the movement known as *taiqing dao*, the Way of Great Clarity, beginning in the second century C.E. This religious community established the first ritual procedures for what is called external alchemy (*waidan*). Ge Hong, author of the *Baopuzi* (*The Master Who Embraces Simplicity*), was a well-known member of this movement. Alchemy is the search for an elixir of immortality. The goal is to formulate a body within the body (*shen wai shen*), an immortal embryo (*xiantai*) less susceptible to corruption than the body we are born with. Among the various ideas about how to do that are methods that involve ingesting laboratory concoctions—the *waidan* of the Way of Great Clarity—and methods of inner cultivation, which teach that everything we need to concoct the pill of immortality is already inside the body. We need only cultivate the body according to a regimen that these adepts work out in detail. This is "inner" alchemy (*neidan*).

These two approaches are not coeval, owing to the interval of some five hundred years between the first external alchemy and the internal practices, which began in the Tang dynasty (618–906). Internal authors describe the alchemical process as happening entirely within the body, with no dependence on minerals or metals, instruments, or fire. All the while they use the terminology, imagery, and symbolism of the "external" textual tradition. Our bodies are composed of diverse elements and are swept up in multiple currents of *qi*—celestial and terrestrial, the vital *qi* of birth and the local environment. The internal aim is to concentrate these flows through inner smelting and fusion into a single unified entity capable of transcending the death of the natural body. At first it seems that the internal practitioners felt theirs was the superior method. Everything can be done through the internal cultivation of the body. But as the alchemical tradition develops, so does the awareness that these two ways of working on the self are better combined. A writer on alchemy in the twelfth century observed that "the internal and the external cannot be separated even for one instant; if they are separated, that is not the *dao*." By the Song dynasty (960–1279), Daoist alchemy had become a synthesis of medical knowledge concerning natural materials, especially metals and gems; internal meditation and especially visualization; and ancient practices of breathing and stretching, such as the *daoyin*.[58]

This synthetic approach to internal and external makes sense in terms of the Daoist teaching on yin-yang. Everything it says about yin and yang concerns their interaction. Any yin is a bit yang, and vice versa for that bit of yang and for its bit of yin and so on ad infinitum. Any yin is the true yin of the esoteric adept only if it is also somewhat yang. Only then is it still energized by opposition, still chaotic and empty, not finished and full. Identity, such as it is, reifies this interminable yin-yang oscillation. No so-called thing is perfectly consistent, identical to itself. Every "thing" contains its opposite. The only way to conceive such a thing is as a process. There is no principle of contradiction for time or becoming and, consequently, neither for the *dao*. Becoming is a duration, and any duration embraces what is present and what is past, that is, not present. There is no duration too brief to divide into a present and its past. What common sense regards as a thing, an entity, the bearer of a name is a conventional freeze-frame imposed on such becoming, primarily by the artifice of language.

Alchemy has to undo as much of that rigidity as possible, endeavoring to concoct a small body (a pill) of matter such as it was in the epoch before the ten thousand things. The achievement requires both an external work and an internal work, carefully integrated, as this fourteenth-century Daoist alchemist explained: "One should begin with action, which is related to existence (*you*), and with life force; only then can one give way to non-action, which pertains to the non-being (*wu*) that is true existence (*zhenyou*)." The second part of the work is interior. This is the slow heating, when the adept nourishes and hatches the embryo: "At the external stage, one obtains only earthly immortality; at the internal stage, one reaches celestial immortality." What this author calls the alchemical path or *dao* of non-action allows the practitioner to join his breath to the cosmic breath, to make his heels a conduit for terrestrial *qi*, and become an immortal bird-man.[59]

The Ming dynasty saw a move to synthesize, simplify, and popularize inner alchemy, including the publication of once closely guarded texts. Esoteric language was either defined and explained or discarded, and inner alchemy became accessible, intelligible, and widely disseminated. It was at this time and in this form that the Chinese martial arts encountered Daoist inner alchemy. The first proof of the encounter is our beginning to hear of internal and external martial arts, newly invented analogues for internal and external alchemy. When some martial masters reconfigured their practice as inner alchemy, they felt obliged to discover an "external" within their own tradition. Hence the appeal in martial arts writing of dichotomies like Northern and Southern, Shaolin and Wudan, Buddhist and Daoist, and hard and soft styles. These are avatars of the alchemical external and internal, a difference that the Chinese martial arts interpret in terms of the *Daodejing* teaching on the hard and the soft adapted to their corporeal art.

Modern martial arts writers usually say that external styles are hard and are learned by fighters for fighting, without concern for self-cultivation, which is what the internal martial arts are all about. The explanation retroactively rationalizes less tidy history. Paradigmatically internal martial arts systems like bagua and xingyi were the arts of choice for men working in traditional China's private security services. "The problem with the internal versus external scheme," a pair of Taiwan-based scholars point out, "is that it is a false dichotomy. Xingyi practitioners do a lot of push-ups and sit-ups, both of which are external strength exercises. In a similar vein, Hung Gar—ostensibly an external system—has an entire set, the Iron Wire set, devoted to internal development." In reality, they conclude, "any complete Chinese martial arts system has both internal and external elements," as it was for Daoist alchemy in the form in which the martial arts encountered it.[60]

Consider what is probably the best known of the internal martial arts, taiji. We have a record of how the innovators of this art understood their quest for softness. The uniqueness of taiji among martial arts lies in the belief that long practice in softness ultimately produces internal hardness. Taiji is soft, yes, but the softest soft is always a bit hard, always on the verge of hard, becoming hard without ever being hard, at least not until the other resists. The "Yang Family Forty Chapters," a taiji classic, offers the following explanation of internal and external in terms of hard and soft:

> If we are externally soft, after a long time we will naturally develop internal hardness. It is not that we consciously cultivate hardness, for in reality our mind is on softness. What is difficult is to remain internally reserved, to possess hardness [virtually] without expressing it, always externally meeting the opponent with softness. Meeting hardness with softness causes the opponent's hardness to be transformed and disappear into nothingness. . . . The external becomes concentrated in the internal, and the internal expresses itself externally. In this way we develop within and without, the fine and the gross, and with penetrating understanding, we realize the work of wise men and sages.[61]

The Qing-dynasty internal master Chang Naizhou enjoined practitioners to "be hard with softness, and then the *qi* will accumulate but with no negative effects" and to "be soft with hardness, and then the *qi* will scatter but with no negative effects." Otherwise, he explained, "you will not achieve the marvel of the complementary interaction of hardness and softness." "Be soft passing energy; hard dropping to a point. Each must mutually complement, and thus never lose sequence." This take on hard and soft in martial arts is a variation on the art-of-war teaching about orthodox and unorthodox tactics. As with internal and external, the art is to know how to play these off each other and achieve sublime effects with minimal exposure. That is what the alchemist author called the way of non-action. In the fourteenth-century *Romance of the Three Kingdoms*, this strategic concept is attributed to the Han-dynasty warlord Cao Cao: "Always, if you wish to be a general, let hard and soft mutually complement. You may not simply rely on your courage. If you simply rely on courage, then you are one fellow's match."[62]

We first hear of internal and external martial arts when the martial arts and Daoism began to draw together and martial arts authors started using alchemical terms to elucidate their practice. This rapport between Daoism and martial arts did not occur until much later than martial arts legend says it did. Although the "Yang Family Forty Chapters" uses a Daoist language of internal and external, it does not actually claim to describe a Daoist ritual practice. The earliest self-conscious attempt to connect a martial art with Daoist teaching and practice is found in a "postscript" added to the "Yang Family Forty Chapters" in the mid-nineteenth century. The postscript's author presents the martial arts as a practice for realizing the *dao*. He places the martial arts in the service of martial (*wu*) rather than literati (*wen*) methods to harmonize the body, regulate the *qi*, and produce the golden elixir of Daoism's inner alchemy. He explains that the practice of taiji is "based on the sinking of the *qi* and the *dantian* and moving solely with the spirit; it has nothing to do with native physical strength. Getting the best of an opponent seems to be effortless. Although allowing one to demonstrate great skill, it also contains the highest philosophical principles." In particular, this author says, "the emphasis on 'concentrating the *qi* and developing softness' in this art corresponds to the teaching of the Daoists."[63]

This association of Daoism and Chinese martial arts is new in the mid-nineteenth century. The interval exposes the fiction of an ancient relationship between these quintessential Chinese traditions, which is confirmed by the *Baopuzi*, a classic of external alchemy. The *Baopuzi* is divided into Outer and Internal Chapters. The Outer Chapters discuss success and failure in affairs from a Confucian perspective. We learn that the author, Ge Hong, was a martial arts practitioner, as he described in some detail. The entire discussion, however, is an appendix to the Outer Chapters and is not part of the Internal (Daoist and alchemical) work. Although we have Ge Hong's record of training in the martial arts, he inadvertently makes clear that he did not connect what he was practicing with any influence of Daoism on him.[64]

Daoist alchemy and Chinese martial arts were practiced for a thousand years before anyone thought of bringing them together. One of Daoism's strong points is incorporating practices that were not originally part of its tradition. That is what happened with *daoyin* and *yangsheng* (nourishing life) practices, *fengshui* geomancy, and Chinese medicine, which became established dimensions of Daoist practice only in the Tang dynasty. Most of the health and longevity practices are not "Daoist" in origin but were subsequently made part of Daoist training regimens. Likewise, *waidan*, "external" alchemy, also did not become a Daoist practice until some three centuries after its inception. We might expect that the same thing happened to the martial arts, and to an extent it did. But perhaps more surprising than the relatively late date of their association is that the impetus to remodel martial arts as "Daoist" practice did not come from the Daoists. Instead, the modern connection between Daoism and martial arts turns out to be a Confucian construction, undertaken for reasons remote from the Daoist's lofty aspiration to immortality.[65]

CONFUCIANISM AND THE MARTIAL ARTS

Scholars who try to lift the veil of myth over the history of the Chinese martial arts have found their origin in the military. Martial arts, including archery, sword, and many of the empty-hand techniques still practiced, were widely studied by all ranks and elements of ancient society. This is not surprising, as these arts were fundamental to the function and identity of China's ruling class starting with the Zhou dynasty, if not earlier. The martial arts would have been ordinary skills for Shang- and Zhou-dynasty aristocrats, and it seems likely that their association with nobility would affect later generations' attitude toward these arts. What is apparently the earliest term to describe bare-hand combat is *shoubo*—*shou*, "hand," and *bo*, "strike or seize." The expression used in this way is found from the Spring and Autumn period (722–479 B.C.E.) until the Song dynasty, when it was displaced by *quan*, the still usual term for "boxing." A Han bibliography from the first century C.E. classifies works on *shoubo* (none survive) under military writings, distinguishing them from wrestling (*jueli*) and defining them as skills or techniques to train the hands and feet and to facilitate the learning of weapons.[66]

The military had long been a presence in China's culture. From the Han dynasty, able-bodied men aged twenty-three to fifty-six owed two years of military service, one year in training and one year posted. Commoners were constantly cycling through the military, training, retraining, and returning to their villages. No information survives about the training that the recruits received, but it seems plausible to suppose it included something like techniques we know as the Chinese martial arts. We can imagine that discharged soldiers and retired officers brought these arts home from military service, where they may have been subject to generations of development at the family or village level. That would liberate martial art practice from the imperative of battle, leaving practitioners free to explore virtualities, discover virtuosities, and take the step from an ensemble of techniques toward an ethical technology for self-cultivation.[67]

No currently practiced style of the Chinese martial arts has a lineage claim to these ancient origins; rather, over a long evolution, systems morphed into systems, with new selections pruning and perfecting a constantly growing inventory of techniques. It is the techniques that are ancient in the Chinese martial arts, not the styles or systems. These techniques, transmitted to the civilian population by imperial officers and discharged soldiers, became what one scholar called "the source of all the postures, gestures, and implements associated with the martial in every imaginable mode of representation in Chinese culture."[68]

The idea that the practice of martial arts can be a method of ethical self-cultivation seems to go back to Warring States times. For example, according to the Confucian *Record of Rites* (*Liji*): "Archery is the best way to practice rites and music to their perfection, and can be frequently performed so as to cultivate one's moral character. That is why all the sage kings went in for it." The Confucian *Analects* says that a young man should be filial at home, respectful of elders in public, conscientious, trustworthy, and especially affectionate toward the good. If he has strength left after seeing to all that, then "let him devote it to learning the cultural arts (*wen*)" (A 1.6). The reference is to the so-called Six Arts: ritual, music, archery, charioteering, calligraphy, and mathematics. The commentaries agree that these arts are branches of a tree whose root is virtuous character, so a person would have no reason to practice them apart from a contribution to ethical self-cultivation and virtue.[69]

The *Analects* has Confucius say, "Set your will upon the *dao*, rely upon virtue, lean upon goodness, and explore widely in your cultivation of the arts" (A 7.6). Some commentators read this series as ranked, placing the practice of arts last and least. This reading is perhaps optional. The great Ming-dynasty Confucian teacher Wang Yangming had this comment on the text: "If you set your will upon the *dao*, then you will become a scholar of the *dao* and virtue, whereas if you set your will upon the cultural arts, you will become merely a technically skilled aesthete." It would, of course, be a blunder to *set your will* on the arts. The will should be set on the *dao*, which, for Confucians, means *ren* (benevolence or humanity). Yet that determination does not discredit the arts so much as show where their value lies, which, for Wang, is their contribution to a person's effort to be a sage. This use of cultural arts goes back a long way, for instance, to the Discourse on Archery in the *Record of Rites*:

Archery implies in it the principles of humanity. For to prepare oneself for arrow-shooting, one is required to be quiet in mind and upright in posture before one can let the arrow go. When he fails in hitting the target, he cannot blame or resent those who have succeeded; he has to make introspections.[70]

As the fundamental battlefield skill, archery, was China's premier martial art. An association with aristocratic accomplishment and ethical self-cultivation gave it a luster that the otherwise grisly association with war might exclude. As one of the Six Arts, archery has its own component Five Excellences, of which skill in hitting the target is but one, along with lack of contentiousness, correct ritual deportment, singing, and dancing. The incongruous (to us) reference to song and dance probably alludes to the military's practice of martial dancing. A Han-dynasty dictionary explains: "Martiality (*wu*) means 'to dance' (*wu*); the movements of an assault are like the drumming out of a dance." That is not merely a learned pun. China's military has an ancient tradition of weapons dancing, with swords, bows, and other arms. Training forms, presumably repeated en masse with an instructor, were at some point reconfigured for a dance that could be performed as an aesthetic spectacle. According to a historian of China's military, these dances "were the earliest displays of martial skills that did not serve a competitive purpose, but rather an aesthetic and spiritual one." With prescribed forms and lineages of practice, these dances "were not just physical training but also emotional, mental, and spiritual training as well." These qualities, which return in the Chinese martial arts as we know them, were active from an early time and have persisted in various forms down to the present.[71]

The Chinese discovered that unarmed combat techniques like those of contemporary Asian martial arts were good for more than merely preparing men for weapons and war. They recognized boxing as a developmental rather than fundamental combat skill. The oldest known martial arts training manual is the *New Book on Effective Military Techniques* (1584), by the Ming-dynasty general Qi Jiguang, who wrote, "Unarmed combat would not seem to be a preparation for war, but the study of unarmed combat makes your body used to action, so in fact it is the basis for all further training." It may be that, as the military historian Peter Lorge believes, "the long Confucian tradition of self-cultivation through archery practice points to a deep acceptance of the spiritual and intellectual power of the physical practice of martial arts." However, Confucians had ideas about these arts that would dismay those more deeply involved than literati want to be in fighting and violence. Confucians separate the intelligence that aims the arrow from the force that pierces the target (A 3.16). Archery holds up to the self a mirror that does not flatter. Only this sublimated archery contributes to Confucian self-cultivation, not the barbaric power of one who can penetrate seven shields shooting from horseback. For Lorge, the Confucians were not repudiating martial arts but wanted to put them in their proper place. They were aware of the use of these arts for self-cultivation, yet they also needed to discredit violence and maintain the superior value of virtue and goodness over strategy or other military arts.[72]

The few references to military themes in the *Analects* substantiate this conclusion. Confucius expresses admiration for the man who said, "Yi was a skillful archer, and Ao was a powerful naval commander, and yet neither of them met a natural death" (A 14.5). On one occasion, the Master and some disciples were surrounded by murderous thugs and held captive, awaiting orders to kill them. Zilu, one of the oldest disciples and a former soldier, wanted to fight. But Confucius said that it would be better to sing and took out his *qin*-zither. So intense was the music that the captors, realizing he was a sage, fell to the ground in submission and allowed him to depart. Apocryphal as it must be, the story illustrates the Confucian order of values: goodness is a greater power than violence.[73]

The *Analects* recounts a visit by Confucius to the duke of Wei, who asked the sage about military formations. "Confucius replied, 'I know something about the arrangement of ceremonial stands and dishes for ritual offerings, but I have never learned about arrangements of battalions and divisions.' He left the next day" (A 15.1). The duke should have known that Confucians disdain what the military has to do to be successful. For Mencius, the second sage of classical Confucianism, "those who are good at war deserve the greatest punishment." He allowed that there was something to their art of strategy, agreeing with Sunzi that "heavenly omens are not as good as advantages of terrain," an allusion

THE *DAO* OF ASIAN MARTIAL ARTS

to the signature art-of-war theme of strategic position (*shi*). But these strategic advantages and knowing how to manipulate them "are not as good as harmony with the people." An art of war is superfluous. "If the ruler of a state is fond of benevolence, he will have no enemies in the world."[74]

That is also the argument in a chapter of the *Xunzi,* another great source of classical Confucianism, which stages a debate between Master Xun and Lord Linwu, an art-of-war strategist. Linwu's first point was to praise the advantage of strategic position. Xunzi replied that the best rule in war is the same as in kingship, namely, humanity and righteousness. Strategic advantage is a by-product of benevolent government. Only when the king is virtuous and the officials sincere will a favorable strategic disposition enable rulers to overcome their enemies. A righteous king is more powerful than any army. The *Record of Rites* states, "The army has ritual propriety (*li*), therefore it accomplishes military merit," while the *Zuo Commentary* says, "Having ritual propriety there will be no defeat."[75]

The mistake of the military philosophy is to think that virtue is superfluous to command, as if knowledge of strategy were enough. These Confucians do not scorn the military altogether but insist on military subordination to scholarly-official *wen* culture. *Wen zhi wu gong,* as a later motto has it: "Use the military to *get* something, use culture to *keep* it." Confucian thought tends to assume that warfare is inevitable, having existed since the beginning of civilization, and that no ruler can renounce it. War is justified as the ultimate punishment through which a ruler suppresses large-scale deviance or criminality, ensuring the peace of the people and the order of the world. As Dong Zhongshu, the leading Confucian of the early Han, put it, "War is not as good as no war, but there are also good wars. There is justice in injustice and injustice in justice."[76]

Confucian thought does not ignore violence and even tries to make it conform to ritual civility. The *Record of Rites* records Confucius as saying, "There are rules of propriety even in killing people." We find some of them in the *Zuo Commentary* on the *Spring and Autumn Annals,* in a veritable "just war" (*yi bing*) theory, parallel to the European version. The *Commentary* articulates a number of conditions under which a gentlemen may or must sanction war:

- Proper aim; for example, justified retribution or revenge. In an ideal world (*taiping*), the Son of Heaven would see to punishments. Until that day, we have the principle of *da fuchou*, glorifying revenge. Gross injustice should not be left unrectified.
- Proper agent. It is right (*yi*) to launch war to stop or punish injustice, but only provided there is no duly constituted higher authority. Not just anyone has the right to intervene, but if there is no one else to do it, then anyone has the right.
- Proper provocation. The fight must be defensive. A gentleman waits for the other's violence.
- Proper declaration. No surprise attacks, though preemptive attack is justified against barbarians, according to the principle of *yuyu*, advance defense.
- Proper timing, not strategic but ceremonial; for example, there should be no war when the enemy is in mourning.
- Proper location, far from settlements, to minimize civilian casualties.
- Proper weapons. Incendiaries should not be used because they are too difficult to control, leading to the indiscriminate killing of noncombatants.
- Proper violence. The point of war is to defeat the enemy, not to destroy it.
- Proper humanity. War does not cancel the obligation of benevolence. The best reason to go to war is in defense of humanity (*ren*). The worst reason is self-interest.[77]

We see the effort to subordinate force to righteousness. Force has no principle of its own. On its own, force is thuggish and contemptible. The same ethical determination appears in the Confucian teaching on courage, the battlefield virtue par excellence. Although courage—whether Greek (*andreia*) or Chinese (*yong*)—is a good thing, a virtue, philosophers both East and West remind their readers that courage is not mere fearlessness, which can be rash and counterproductive.

Confucian thought relocates courage in righteousness, a field in which scholar-officials make a better showing.

The *Analects* discusses courage in several places. The gist of these passages is to reconfigure courage from *wu*, "the military," to *wen*, "the civilian administration." Courage is distinguished from rashness (A 7.11) and is pronounced as consistent with trepidation, perhaps even fear (as Aristotle also thought). Courage is not fearlessness; it is self-control under conditions of fear. The paragon of Confucian courage is not the brave warrior; it is a good man trying to do the right thing despite opposition. "To see what is right but fail to do it is to be lacking in courage" (A 2.24). The disciple Zilu asks the Master, "Does the gentleman admire courage?" Confucius replies, "The gentleman admires rightness above all. A gentleman who possessed courage but lacked a sense of rightness would create political disorder, while a common person who possessed courage but lacked a sense of rightness would become a bandit" (A 17.23). Mencius reiterates the message that the highest courage is not martial. His models are people who are steadfast and undaunted in pursuit of an ethical or political goal. True courage is the virtue of those who master an unmoved heart.[78]

An assessment of the Confucian perspective on the martial arts has to negotiate the distinction in Chinese between *wen*, "civilian administration," and *wu*, "military." It would be a mistake to take the almost puritanical form that the distinction assumes in Song-dynasty Neo-Confucianism for the historical norm. From remotest antiquity to Han times, aristocratic education included both literary and martial arts. Until the Tang dynasty, these traditions borrowed from each other, despite official disdain. Scholar-officials recoiled from acknowledging the place of military force in the empire. They never permitted the emperor to be depicted with a sword, even though many emperors had been warriors, continued to lead the army as emperor, and even wore swords at court.[79]

The literati seem to have tried to isolate the martial from the force of violence and discipline it by means of civil *wen* culture. Confucians reconfigured courage as doing what one knows is right despite the risk, and they reimagined the martial man as at heart an agent of culture. Without it, he is little more than a beast. A series of passages in a long-lost manuscript unearthed in 1972 offer a good example of this effort.

> To nourish life in accord with the propagating of Heaven is called *wen*. To attack and cause things to die in accord with the killing of Heaven is called *wu*. When culture and martiality are used together, then all under Heaven will obey.

> For movement and quietude to accord with Heaven and Earth is called *wen*. For killing . . . when the season is proper is called *wu*.

> To follow the seasons of Heaven and attack what Heaven would destroy is called *wu*.

The martial is defined not by its violence but by its righteousness. Not just any killing is *wu*, only righteous killing, when it is really Heaven killing through the agency of the righteous warrior. According to the *Zuo Zhuan Commentary* on the *Spring and Autumn Annals*, "Martial activities are those that prohibit violence, end hostilities, protect the greater stability, pacify the people, harmonize the masses, and enable abundance and prosperity." The martial is not just the force of violence but is that force under the command of culture, fighting for culture.[80]

This tendency to diminish the military appears to have peaked with the Song dynasty. Earlier Tang literati could still practice martial arts, especially archery, without compromising their Confucian identity, but Song literati fundamentally rejected the practice of martial arts, archery included, as antithetical to their stature as men of *wen* culture. They redacted the historical record to confirm the bias, creating an elite perception of their civilization as inconsistent with martial values. Power flows from virtue, as Confucius and Mencius maintained, not, as Mao Zedong would have it, from the barrel of a gun. The more the literati attributed to psychology and cunning strategy, the less they had to credit the grisly war machine that kept them in office.[81]

Things seemed to change with the Ming dynasty, or to return as they were before Song scholars put their seal on a dichotomy of *wen* and *wu*. Martial values seeped deeply into the Ming dynasty's civil *wen* culture after China's first experience of foreign conquest (the Mongolian Yuan dynasty, 1260–1368). The blurring of formerly sharp lines—such as between a general and a scholar or between the preparation for military command and the preparation for administrative office—acknowledges the value of military force to the preservation of civilization. Military men began to participate in activities associated with the educated elite of the civil examination system, like scholarship, poetry, painting, calligraphy, and collecting antiquities. High-ranking scholar-officials began to participate in activities characteristic of men from the hereditary military families, like archery and swordsmanship, and to study the military classics. Sword collecting and, it seems, even unarmed martial arts practice became new literati leisure activities in the Ming dynasty, when it became possible for scholars to signify honorable temperament and admirable erudition by fencing with the archaic double-edged sword.[82]

Tan Lun, a minister of war in the Ming dynasty, observed, "To have *wen* and not be *wu* is to be a scholar behind the times / To have *wu* and not *wen* is to be an ignorant man." He inscribed the lines on a sword, a gift to a friend. Swords, especially the double-edged *jian,* which by that time was no longer used in the military, were linked to a lost esoteric knowledge of the sword in antiquity. Such swords came to be regarded as appropriate objects for a scholar's study, penetrating the quintessential *wen* space. What these scholars imagined in that lost lore of the sword was just what China needed. "It is only a pity that the art of the sword has not been handed down," wrote a late-Ming scholar. The loss prevented "a myriad generation of those people who are patriotic and loyal, who have a reputation of preserving filial piety and righteousness, and who graciously repay kindness" from realizing "their true aspirations. . . . As for the ingeniousness and awesome nature of the art of the sword, how can one let historians unfeelingly neglect it?"[83]

The tendency for a dichotomy between *wen* and *wu* to lose consistency continued unabated in the succeeding Qing dynasty, which arose in the second experience of foreign conquest. Mobility between civilian and military offices had never been more fluid. The Qing-dynasty's Kangxi emperor had military questions added to the civil examinations, in what one scholar described as an experiment in creating Confucian generals. He also added questions on the Confucian classics to the military examinations, which previously had been limited to tests of martial capability. The hope was that *wugong*, or military achievement, and *wende*, scholarly virtue, would perfect each other to the advantage of imperial power. This sublime synthesis of force and virtue was also the promise of the spiritualization of martial arts practice, presaged at Shaolin Temple and consolidated for elite secular culture in the unsettled time of the Ming-Qing transition, when Manchu invaders conquered China's last endogenous dynasty.[84]

Shaolin was certainly not the birthplace of Chinese martial arts. But what happened to the martial arts there marked a notable transformation of these arts' potential for self-cultivation. The ethical formation that became the hallmark of these arts evolves from the Tang and Ming dynasties and especially the unsettled time of the Ming-Qing dynastic transition, when politically motivated scholars sought signifiers of Sinitic identity. Scholarly interest in China's martial arts began in the seventeenth century as an expression of loyalty to the extinguished Ming dynasty. Literacy in China had never been greater. Its growth outpaced the expansion of the imperial administration, creating a new literate class without the chance of an official post. The popularity of private study surged, creating a market for new books in all genres, including commentaries on the military classics and the appearance of martial arts manuals. Scholars began to use literary and historical erudition to legitimize these arts and the elite's interest in them. Learned appraisals of the martial arts' authenticity and effectiveness, and criticism of theatrical but combatively vacuous "flowery boxing" (*hua quan*), expressed the new connoisseurship. Different lineages of martial arts knowledge began to appear in writing, and local traditions long left oral became part of a national martial arts history.[85]

Scholarly imagination invented the idea of a lost art of the sword— a trenchant martial art combined with Confucian virtue and dedication to the Chinese people. These same literati enthusiastically consumed encyclopedias of sword lore and published tales of the *xiashi,* or freelance martial artists, in China's enormously popular *wuxia* literature. The name combines the word for "military," *wu,* and *xia,* "chivalrous spirit." For example, *xia yi* means to protect the weak, oppose injustice, and make sacrifices for loyalty and friendship. The stock plot of these demotic tales involves a hero seeking vengeance or called upon to save a damsel or a village. To prevail he may have to undergo secret martial arts training, or have a secret technique revealed to him by a hidden master, or find some storied weapon like a magic sword. The tales are usually set in the *jianghu*, rivers-and-lakes, a name for the Chinese underworld, populated by kind-hearted outlaws, rogue monks, gangsters, gamblers, and impoverished scholars, as well as ghosts, demons, and fox fairies. Characters are often identified by their martial arts style or special weapons.

Hong Kong's martial arts films made *wuxia* lore international, to the point that much of what the average practitioner, Asian or Westerner, thinks that he or she knows about Chinese martial arts comes from these movies. The quintessential *wuxia* hero of that martial arts cinema is Wong Feihung, modeled on a reputed champion of Confucian virtue who enjoyed an early-twentieth-century reputation as a dazzling martial artist, healer, protector of the underdog against landlords and criminals, and conservative guardian of Confucian morality. After Wong Feihung died, newspapers began serializing novels depicting his exploits. Then, starting in 1949, Cantonese cinema devoted more than seventy films to his character, making him the most enduring legend in Hong Kong's film history.[86]

An early *wuxia* tale appears in the *Spring and Autumn Annals of the Kingdoms of Wu and Yue* (Eastern Han, 25–220), in a passage known as the "Yue Maiden Tale." Gou Jian, king of Yue (495–465 B.C.E.), was warring against the neighboring king of Wu. An adviser told the king about a young woman of incomparable sword technique, urging him to secure her to train his troops. She was duly summoned. En route traveling on a lonely road, she met an old man who had heard of her skill and asked for a demonstration. She offered to let him test her. He picked up a bamboo staff and tried three times to strike her. When he gave up, she plucked the bamboo from his hands with her own sword and struck him, whereupon he turned into a white ape and escaped up a tree. Eventually she arrived at court. The king asked her two questions. First, where did she get her skill with the sword? Her answer: "This little girl was born deep in the mountains and dense forest, and grew up in the unpopulated wilds without a place to study or practice, and I had no association with the nobility. I did not learn from others, but practiced alone and suddenly it came to me." The king then asked whether her sword technique was based on a theory. She replied that it was and offered this explanation:

> The theory is very subtle yet easy to understand. Its true significance is hidden and deep. The theory includes both large [double/offensive] and small [single/defensive] doors, and yin [passive/yielding] and yang [active/ attacking] aspects. Open a large door and close the small one [move from defense to offense], passivity recedes and activity rises. The following precepts are applicable to all forms of hand-to-hand combat: strengthen the spirit within, appear calm without; give the appearance of a proper woman and fight like an aroused tiger; generate energy throughout your body and move with your spirit; remain distant and as obscure as the sun, and quick and agile as a bounding hare; now your opponent sees you [your form], now he does not [pursues your shadow], and the sword blade flashes similarly; breathe with the movement and do not break the rules; side-to-side, back-and-forth, direct attack or reverse blow, the opponent does not hear these [your movements are not telegraphed]. This body of theory will allow one person to resist one hundred and a hundred to resist ten thousand.[87]

The kingdoms of Yue and Wu were famous in antiquity for the quality of their swords. The principal literary remains of these ancient states are two historical texts, the aforementioned *Spring and Autumn Annals* and a second chronicle, *Historical Texts from the Kingdom of Yue*, covering the same period. These volumes apparently contain all the important sword legends from antiquity, which are the origin of many conventions still used to describe weapons. The *Historical Texts from the Kingdom of Yue* was compiled by Ruist scholars who, despite residing in the southern kingdom of Yue, identified with the Central States lineages of literati for whom the study of history was a means of understanding the present. It seems likely that the composition, redaction, and preservation of the Yue Maiden text would be the responsibility of like-minded literati.[88]

The Yue Maiden's theory of swordplay appears to be a competent explanation by someone who knew what she was talking about, and it was read that way, for instance, by Chang Naizhou, who quoted the passage in his martial arts writings. What might have encouraged *wen*-loving Confucian scholars to preserve the story? Her skill contains something daimonic, which resembles the charisma of the Confucian sage. *Xunzi* explains this sage as good at blending and orchestrating things, making different things work together. Mencius praised Confucius as a master of timing. He knew just when to engage with a thing and just when to stop. The sagacity of the sage is an art of timeliness, knowing when to open, when to close, when to move right, left, and so on.[89]

Those terms also characterize the Yue Maiden's skill. She discerns the forces in play and their phases, which she masterfully blends, differentiating movements into large and small, double and single, offensive and defensive, side to side, back and forth, direct and reverse. Each has its yin-yang valence, predominantly yin or yang, but never one to the exclusion of the other, which is the source of their power. At any moment, all these elements are interacting. What is passive is becoming active, what is rising is beginning to fall. The movement flows in one beat and does not stop, so nothing is heard, that is, perceived by the opponent. Her work with the sword expresses the uncommon harmony of a proper female and an aroused tiger. Her technique synergistically generates energy throughout the body. You "move with your spirit" and "breathe with the movement." These words must be the earliest version of a mantra repeated to this day in the philosophy of the Asian martial arts. Some think the mantra is Daoist. Others think it is Zen. But we see it first in a passage from this minor Confucian chronicle.

The Yue Maiden tale depicts invincible martial art under the control of a demure female of unimpeachable virtue. We see this mixture of virtue and martial expertise again in the emergence into cultural prominence of the so-called internal martial arts, including bagua, xingyi, and taiji. All these arts have the reputation of an association with Daoism, but they initially were promoted by Confucian literati. A foundational text for the philosophy of internal martial arts is the "Epitaph for Wang Zhengnan," which was composed by Huang Zongzi (1610–1695) shortly after the Manchu conquest and the establishment of the Qing dynasty. Huang was a degree-holding scholar and Ming loyalist. His father had been a prominent Ming official and Confucian reformer. The son earned an examination degree under the Ming and fought against the Qing until 1649, when, refusing to serve the new dynasty, he retired to study and write.

It was this Confucian literatus and disgruntled Ming loyalist who invented the myth of taiji's revelation to the Daoist immortal Zhang Sanfeng in a dream on Wudang Mountain, a tale that he publicized as a covert political statement against foreign rule. In the first text to mention an "internal" martial art, he wrote, "Shaolin is famous for its boxers. However, its techniques are chiefly offensive, which creates opportunities for an opponent to exploit. Now there is another school that is called 'internal,' which overcomes movement with stillness. Attackers are effortlessly repulsed. Thus we distinguish Shaolin as 'external.'" This reference to the Buddhists of Shaolin is anti-Manchu code; like the Buddhists, the Manchu were foreigners and not really Chinese.[90]

Something similar happened about a century later in the writings of Chang Naizhou, which have been described as the most complete premodern treatment of martial arts theory in any language. Chang, who obtained the *mingjing* examination degree under the Qianlong emperor, is known as the scholar-boxer (*ruquanshi*). The Qing-dynasty *Sishui District Gazetteer* described him as "an accomplished poet and essayist. He taught Classics, and disciples were numerous. In spare time he gave instruction in fists and staves. Men, expert in one art, all achieved spiritual marvels." Chang created the earliest-known explanation of martial arts to employ the Song Neo-Confucian concept of the *taiji*, or great pole, and the opposition of yin and yang. He very influentially, though at the time counterintuitively, explained that the value of practicing martial arts is not success in combat; it is longevity, health, and spiritual realization. Combative movements are a method for an inner cultivation of *qi* energy:

> Martial defense is like this: refine the form to coordinate externals; refine energy to solidify internals. "Hard and tough as iron" [*Change Muscles Classic*], you will naturally complete a "Gold elixir indestructible body"

[Nirvana Sutra]. You will then transcend laity and enter sagehood. The supreme vehicle may be attained. To speak of "facing men fearlessly" is the least of it.[91]

As this passage suggests, Chang synthesized Confucian sagehood with the pursuit of the alchemical elixir and the adamantine *vajra* body of esoteric Buddhism. Martial arts practice is an alchemical synthesis of *wen* and *wu*: "Through *wen* refinement, it contrives the internal elixir. Through *wu* refinement, it contrives the external elixir. Internal elixir invariably borrows external elixir to be completed." This farrago of postclassical sources comes with the expected approbation of Confucius and Mencius. A motif in Chang's writing is a line from Zhu Xi's Song-dynasty commentary on the Confucian classic *Zhongyong*: "Not partial nor leaning/Without excess or insufficiency." He also found Mencius's pronouncement on floodlike *qi* to be a valuable martial arts image:

Heaven and Earth's correct energy collects in my center:
Capacity great, flowing dynamic, the whole body fills.
Mencius called it flood-like *qi*.
What other energy can compare with its ability?[92]

Ideas of an internal martial arts practice connected with Mount Wudang and the Daoist immortal Zhang Sanfeng—of the pursuit of Buddhist-cum-Daoist enlightenment and a longevity-inducing alchemy of the *qi*—emerge not among the Daoists but as the invention of literati like Chang Naizhou and Huang Zongzi. For these writers, playing up the "Daoist" qualities of something became a way of saying that it was Chinese and did not belong to foreign conquerors. In the later Republican period (1912–1949), after the collapse of the Qing dynasty, literati again reached out to the increasingly mystified Chinese martial arts for signifiers of Sinitic identity.

The dissemination of martial arts knowledge and practice became official Republican government policy. The culmination of this effort was the founding of the Jingwu meng (Essence of the Martial Arts Association) in Shanghai in 1909. This was the world's first public martial arts association, where anyone could walk in, register, pay a fee, and receive instruction. Its foundation marked a turning point when the Chinese martial arts graduated from being a disreputable manual trade associated with soldiers, bodyguards, and theatrical charlatans to being an ideologically charged middle-class recreation and the answer to China's reputation as the "sick man of Asia." It was at this time that the Chinese martial arts began to be referred to as "national arts" (*guoshu*), an expression still in use, for example, in the name of my wing chun school in Hong Kong (Shun ching ving tsun guo shu hui).[93]

In support of the Republican cause, influential literati tried to dispel the secrecy that had long enveloped these arts. Every Chinese who cared about the country should take up their practice. In his *Study of Xingyi Boxing* (1915), the enormously influential Sun Lutang stated:

A strong country cannot be composed of weak people. We cannot make people strong without physical training. To brace up the people though physical training is the way to strengthen the country. . . . Martial arts has been put into the curriculum in schools so that the students can be trained in both literary and military arts.

In a later foreword to *Xingyi's Fist and Weapon Instruction* (1928), Sun declared: "A country's strength or weakness lies with its people. Strength or weakness of its people lies in their physical prowess. This determines winning or losing, surviving or perishing. This is why martial arts must be revitalized."[94]

One scholar called the internal arts of bagua, xingyi, and taiji "a metaphor in body movement," an image that is meant to capture the culture's spiritual essence and provide a plan for its survival. For instance, professing his "desire only to hear the true *dao* of Confucius," Zheng Manqing, in his *Thirteen Treatises on Taijiquan* (1947), enrolled taiji in a national program of self-cultivation: "Today people want to emulate Mencius, but they do not know how to cultivate the *qi* or to practice *taijiquan*. They are not able to emulate him." The practice of martial arts is at once a care of the self and a preparation for civic duty. As "the premier martial art," he explained,

[Taiji helps] the weak to become strong, the sick to recover, and the timid to become brave. Its practice strengthens the body, the race, and the country. Those who deal with national and civil affairs should not neglect this. . . . If you cannot improve yourself for the benefit of yourself and your family, you will betray your country just as corrupt government officials do. For you commit these acts even though you know they are wrong. There must be a reason—it is because your body is weak.[95]

The effort to merge Confucian self-cultivation with corporeal praxis seems to have had a classical precedent. Xunzi, the last of the great Confucians of the classical period, deplored the popularity of the *daoyin* techniques I mentioned earlier, which were new in his time. He did not doubt their effectiveness in strengthening and harmonizing the *qi* but was suspicious of the—to him, morally dubious—motives that people have for practicing them. Accordingly, he presented an alternative cultivation praxis that promised similar rewards without the selfishness of the *daoyin* cult that he criticized.[96]

Xunzi's program relies on self-examination and moral commitment, staples of Confucian discipline, but also teaches physical deportment and corporeal habits. Xunzi called the process "accumulating goodness" (*ji shan*) and described its result as the attainment of divine insight (*shenming*), a term also used in the *daoyin* texts, including the *Stretching Book* discussed earlier. For Xunzi, the Confucian discipline of ritual and its proprieties was the most efficacious way to control the *qi* and harmonize emotions and desires, promoting righteousness no less than longevity and producing a person who is at once benevolent and vigorous, a Confucian Ancestor Peng as it were. "When one identifies the measure of goodness and uses it to control his *qi* and nourish life (*yangsheng*), he will live longer than Ancestor Peng. When he uses it to cultivate his body and make a name for himself, he will become equal to [the sage-kings] Yao and Yu."[97]

An American with extensive martial arts training in Taiwan was asked by his *shifu* how he would guard his back. He came up with several clever answers. Then it occurred to him to ask the teacher. How would *he* guard his back? The master answered, "The way to guard your back is to act in such a manner that the people about you love you so much that they would never allow you to be attacked from behind." That was an important lesson for him. "The ultimate power of the boxer," he says, "is not his advanced skill but his righteousness." This martial artist, like the *xiashi* hero in China's beloved *wuxia* literature, "possesses what his adversary cannot: an unwavering knowledge that his purpose and behavior are correct." The aforementioned American believed that this idea was Daoist wisdom going back to China's most ancient martial arts tradition in the Shang dynasty if not earlier. But his moral rendition of Chinese martial arts seems to me more intelligible as an example of the political literati attitude of Republic-era martial arts practitioners like Sun Lutang, who synthesized Confucian morality and martial arts practice. There is no contradiction, they say, between training martial arts and being a benevolent, righteous human being. A king "watches his back" by practicing benevolence, which will make him so loved by the people that he has no enemies. That was Xunzi's answer to the art-of-war general in their debate over the value of strategy. The best principles of war are no different from those of Confucian rulership, namely, humanity and ritual propriety. The best kings have no enemies. "The army of a true king is not tested."[98]

A passage of the Confucian *Analects* reads,

> When it comes to the practice of ritual, it is harmonious ease (*he*) that is to be valued. It is precisely such harmony that makes the *dao* of the former kings so beautiful. . . . Yet if you know enough to value harmonious ease but try to attain it without being regulated by the rites, this will not work. (A 1.12)

The restriction of harmonious ease to the *li* rites was resisted—by Daoists, military thinkers, and eventually martial arts masters too. They found other theaters for the practice of harmonious ease, whether in meditation, strategy, inner alchemy, or the martial arts.

Classical Confucians might be expected to resist this expansion of their ideal and would be unlikely to find ethical value in *wushu*. Yet martial arts practice acquired Confucian acceptability at the same moment as these arts emerged in the form that we now know them, as spiritual practices, methods of self-cultivation, and middle-class rec-reations. All that happened first in China and then gradually spread throughout the world. The emergence of Chinese martial arts into cul-tural prominence and middle-class acceptability is a Confucian, not a Daoist or Buddhist, event. The association between these martial arts and, especially, Daoism began as a construction of the Confucian lite-rati. Martial arts practice was appropriated for Daoism not by Daoists but by Confucian scholars bitterly opposed to what had become of their class and tradition under foreign conquerors.

2

FROM DUALISM TO THE DARWINIAN BODY

Themes from Western Philosophy

So long as we keep to the body, and our soul is contaminated
with this imperfection, there is no chance of our ever attaining
satisfactorily to our object, which we assert to be truth.

PLATO, *PHAEDO*

Oppositions of mind and body, soul and matter, spirit and flesh
all have their origin, fundamentally, in fear of what life may bring
forth. They are marks of contraction and withdrawal.

JOHN DEWEY, *ART AS EXPERIENCE*

I say little in this chapter about the
Asian martial arts. Instead, I explain why a chapter on Western philosophy *cannot* have much to say to these arts, not for accidental reasons
of language and geography, but because this philosophy tends to be
struck mute before anything as corporeal as the martial arts. Philosophy began in the West as a movement of nature rationalism, conceiving
nature as a rational order, a cosmos with a principle that is both intelligible and intelligent. The early Greek philosophers, figures like Xenophanes, Heraclitus, and Parmenides, invented the idea of knowledge as
the Truth of Reality. This is the pure knowledge that sets philosophers
apart from the traditional masters of knowledge, the poets and orators,
and distinguishes the philosopher's way of life from traditional norms
of human excellence, epitomized in the victorious athlete. Theoretical
philosophy was advanced and explained through a dual polemic against

rhetoric and athletics. While Plato's attack on rhetoric and poetry is well known, the animus against athletes requires an explanation.

GREEK ATHLETICS

Every major Bronze Age cultural group in the world seems to have enjoyed some form of physical entertainment, such as fights, feats, contests, or military dancing. The earliest of these usually suggested a royal audience. It was first in the post-Mycenaean culture of Greece that such physical entertainments evolved into the distinctive character of *sport*, distinguished by the law of victory. The prize went to the winner, not to the one who most impressed a royal patron. The terms of competition, not the sentiment of the sponsor, determined the victor. The Greek innovation was to make a sport of athletics under the law of competitive victory. The pillars of Greek athletics were the gymnasium, where athletics were taught and practiced, and the ritual cycle of the Panhellenic games, the premier athletic competition. Athletic contests in Greece were associated with religious rites, especially funerals. The oldest written source, Homer's carefully detailed rendition of funeral games to honor Patroclus at Troy, describes an already well developed culture of competitive athletics. In the *Odyssey*, a royal prince asks the newly arrived Odysseus to join their contests:

> Friend, Excellency, come join our competition, if
> you are practiced, as you seem to be.
> While a man lives he wins no greater honor
> than footwork and the skill of hands can bring him.[1]

Olympic games were held every four years, from 776 B.C.E. to Roman times (the emperor Nero triumphed in every contest he entered). Sheltered under a ritual ban on hostilities, the games gathered Greeks from all provinces and social ranks to compete for glory. Although Olympus was the site of the first and always most prestigious games, Panhellenic games also were held at other locations. Already by the first Olympiad in the eighth century, athletic victory was the epitome of human achievement. The Greek word for that epitome, the virtue embodied in the victorious athlete, is *arete*, "excellence," the human being at its utmost.[2]

Greek athletic contests included racing, discus throwing, jumping, and javelin throwing. Running on a straight track was the athletic event par excellence and the original contest at the first Olympiad. The people's choice for excitement and adulation, however, was wrestling, whose name, *palaestra*, was lent to the place for all athletic training and competition. The object of Greek wrestling is to throw the opponent to the ground without falling oneself. Opponents must fall completely, not merely to their knees. Tripping is allowed but not leg holds, although arm, neck, and body holds are allowed. Those ancients who left their view of it regarded wrestling of all games to have the best balance of skill and strength. It was not just a fight but had something canny and daimonic about it, as its origin testifies: "Theseus first invented the art of expert wrestling (*palaistiken technen*), and through him afterward was established the teaching of the art. Before him men used in wrestling only size and bodily strength." A credible ancient source tells us that Plato was a champion wrestler, and his *Dialogues* bristle with allusions to the sport.[3]

Other fighting sports were popular, too. By the fourth century B.C.E., boxers were using gloves, probably leather, with exposed fingers. Without a ring or rounds, the fight continued until the competitors were exhausted or one submitted by raising his arm. The mythical founders of Greek boxing—Onomastos, who drew up the first rules, and Pythagoras of Samos (not the philosopher)—both worked in Ionia, the Asian province where also Greek philosophy and science were born. Like wrestling, boxing emphasizes intelligence over strength. Apollo, the divine patron of boxing, defeated Ares, the god of war, in boxing at the first Olympiad, vindicating skill over brutality. His cult name at Delphi was Apollo *pyktes*, Apollo the Boxer. Another combat sport, and the last new competition added to the Olympic roster in classical times, was *pankration*, or all-in wrestling (from the thirty-third Olympiad, 648 B.C.E.). The name means "complete strength" or "complete victory" and has the synonym *pammachon*, "total fight." Such contests are not described in Homer or any literature before the fifth century, but in the fifth century Pindar left this epitome: "One must wipe out his rival by doing everything." *Pankration* was the most violent event of ancient athletics, as its aim was to knock an opponent unconscious or force him into submission. Anything was allowed except gouges to the eyes, mouth, or nose.[4]

An ancient traveler left an account of the stadium at Olympia, now long gone, that described a ceremonial entrance flanked by two altars. One was dedicated to Hermes *agonios*, Hermes of the contest, the divine patron of athletics. The other altar was dedicated to *kairos*, the divine epitome of timing, the propitious moment. This time is an intensive quality rather than a quantity or chronological time. *Kairos* is the time in good timing, the opportune moment, the strategic timing of a move or play. In a line from Sophocles, "for the right time (*kairos*) has come, and this is what holds the greatest sway over all human action." A sculpture by Lysippus adorned the Kairos altar, which the traveler described. It depicted Kairos as now a god, a winged deity balanced on a stick, holding a knife, edge up, on whose blade was balanced a pan-balance—balancing a balance on a balanced balance! A time so subtle, so effective! All contestants had to time their exertion in order to stay the course and finish strong. Boxers use timing to dominate their opponent; wrestlers have to seize fleeting openings. In the *Peri gymnastikes* (*On Gymnastics*) of Philostratus, the ancient author says: "How many different kinds of wrestling holds are there, the *paidotribe* [gymnasium master] will show, laying down the principles of the opportune moment (*kairos*), the attack, the extent of practice, and the rules of defending oneself or for breaking though another's defense."[5]

Since the philosophers launched a parallel polemic against athletics and rhetoric, we should remember that these two already were associated in the culture and shared ritual occasions and venues. Gorgias became a famous Sophist for his speeches at the Olympian games, and Sophists claimed the athletic virtue of opportunity (*kairos*) for themselves. Protagoras was the first to "expound on the power of *kairos*" and to initiate competitive debate (*logon agones*). The title of his best-known work is *Aletheia e kataballontes* (*Truth, or the Wrestlers*). Socrates compared hearing a speech by Protagoras to boxing: "His speech really produced noise and approval from many of the listeners; and at first I felt as though I had been struck by a skillful boxer, and was quite blind and dizzy with the effect of his words and their shouts of approval."[6]

The first schools of any kind in Greece were the *gymnasia*, schools for athletic training. Before the seventh century B.C.E., the system already was well developed, and it spread wherever Hellenism did. The training was primarily physical education accompanied by literature and began at age seven or eight. Gymnasium pedagogy was entirely separate from the training of professional athletes. Besides athletics, these schools practiced a system of health exercises, including loosening-up exercises based on anatomical analysis. A characteristically Greek feature was to accompany exercise with the music of the *aulos* flute. A trainer (*paidotribus*) supervised the practice, clad in a purple cloak to emphasize his authority and carrying a staff with which to strike those who were clumsy or inattentive or broke the rules of competition (a popular depiction on ancient vases). This *pedotribe* was expected to be knowledgeable in hygiene, bodily development, diet, the effects of different exercises, and the suitability of different training for different temperaments.

Greek athletes always practiced naked. First they carefully oiled their body, which was considered important and subject to precise rules. The justification for the oil was hygiene, not to make the body slippery for wrestling. In fact, after oiling his body, the athlete covered himself with a fine layer of dust sifted through the fingers over the skin. Nudity is a post-Homeric innovation from the sixth century B.C.E., and Greeks, acutely aware of its singularity, defended the custom from ridicule. A modern scholar explained the appeal of the practice: "To be naked, it seems, was to be worth seeing; it was a costume rather than an assertion of sexuality or an invitation to eroticism." It also was a way of signifying one's identity as Greek and not barbarian (or Roman). The naked body, too, was an expression of self-assurance, the athletes visibly relying on nothing but themselves, with nothing up their sleeve. This absence of fakery remains an attraction of athletics today.[7]

The pedagogy of the gymnasium lasted for a thousand years. But by Hellenistic times, in the epoch after Alexander the Great, physical education had lost its leading part, supplanted by literary study, and by Christian times, physical education had disappeared. The lost ethos of

Greek athletics was one of seriousness, evident in the honors and the status of victors; the high value of winning, with no prize for second place; the mostly individual competition, with few team sports; and participation open to all classes. Anyone could participate in the Panhellenic games. Although expense was an obstacle, we have numerous accounts of humble men triumphant at the games.[8]

What did Greeks admire about athletics? Our best answer comes from the poets of athleticism. One, relatively late, is Lucian, whose *Anacharsis* (ca. 170 C.E.) is a conversation set in sixth-century B.C.E. Athens, in which Solon explains athletics to a visiting sage. He says that the games bestow health on participants, delight athletes and spectators alike, and ennoble all society by inspiring achievement. He rationalizes athletics as a form of military preparedness, despite the ever present skepticism about the training's combat value. Clearly, the aesthetic pleasure in the spectacle was the main attraction:

> I cannot, just by telling you about it, convince you of the pleasure of what happens at such a festival, as well as you would learn for yourself, sitting in the middle of the crowd, watching the *arete* of men and physical beauty, amazing conditioning, and great skill and irresistible force and daring and pride and unbeatable determination and indescribable passion for victory.[9]

The most profound approbation of athletics comes from Pindar, whose *epinikia* poems commemorate victory in the games. In his telling, what matters for *arete*, "excellence," is not victory per se but the passion of the victory, the courageous *agon*, "a profound and questing pursuit": "Work and expense, always in the company of excellent accomplishments, struggle for a deed wrapped in risk." Pindar lived in the early fifth century B.C.E. in mainland Greece, removed from the intellectual center of Ionia in Asia Minor. He seems to have been unaffected by the rise of Ionian rationalism and natural inquiry from about a century earlier. Neither did he follow the epic tradition of Ionian bards like Homer. Homer's epic relates and adorns, whereas Pindar's hymns are a solemn religious invocation. His songs, celebrating the greatest moment in the athlete's life, express what Werner Jaeger calls "the religious meaning of the athletic contest."[10]

Pindar appears to have been the first to use the form of the hymn, previously reserved for addressing the gods, in praise of athletic victors. In *their* deeds, he seems to say, more than in the legends of the gods and heroes of epic, we see the ideal by which to measure *arete*:

> If ever a man strives
> With all his soul's endeavor, sparing himself
> Neither expense nor labor to attain
> True excellence, then must we give to those
> Who have achieved the goal a proud tribute
> Of lordly praise, and shun
> All thoughts of envious jealousy.[11]

Poet and athlete belong to each other. Victory demands a song: "One thing thirsts for another, but victory loves song best, song the readiest companion of crowns and virtues." A motif of Pindar's hymns is the difficulty of successful competition. The victories he praises are consummate *arete* and must be recorded for posterity, not "silently hidden in the ground":

> To a poet's mind the gift is slight, to speak
> A kind word for unnumbered toils, and build
> For all to share a monument of beauty.[12]

The fine-tuned body of the athlete and the poet's musical mind are two sides of one *arete,* with no allowance for a mental excellence divorced from the body, or vice versa. The poet would be speechless without the athlete's victory, and the athlete's *arete* would be "silently hidden in the ground" without the song. To supplant this ancient evaluation of *arete*, Plato had to attack both athletics and its poetry. Poetry is momentary madness, he would say, a bad mind, and athletics is all body, which, for Plato, was all bad.

PHILOSOPHY AND ATHLETICS

The utopia that Plato describes in his *Republic* includes a reformed athletics. Traditional methods merely train the body. His improved and philosophical physical education uses the body to train the soul. A pupil is to "work at physical exercises in order to arouse the spirited part of his nature rather than to acquire the physical strength for which other athletes diet and labor." Plato is not saying that education should train the soul no less than the body. *All* the training should address the soul, despite an instrumental passage through the body:

> A god has given music and physical training to human beings not, except incidentally, for the body and the soul [respectively], but for the spirited and wisdom-loving parts of the soul itself, in order that these might be in harmony with one another, each being stretched and relaxed to the appropriate degree.[13]

There is no good in the body per se. Anything we do with the body is good—if it is—by having a good effect on the soul. The philosophers compelled athletics to be rationalized according to the new dichotomy of body and soul. Plato's contemporary Isocrates declares,

> I have often been astonished at those who hold festivals and set up athletic contests, that they consider physical success worthy of such great rewards, but have not given any honor to those who personally labor for the common good or so prepare their souls that they are able to benefit others.

Note the binary values: soul over body, polis over person. These are the new values of the philosophers in their contest with the earlier paragons of wisdom and excellence, the poets and athletes.[14]

Philosophers of the Cynic school attacked athletes for a completely mistaken understanding of excellence, cynically borrowing and bending the athletic vocabulary to a new use. Athletes trained for victory in the stadium, but philosophers trained for victory in life, for tranquillity and happiness. Cynic philosophers came to the Panhellenic games and demanded a prize for their *arete*. An ancient source left an account of the Cynic Diogenes haranguing the crowd at the Isthmian games:

The man who is noble is the one who considers hardship as his greatest competitor and struggles with it day and night, and not, like some goat, for a bit of celery or olive or pine [the material of victory crowns at the games], but for the sake of happiness and *arete* throughout his whole life.[15]

The physicians joined in to discredit athletics, at least the philosophically ambitious Galen did. He flatly denied a health benefit. Overexertion impairs health as much as overeating does, and competition ruins beauty: "When they finally smash or wrench some part of the limbs or strike out the eyes, then, I suppose, then especially is the beauty of their completed training clearly seen." The doctor diagnosed athletes devoted to the petty virtues of the body, oblivious to intellectual virtue:

It is crystal clear to everyone that the athletes have never even had a dream of intellectual virtues. . . . Always gaining bulk in flesh and blood they keep their intellect smothered as if in a mass of mire, unable to discern anything clearly, but instead devoid of understanding like that of the brainless beasts.[16]

Euripides, the most rationalistic of Athens's tragedians, came right out and asserted, "Of the thousand evils which exist in Greece there is no greater evil than the race of athletes." They are slaves to their mouth and servants to their belly. They cannot bear poverty yet cannot acquire wealth. They lack good habits and cannot cope with difficulties. They are beautiful in their prime but wrecks in old age. Those who encourage athletic contests honor useless pleasures. The claimed military value of the training is a fraud. "Do men drive the enemy out of their fatherlands by waging war with *diskoi* in their hands?" The values of athletics are completely misplaced:

We ought rather to crown the good men and the wise men, the reasonable man who leads the city-state well and the man who is just, and the man who leads us by his words to avoid all evil, deeds and battles and civil strife. These are the things which benefit every state and all the Greeks.[17]

Scholars think that in this passage, Euripides was imitating an earlier poet-philosopher of rationalism, Xenophanes of Colophon (ca. 570–475 B.C.E.). Xenophanes seems to have launched the criticism that athletics is limited to the body, that it fails the mind, which makes it unworthy of the wise, whose highest value is understanding. A contemporary of Pindar, Xenophanes was an Ionian poet-philosopher who was violently transplanted to mainland Greece when his city fell to the Persians in 546. He may have known Anaximander and Pythagoras and was the legendary teacher of Parmenides. Werner Jaeger credits Xenophanes with giving Greeks their first lesson in how to use the inherited language of poetry to express philosophical rationalism, which it does first in the writing by Xenophanes, followed by Parmenides and Empedocles. That makes Xenophanes the pioneer poet of Greek rationalism. He linked the natural speculation of early Ionian thought (Anaximander and others) to the moral authority that Greek tradition vested in poetic ideals of wisdom and *arete*, and he discovered an "intellectual virtue" (*sophia*) entirely unlike athletic accomplishment.[18]

It seems acceptable to describe Xenophanes as a rationalist (*logikoi*), even though that word was first used more than a century later in the different context of Greek medicine. In calling Xenophanes a rationalist, I do not mean that he anticipated a Cartesian epistemology of the a priori and innate. I mean that he solemnized rationality. What is, and what ought to be, is logical. Reason rules. Nature is a rational cosmos. Centuries before Plato, Xenophanes introduced the distinction between genuine knowledge—an apprehension of things based on clear and reliable indications—and opinion. He stripped phenomena of their supernatural aspects—"For all things are from the earth and to the earth all things come in the end"—and sought a naturalistic explanation for events that credulous people invested with supernatural significance, like rainbows, clouds, and winds. He deplored the disparity between the people's intellectual resources and the requirements of the best knowledge, which is rarer and more difficult than people, and especially poets, appreciate. Xenophanes took the first step toward the idea of a special kind of knowledge (eventually to be called *episteme* [science]), which is preeminently interesting to philosophers and defines their distinction from poets and sophists, and all the more from athletes, the brutes![19]

Xenophanes is remembered as an early critic of traditional ideas about the gods. He ridiculed poets who thought they could describe a god. If oxen could paint, they would depict gods as oxen. Poets are no less naive than ordinary people when they interpret things like rainbows and winds, which have completely natural causes, as messages from the gods. Civilization is not a gift from Heaven. It was built up by people's own discoveries and gradually improved by their labor: "The gods have not revealed all things to men from the beginning, but by seeking [men] find in time what is better." The consistency of this criticism calls forth a polemic against the poets, who retail nonsense about the gods. Hence another memorable first in Xenophanes: his attack on poetry. A satiric fragment reads, "Homer and Hesiod have ascribed to the gods all things that are a shame and a disgrace among mortals, stealing and adultery and deceiving one another." Here began that ancient enmity, as Plato called it, between philosophy and poetry.[20]

Consistency also made Xenophanes an ardent critic of athletics and its cult. When his native Colophon fell to the Persians, he found himself unexpectedly thrown into the cultural ambit of the Pindarian ideal, the old mainland aristocracy, among whom Xenophanes gained his first reputation as a poet of the new *sophia* that eventually became philosophy. He confronted the culture of athletics, demanding of its adherents a choice they did not know they had to make. What do they value, mind or body, divine reason or brute strength?

What if a man win victory in swiftness of foot, or in the pentathlon, at Olympia, where is the precinct of Zeus by Pisa's springs, or in wrestling; what if by cruel boxing or that fearful sport men call pankration he become more glorious in the citizens' eyes, and win a place of honour in the sight of all at the games, his food at the public cost from the State, and a gift to be an heirloom for him; what if he conquer in the chariot-race, he will not deserve all this for his portion so much as I do.

> Far better is our art than the strength of men and of horses! These
> are but thoughtless judgements, nor is it fitting to set strength before
> wisdom (*sophie*). Even if there arise a mighty boxer among a people,
> or one great in the pentathlon or at wrestling, or one excelling in swift-
> ness of foot—and that stands in honour before all tasks of men at the
> games—the city would be none the better governed for that. It is but
> little joy a city gets of it if a man conquer at the games by Pisa's banks;
> it is not this that makes fat the store-houses of a city.

The *sophie* referred to is presumably the knowledge of the poet, but how
are we to understand that? Is this poet's *sophie*-knowledge a *techne*, the
traditional term for the poet's art, or does it refer to *philosophia*, the
emerging term for a new sort of *arete*? The learned Bowra thinks that either reading was possible in the sixth century but that Xenophanes probably meant to praise "the philosophical and critical poetry which he himself
wrote and which he believed to be worthy of better rewards than it got."[21]

The criticism is not merely that athletes were given honors that
philosophers should receive but that the athletes do not deserve their
honors, for it is wrong to celebrate their values. Rather, the merit should
be transferred to the philosophers, who deserve to win the prize for
their tangible political accomplishments. The problem with athletes
is that their glory does not benefit the polis. Although the cities feel
honored by their victorious sons, they should not, because the polis
does not truly benefit from their deeds. Athletic victory is the private
accomplishment of vainglorious individuals, and reverence for athletes
is *adiakos* (not right, without justice), because it goes against rational
economy. As a modern editor explained,

> Xenophanes must have believed that his *sophie*—his expertise as a
> moral and spiritual advisor to his fellow citizens—could help to produce
> and preserve *eunomie* [good order] for a city as athletic competi-
> tion—even at its highest levels of achievement—never could, because
> his words could help to bond the citizens together in harmony.

Xenophanes appealed to the welfare of the polis to prove the value of
his new conception of *arete* as rationality and intellectual knowledge, a

new and better wisdom (*sophia*). Right order in the polis is a product of this rationality, to which the cult of athletics is an affront. A forceful assertion of economic rationality as the criterion of value apparently was original with Xenophanes and was canonized only later as a norm by Plato and Aristotle.[22]

To Xenophanes, discrediting athletics was no less important to his rationalist reform than discrediting poets. Poets lend credence to the values that athletes monopolize. The city is more important than any individual, however glorious. Athletics is simply economic irrationality. We should either get rid of it or make it contribute something to the polis, make it political. Because the Greeks remained no less in love with athletic beauty, despite the philosophers' criticism, they politicized athletics instead. The new politics of the polis, urged by the philosophers and fortified by their implacable dichotomy of body and soul, reduced athletics to a policy instrument. Participants in the games became representatives of a city, advertisements and propaganda to buff the city's reputation and competitive edge. Jaeger wrote, "As soon as Greeks began to feel that the spirit was different from or even hostile to the body, the old athletic ideal was degraded beyond hope of salvation, and at once lost its important position in Greek life, although athletics survived for centuries more as mere sport." In *The Birth of Tragedy*, Nietzsche depicts the subversion of tragic drama by Socratic rationalism and its afterlife as entertainment. We also see a parallel subversion of athletics by rationalism and its afterlife as professional sport.[23]

Cynic philosophers presented themselves at the games and demanded a prize for their virtue. A different image inspired by the games associated philosophers with a superior sort of spectator, observing the games with serene disinterest. The invention of these ideal spectators led to the birth of Western "theory," a word that originally meant "to witness." According to Heraclides of Pontus, from Plato's Academy,

The life of man resembles a festival [at Olympia] celebrated with the most magnificent games before a gathering collected from all of Greece. For this festival some men trained their bodies and sought to win the glorious distinction of a crown. . . . But there was a certain class, made up of the noblest men, who sought neither applause nor gain, but came for the sake of spectating and closely watched the event and how it was done.

These are the philosophers, masters of pure theory.[24]

Since well before the rise of philosophy, *theoria* was a venerable cultural practice, characterized by a journey abroad to witness an event or spectacle on behalf of one's home polis. These could be visits to oracles, attendance at religious festivals or games, or travel abroad for the sake of learning. Individuals selected to be such *theoroi* generally were wealthy aristocrats from the highest rank, lending their prestige to the practice of theory. Their *theoria* was a distinct kind of seeing: a formal, sober, quasi-religious, ritual-centered visuality, witnessing objects made sacred by the act of contemplation (*contemplatio* is Cicero's Latin translation of *theoria*). To attribute such value to sight probably reflects Plato's fascination with the Eleusinian Mysteries, which he bequeathed, appropriately sublimated, to later tradition. The heart of these mysteries is the promise that initiates will *see* something that will save them from death. In the words of the Homeric Hymn to Demeter (the goddess that the Eleusinian Mysteries celebrate), "Blessed among mortals on earth is he who has seen; but the uninitiated never has the same lot once dead in the dreary darkness."[25]

Before the fourth century B.C.E., the word *philosophein* and its cognates referred to intellectual cultivation in a broad sense and not to a special discipline or mode of wisdom. It was Plato, preeminently in *The Republic*, who first appropriated the term for a specific sort of discipline and concept of wisdom, identifying *theoria* as its defining activity, the distinctive way in which philosophers love wisdom. Philosophers love seeing, especially one kind of seeing, one special spectacle; they love the sight of truth. A visit to a religious festival or oracle is the model of philosophical *theoria* and its truth, the truth of being. Disinterested, objective, situated in a Panhellenic space divested of political differences, the contemplative philosopher enjoys the righteous sight of a sacred object, the idea, the form, the essence, liberated from perspective—a view of what is as it is, a view from nowhere in particular, the divine spectatorship of a god.[26]

Plato and other writers contrasted philosophy with all banausic activities, from the word *banausoi*, a derogatory label for people who live by the use of their hands. The term connotes the mercantile and servile, labor for hire. Theirs are the "bodies deformed by arts and crafts" that Plato deplored in *The Republic*. Aristotle wanted to revoke their citizenship. "Why is it," Plato has Socrates ask,

> that *banausia* and working with one's hands is a matter of reproach? Shall we not say that it is because that part which is by nature the best in a man is weak, with the result that it is unable to rule the beasts within him, but serves them, and can learn nothing but the means of flattering them?

To confuse a philosopher with an skilled technician is to confuse the knowledge of reason with the insipid mechanics of a docile body.[27]

THE PHILOSOPHERS' BODY

Perhaps we do not appreciate the novelty in the idea of *intellectual* virtue—the idea that intellect, *nous*, can be a field of *arete*, human excellence, no less than the battlefield or athletics. Its vogue coincides with the rise of philosophy in Greece, with Plato and Aristotle the summit of this development, not its source. They followed some two centuries of philosophical polemic debasing athletics and advocating for the new idea of intellectual virtue. Their weapon in this war of words was philosophical dualism, the dichotomy between mind and body, refined and elaborated in Plato's dualism of body and soul, and then again for modern thought in Descartes's dualism of mind and matter. Descartes did not invent this dualism and neither did Plato. It is nearly as old as philosophy itself, as we see in Xenophanes and again in Parmenides.

The philosophers compelled their adversaries—poets, orators, and athletes—to answer a question that had never been asked before. Are you caring for your body or your mind? For Pindar, excellence, *arete*, belonged to the whole person, indeed, to the whole genealogy of noble ancestors. He did not value the body over the soul. How can you separate them, as if *arete* itself were split! It was the philosophers who confronted their tradition with this demoralizing alternative. The whole *arete* of a whole human being was all that Pindar saw, and its paragon was the victorious athlete.

"Soul" in Greek is *psuche*, "psyche." The specifically intellectual mind is *nous*. In the oldest use, *psuche* is a concept of life force. Soul is what living things evince in their every appearance of vitality, especially movement and breath. In the late eighth or early seventh century B.C.E., this concept was unexpectedly shaken. Greeks started hearing about a strange new idea of the soul. They heard this new idea from travelers returning from remote lands to the north and east. The accounts tell of an immortal soul capable of mystical adventures (for instance, journeying to the land of dead) and foreseeing the future. This soul is not a principle of life for the body but a living thing in its own right, independent of the body, and continues living even after the body perishes. Possessing such a soul makes one not merely alive but godlike and divine.[28]

The source of these ideas lay beyond Greece, possibly in India, or among the shamans of the Eurasian steppe. They were taken up in a philosophical teaching in the school of Pythagoras. An immortal soul removes the barrier that Olympian religion placed between the gods and humans. For the Greeks, to describe something as a god or as divine basically meant one thing: immortality. Gods, divine beings, do not die. Except in this respect, they are a lot like people. But with an immortal soul, a human being (or its soul) becomes godlike. With that, all the rituals of traditional religion, including prayers and sacrifices to gods, were revealed as a childish misunderstanding of the true facts about divinity, especially the divinity within us. Worship and prayer cannot be the spiritual heart of religion. What is more important, and must occupy the attention of the wise, is taking good care of the soul. That became the problem of Pythagorean thought: how should we care for this immortal soul of ours? They sought their answer partly in ascetic practices of purity, but mainly it was rational understanding that should set the soul straight. A good future for the soul requires eliminating the disorder that infects it with bad character. The key is a lucid understanding of nature, as such knowledge brings the soul into its best condition and prepares it for immortality.[29]

Socrates powerfully affirmed this Pythagorean thesis in his famous speech to the Athenian jurors. He told them that the soul is something to care for, that such care is the most important thing a person can do, that the value of everything else depends on that. Its good is the highest good, distinct from bodily goods: "For all good and evil, whether in the body or in the whole person, originates in the soul and overflows from there." In *Gorgias*, Socrates proposes a specific technique for the care of the soul, distinct from the care of the body. For the body, gymnastics and medicine; for the soul, politics, including knowledge of law and justice. He refers to the binary body and soul as "two things" (*duoi pragmatoin*) and advises that the soul supervise (*epistatein*) the body. *Sophrosune*, moderation or self-control, is the virtue of the soul that is properly in charge of its body. We are more our soul than we are our body. The body is something the soul uses, but your soul *is you*. The excellence of the intellectual soul is therefore the highest, even exclusive, virtue of the wise.[30]

A second source after Pythagoras for this new psychology is Parmenides. Plato called Parmenides "venerable and awesome." He invented a brilliant new poetic-philosophic image, one that Plato reused in his Myth of the Cave. Parmenides imagined ignorance of truth as a kind of darkness and knowledge of truth as light. Because this trope is so trite, we forget that someone had to invent it, and it appears to have been Parmenides; according to scholars there is no earlier example. He used the figure to advance a new sort of claim, which is to speak with the quasi-religious authority obtained through a personal relation to something transcendent, like the revelation of a god. That is the kind of claim that prophets make in the Bible, but it was not something that Greek poets had done before.[31]

Parmenides used this self-conferred authority to impart a religious seriousness to the intellectual mind and the search for truth. That is how you take care of your deathless soul—by caring for your mind, your intellect, your *nous*, and its *logos*, caring for them by caring about the truth. Parmenides stressed, as did his near contemporary, Heraclitus, the ritual propriety of this devotion to truth. It is natural and right, offending no moral or religious prohibition, and is necessary for *arete*. Truth is the perfection of knowledge and the spiritual dignity of the human soul.

In the surviving fragments of Parmenides's poem, traditionally entitled *On Nature*, a goddess shows the poet the Way of Truth. This poet describes himself as "one who knows," that is, has knowledge, not mere opinion or belief. Such knowledge knows the truth, the truth of being, what is and never changes. This knowledge elevates the knower above the usual run of men, who are stuck on the path of opinion. Those rare few who travel the path of Truth live for *nous*, intellectual understanding. This intellect is entirely different from the senses, which are confuted by the body. Intellectual intuitions are complete and perfect in an instant. Sensory perception, by contrast, is a duration, always involved with the past, with what is not present, with what is not, and therefore, according to Parmenides's famous argument, is illogical and cannot truly exist or even be thought. This was the beginning of the idea that sensory perception is confused and has to be suspended for the sake of pure knowledge. Intellectual intuitions, or what later Stoics and then Descartes called clear and distinct ideas, are completely different from sense perception and completely different from anything a body can do. Their instantaneous intellection is exactly what we need to know the truth of being, because *What Is* is without perspective. *What Is* maintains the same character throughout. To grasp any of it is to grasp all of it. To achieve such unity of thought is an ascent to divinity. One becomes godlike or discovers one's godlike essence.[32]

Parmenides offered his Greek audience a momentous choice that no one before him knew they had to make. Which path do you follow: The Way of Truth or the Way of Opinion? What do you value: Being or appearance? Knowledge or ignorance? Intellect or sensation? Plato condensed all these oppositions into the great dichotomy of body and soul, which is why the "battle of gods and giants," the argument between *soma*-centered materialism and spiritual idealism, is the most decisive in all philosophy. Before Plato could deploy the dualism of body and soul, however, he needed more than the idea of soul he learned from the Pythagoreans. He also needed the idea of *body*, which he learned from the new medicine of the Hippocratics. Pindar was not a champion of body *over* soul. His thinking is innocent of the idea of body no less than that of soul. All he knew was the person, the human being, *ho anthropos*. The idea of body as a distinct reality was invented by the ancient physicians, who identified this body as the site wracked by causes about which they had expert knowledge. A philosophical concept of soul emerged as the place for everything the philosophers believed the physicians' *soma*-centered thought overlooked.

The distinction of the new medicine in the fifth century B.C.E. from older healing traditions is the great idea of disease as a natural process that happens inside what these physicians called the *soma*, the body. By explaining disease in terms of a physical body rather than daimonic agents, these physicians facilitated the emergence of the body as something about which they could have special knowledge. This body is the impersonal, largely unfelt physical reality of the human being. Its workings are hidden, though a physician can reconstruct them by reasoning, deduce a diagnosis, then intervene and cure. For the Hippocratic authors, *soma* (living medical body) and *phusis* (natural body, human nature) were interchangeable terms. The body that medicine knows is the source of everything that matters to the value and dignity of our lives. The more that medicine claimed to know about human nature, the more urgent the concern became with what critics thought the physicians' *soma*-centered thinking left out of the account.[33]

Doubt about the consistency of the doctors' account focused on our social and ethical nature and the powers of learning, thinking, and self-mastery. In *The Republic*, Plato has Socrates criticize excessive care of the *soma* as a distraction from due attention to learning and thinking, activities of *psuche*. The physicians' body is unconscious, irrational, more animal than human. The source of human distinction, therefore, must lie elsewhere. *Psuche*, "the soul," emerges in Greek philosophy as a name for what *soma*-centered naturalism could not explain. Our social and ethical nature requires reference to an entity that is categorically different from the body. The soul is just like a body except it is not a body. It is like a body in being effective, having a power to act. It is unlike a body in being ethical, social, rational, *incorporeal* (*asomatos*), a word that is new with Plato.[34]

Plato's dialogue *Phaedo* contains his most uncompromising disdain for the body. The setting is Socrates's last day of life in prison, when he talked with friends one last time and then drank the fatal poison. In that last conversation, he proved to everyone's satisfaction that the soul is immortal. He was not going to die, that is, cease to exist. He would undergo no more than a change of location, and the new place to which he would travel was bound to be better for his soul. The body is an obstacle to the highest good. That good is truth, and truth requires as much distance as possible from everything corporeal, including the senses and embodied perspective. When the soul tries to investigate anything with the help of the body, "it is obviously led astray." The soul thinks best "when it is free of all distractions such as hearing or sight or pain or pleasure of any kind—that is, when it ignores the body and becomes as far as possible independent, avoiding all physical constraints and associations as much as it can, in its search for reality." "So long as we keep to the body," Socrates added, "and our soul is contaminated with this imperfection, there is no chance of our ever attaining satisfactorily to our object, which we assert to be truth."[35]

The body is obstacle, nothing but obstacle. Socrates told his friends, "Every seeker after wisdom knows that up to the time when philosophy takes it over, his soul is a helpless prisoner, chained hand and foot in the body, compelled to view reality not directly but only through its prison bars, and wallowing in utter ignorance." By obstructing the knowledge of truth, our whole soul is obstructed, oppressed, and alienated, as if sent in exile to a foreign land. The body distracts the soul with incessant demands and an appalling penchant for disease. It fills the soul with desires and fears and all sorts of passions that distract contemplation. Even those with leisure experience the body as an obstacle. Contemplative minds are plagued by images, sights, appearances, the appalling legacy of corporeal birth, which hinders ascension to the plane of incorporeal essences. On that grave day, Socrates pronounced himself convinced that "no pure knowledge is possible in the company of the body" and that "if we are ever to have pure knowledge of anything, we must get rid of the body and contemplate things by themselves with the soul by itself." Quite logically, he named philosophy as a preparation for death. It should mortify the body to the point that it all but fades away, so that the greater part of life can attend to logical things, things of *logos*, rationality, and the contemplative excellence of purely intellectual theory.[36]

A dialogue known as *Alcibiades* was uniformly attributed to Plato in the ancient tradition, though modern scholars believe it to be a product of Plato's school, written shortly after his death. The conversation is between Socrates and his notorious friend and would-be disciple Alcibiades. At one point the discussion turns to self-knowledge, which Plato (in *Symposium*) presents as a challenge for Alcibiades, who is good at everything except self-knowledge and therefore is no good for the city. It was Socrates's constant experience that self-knowledge was harder than people suppose. We make a mistake about ourselves. It is the mistake of the athletes and those who share their idea of *arete*. We think that by caring for the body, we can care for our soul. The idea that one can achieve something great through physical training is the foundation of Greek athletics, and as this text argues, all care for the body is a kind of extended athletics. "The skill that makes the feet better [is] the same as what makes the rest of the body better. . . . Isn't this skill athletics?"[37]

Socrates nullified the value of this athletic art. Care for the body evades self-knowledge and does not achieve it: "Someone who knows certain things about his body knows about what belongs to him, not himself." Physical training is pointless, even counterproductive: "If someone takes care of his body, then isn't he caring for something that belongs to him, and not for himself?" The self we need to know cannot be identified with the body and must instead be the soul that uses the body. "A man is different from his own body," Socrates explained, "the command that we should know ourselves means that we should know our souls." In knowing the soul, we know that we are immortal, spiritual beings:

> Can we call anything in the soul more divine than that part in which knowing and thinking take place? . . . This part of it resembles the divine, and someone who looked at it and grasped everything divine—vision and intelligence—would have the best grasp of himself as well.

If you want to know yourself, you have to know that you are not a body, you are a soul, what is more, an immortal, spiritual soul, existing on a plane discontinuous with the ruction of a rumbling, ravenous body.[38]

Aristotle did not follow Plato in his dualism, which is not to say that Aristotle was not a dualist, only that his dualism was not Plato's. Aristotle resisted the Indic dualism that Pythagoras introduced to philosophy and that seduced Plato. Aristotle reaffirmed the Homeric idea of the soul as the life principle of the living body. A human soul cannot be what it is or do what it does apart from a human body. But this soul still is immaterial and ranks higher in power and reality than the body. Aristotle identified the soul with the form or organization of an organism, the life, vitality, and metaphysical actuality of the living body. Body considered in abstraction from soul is nothing actual. By itself, body is merely the potential that materializes when soul (form, organization) enters with matter in some actual living being.

"It is not necessary to ask whether soul and body are one," Aristotle insisted, "just as it is not necessary to ask whether wax and its shape are one." Body has no autonomous agency. It is a tool and needs a user. "The saw is made for sawing. . . . Similarly, the body too must somehow or other be made for the soul." "Each art must use its tools; each soul its body." Having come this far, it seems plausible to infer that the body is inferior to the soul. A body is indispensable to this soul, just as weapons and slaves are indispensable to a great man, but that does not make the good of the body the soul's good too. The good of the soul, its intellectual virtue, belongs to an entirely different order than that of the body and what serves it. "Those occupations are . . . the most servile in which there is the greatest use of the body." "Men ought not to labor at the same time with their minds and with their bodies; for the two kinds of labor are opposed to one another; the labor of the body impedes the mind, and the labor of the mind the body."[39]

In Roman and Christian times, the later school of Plato intensified the philosophers' contempt for the body. Plotinus reiterated the argument in *Alcibiades* that the body is an instrument of the soul and must therefore be completely separate, a wholly other kind of being. "The soul uses the body as an instrument. . . . As long as we have agent and instrument, there are two distinct entities; if the soul uses the body, it is separate from it." As did Plato in the *Phaedo*, Plotinus saw the body as a source of contamination and an obstacle. The body makes the soul ugly: "The soul becomes ugly by mixture and dilution and in-clination toward the body and matter." It prevents knowledge: "Purified [of body], the soul is wholly idea and reason" and is a moral danger: "Someone who clings to beautiful bodies and does not let go will sink, not with his body but with his soul, into dark depths in which the intel-lect takes no pleasure, where he will remain, blind in Hades, and will spend his time with shadows both here and there." Plotinus's disciple Porphyry explained the argument in a letter to his wife:

> What was it then that we learnt from those men who possessed the clearest knowledge to be found among mortals? Was it not this—that I am in reality not this person who can be touched or perceived by way of the senses, but that which is far removed from the body, the colorless and formless essence which can by no means be touched by the hands, but is grasped by the mind alone.[40]

THE BODY STRIKES BACK

Western philosophy tends to assume that it has nothing to learn from athletics, or indeed from any art or *techne*. The only practice of knowl-edge that counts is scientific theory. Not surprisingly, then, this phi-losophy has almost nothing to say to a student of the martial arts. But Western philosophy is no more homogeneous than the Chinese tradi-tion. Not all the Greek philosophers were idealists contemptuous of the body. In fact, some of them invented materialism, the theory that everything is body, that even the soul is an ultrafine body.

Plato described the argument between idealism and materialism as a battle between gods and giants, the giants being the materialists (Empedocles, Leucippus, Democritus) and the gods, the idealists, in-cluding Pythagoras, Parmenides, Anaxagoras, and Socrates. The Gi-gantomachy, depicted on the east metope of the Athenian Parthenon, pitted the brilliant Olympians against the dusky children of Ouranos and Gaia (Heaven and Earth). To Plato's audience in Athens, the strug-gle symbolized the victory of light and order (the gods) over darkness and chaos (the giants) and recalled their own struggle to repel barbaric foreign invaders. Plato thus aligned the idealism he favored with the luminous force of truth, and materialism with a chaotic and barbarous darkness.[41]

In the early fifth century B.C.E., Empedocles invented the first corpuscular theory of nature. Everything in nature mixes four kinds of bodies: earth, air, fire, and water. Driving their interaction are two fundamental forces, Eros and Strife. In a fragment on these elements, Empedocles commented, "These are the only real things, but as they run through each other they become different objects, at different times, yet they are throughout forever the same." By the end of the century, Democritus had enlarged materialism with the first atomic theory. Both these materialists assumed, contrary to Parmenides, that change and motion were entirely real, not mere appearance. Since motion presupposes non-being, the empty place to move to, void must be a reality of some kind, as Democritus acknowledged: "Not-Being is as real as Being." However, void does not produce motion unless it first produces multiplicity. There is no motion for a solitary being in an endless void, because there is not yet any change. This void must penetrate being and shatter it into a non-decomposable multiplicity. Those are the atoms of the Greek *atomos*, "not divisible."[42]

According to Democritus, these atoms come in endlessly many shapes and sizes and are constantly in motion. Motion is original, and seeming stillness is merely unapparent, microlevel change. With multiplicity comes motion and, with motion, collision. One effect of atomic collision is that it sifts the atoms and lets the very finest, smallest, most subtle accumulate. That is how soul arises in a material world. A soul is a body, but its matter is special, being extremely fine and volatile. Here is a signature thesis of Western materialism: The soul is a body. Our mental states, including happiness and virtue, depend on the organism, the vital interaction of body and void.[43]

Democritus eliminated the nonmechanical forces, Eros and Strife, that Empedocles introduced. For the atomist, macroscopic things are systems of atoms, which cease to exist when complex things fly apart. The changes of nature are the outcome of collision among atoms in the void, mindless collisions but not exactly random. The point is that no supervising rationality, no *logos* or law, renders atomic changes reasonable. To their opponents, a problem with materialism was how to explain the beginning of motion. Why would lifeless particles perk up and move? Does the cosmic machine not require animation by a spiritual principle? That is the argument of idealists from Plato onward, but Democritus already had answered it with his principle that what is always the case has no cause. Since atoms have always been moving, there is no cause for their motion and no need for one.[44]

What science must explain is not why atoms move but why they change direction. The principle of sufficient reason, which guarantees a cause for every alteration, applies only to what atoms generate, not to the atoms themselves. In nature at the macroscopic level, we see the usual predictability of experience; at the atomic level, however, the changes are stochastic and lawless. Each atom is different, anarchic, without design, intelligence, law, or a decreed place in nature, and so too are all their effects, which is to say, everything. Hence, another signature thesis of materialism is atheism, for which it already had been denounced by Plato and has been ever since.[45]

Materialism took a new step in the generation after Aristotle with the philosophy of Epicurus. Since Epicurus built on Democritean fundamentals, however, I will not discuss it further. The Stoic philosophers invented a different kind of materialism. They agreed with Democritus that nature is a system of bodies, but with no atoms, no fundamental particles. Matter is continuous, not particulate. Any natural body has two constituents: unqualified, passive matter plus its qualifications, qualities like shape, mass, or color. Passive unqualified matter acquires qualities from the intensity and activity of what Stoics call *pneuma*, the vital cosmic breath that stirs unqualified matter and charges it with qualities.[46]

Pneuma itself is a body, though a very fine one, an ethereal mixture of fire and air. This *pneuma* completely mixes with the matter of all other bodies and makes them qualitatively distinct individual entities. Mixing with *pneuma* imparts intensity to otherwise completely relaxed matter, which becomes not just "matter" ("stuff") but an organized body, an organism, a life. Everything in nature is alive. The material continuum is differentiated by every degree of intensity, producing all qualities and making them interact. The motions of nature are not generated by impact, by particles colliding; rather, they are like waves rolling across the ocean. A body and its changes are like a ripple that eventually grows chaotic and disappears into the mass of water.

That ripple is a Stoic parable for the destiny of any single body and all bodies together. The cosmos is one great body, a cosmic egg that, with time, becomes ever more differentiated and complicated and eventually consumes itself in universal conflagration and then starts over, unfolding in exactly the same way every time. In the words of one Stoic, "There will be nothing different in comparison to what has happened before, but everything will occur in just the same way and indistinguishably, even to the last details." We can understand why the Stoics, with their reputation for rationalism, identifying the *pneuma* with the power of *logos*, reason, insisted on this eternal return of the same. The cosmos is a system of finite matter, thoroughly interconnected, penetrated everywhere by an energy that is at once physical and logical, material and rational, a body, but divine. Since matter is finite, there is a limit to growth, which at some point turns the other way to decline. Given the thorough rationality of nature (animated by the logical *pneuma*), it is impossible for these cycles to deviate. Any difference would imply some lapse of rationality, in either the present or the past iteration. Every cosmic cycle must therefore unfold in exactly the same way. Any other history would be illogical, irrational, and therefore impossible.[47]

The atom theory is friendly to body, friendly to multiplicity, but less friendly to becoming or change, which atomism interprets as a surface appearance of a changeless noumenon. Aristotle tells us that the atomists wanted to reconcile the observable phenomena of plurality and motion with a Parmenidean denial of becoming and ceasing to be. With the atoms, all possible divisions have already been made. There is no original, creative becoming, only the endless repetition of the same atoms, an unchangeable primary reality. In swerving from atomism, Stoic materialism avoids this assumption, and it is to the Stoics that Spinoza and Leibniz look in their reform of the Cartesian idea of body. For Stoics, everything is a mixture. Even *pneuma* is a mixture. There is no fundamental body, no last analysis. That makes the Stoics the friends of becoming and change, but they also are notorious rationalists. Reason is the driving power of nature. Nothing happens without reason. Everything that occurs is rational and good, indeed, divine, a conclusion Spinoza and Leibniz later enthusiastically embraced.[48]

Plato so detested materialism that he supposedly advocated having the works of Democritus burned (friends persuaded him that it would be futile, as so many copies were in circulation). In *Laws*, Plato makes materialism a thought crime, and for a time his campaign to obliterate materialism seemed successful. When, with the passing of the Roman Empire, materialist philosophy also disappeared, it seemed as if the gods had finally won. But materialism was only in eclipse and returned after the fifteenth century with the recovery of the forgotten Roman poet Lucretius and his masterpiece of Epicurean materialism, *On the Nature of Things*. Europeans could now study a carefully worked out atomistic theory of nature, with many new explanations of natural phenomena, written in the masterful Latin that scholars read with pleasure.[49]

As the ideas of the atomists became familiar in Europe, people found a lot to like. Plato and Aristotle detached knowledge from prediction and control, which held no value for them. Modern thinkers tend to be utilitarian and to value application. Atomism intrigues them with the promise of works. Although the ancients considered atoms to be beyond the reach of manipulation, to moderns the theory promised a handle on the forces of nature. Experiments can discover nature's mechanical principles, with which we can engineer a technology that emulates nature's productivity.[50]

By the eighteenth century, the old battle was being fought again, pitting atheistic materialists like Julien Offray de La Mettrie and Denis Diderot against idealistic believers in a spiritual principle. These new materialists modernized the concept of matter—Democritus would hardly recognize atoms after materialism took on the discoveries of Isaac Newton and Abraham Trembley, to say nothing of Niels Bohr and Werner Heisenberg. Yet it was not until Charles Darwin that the contest began to favor materialism. Darwin cleared up what had long been the major objection to materialism, the appearance of intelligent design in nature. After Darwin, there was a scientifically convincing materialist explanation of this seeming purposiveness: There is no real design in nature. It only looks like there is. The appearance of design (for example, in the eye or heart) is like the sky appearing blue—a mere appearance mindlessly produced by natural selection in the struggle for existence over geological time.[51]

The idea of evolution rendered classical materialism at once triumphant and obsolete. After Darwin, we now think differently about the body. The most important quality of anything alive is not its type or essence but its variation or somatic singularity. We explain change genealogically, as the evolution of forms from earlier forms, without postulating a stuff permanently common to all forms, or having to assume, as atomists must, that every purely material difference already exists. Matter is not a changeless substratum of change. It is the multifariously changing stuff itself. Matter changes, new bodies proliferate, acquiring new qualities with new potencies. Matter has no essence, only a history. As Diderot foresaw, the line between organic and inorganic bodies blurs into an evolutionary ecology of human and nonhuman things.[52]

An influential idea in modern philosophy arising from the new materialism is that all knowledge is ultimately knowledge of our own body. Friedrich Nietzsche, William James, and Henri Bergson all developed the idea, but it was Baruch Spinoza who first insisted on it. What we think is knowledge of external things is, in fact, knowledge of our own bodies and how they are affected. As Spinoza wrote in his great *Ethics* (1677), "The ideas which we have of external bodies indicate the condition of our own body more than the nature of the external bodies." The reason is that "the human mind does not perceive any external body as actually existing except through the ideas of the affections of its own body." Indeed, even the mind's own knowledge of itself is just more knowledge of the body. "The mind does not know itself except insofar as it perceives the ideas of the affections of the body." Ultimately there is nothing to the "mind" except the idea of the body: "The human mind is the idea itself, or knowledge of the human body." The soul of the soul is the body.[53]

Spinoza rationalistically interpreted this irreducible corporeality of mind as an obstacle. We never think of things as they are in themselves but only as they affect us, so any idea, however scientific, remains to some degree a confused representation of the body. Science never fully rises above a futile passion. But Nietzsche reversed Spinoza's evaluation.

The body is not an obstacle to knowledge. It is what gives knowledge point and value, especially once we drop discredited ideas of truth and God that Spinoza shared with the idealists. The value of knowledge is the instrumentality with which it endows the body. The more you know, the more you can do, change, and become. Nietzsche was among the first philosophers to weigh the implications of Darwinism against philosophical rationalism. According to Darwin, a living body can only be an evolved organism, an adapted survivor, not a demigod entombed in flesh. This Darwinian body defines the point of view of all our perceptions and of everything we make of perceptions, which are the material of all our concepts. Nietzsche disparaged the realists:

> You call yourselves realists and hint that the world really is the way that it appears to you. . . . That mountain there! That cloud there! What is "real" in that? Subtract the phantasm and every human *contribution* from it, my sober friends! If you *can!* If you can forget your descent, your past, your training—all of your humanity and animality.[54]

Other philosophers rethought the body after Darwin. One of the first, William James, maintained that

> so far as "thoughts" and "feelings" can be active, their activity terminates in the activity of the body, and only through first arousing its activities can they begin to change those of the rest of the world. The body is the storm center, the origin of coordinates, the constant place of stress in all that experience-train.

For the innovative phenomenologist Maurice Merleau-Ponty, "It is no mere coincidence that the rational being is also the one who holds himself upright or has a thumb which can be brought opposite to the fingers; the same manner of existing is evident in body aspects." For Bruno Latour, bodies are affective, historical, and growing through a power to differentiate and survive change. Every body traces a profile of learning, a history of "learning to be affected by hitherto unregisterable differences." A body is not so much *had* as acquired, "not a provisional residence of something superior," but something with a trajectory, being sensitive and changing in response to what the world is made of. Latour suggests that the very idea of the body's "subjective side," an interior of self-feeling that is older or more original than any affection arising in response to external changes, is a myth. We cannot so simply discount "all the extrasomatic resources ever invented that allow us to be affected by others in different ways." We neglect to bear in mind that we do not, and will never, know all that a body can do.[55]

Among the most enigmatic of these new corporealists is Gilles Deleuze, who writes, "The body is no longer the obstacle that separates thought from itself, that which it has to overcome to reach thinking. It is on the contrary that which [thought] plunges into or must plunge into, in order to reach the unthought, that is life." He is saying that thinking is an encounter with its other, with what is not a thought or like a thought. What can thought encounter? As it was for Spinoza and Nietzsche, for Deleuze the answer is the corporeal vitality of the body. Everything we encounter engenders a response from the body. We learn about everything by learning how we respond to it, learning whether we can live with it. The limits of thought are the limits of what we can cooperate with and incorporate. Thought does not judge or evaluate life; life calls thought into being and is the only thing thought thinks. "To think is to learn what a non-thinking body is capable of."[56]

Nietzsche said what Spinoza said, what Hobbes said, what Darwin implied, and what Deleuze and Latour confirm: Spirit, self, creative power—these are corporeal effects. Everything good or bad, all values, exist in relation to the body, its powers, pleasures, and drives. To Nietzsche, "A simple discipline of feeling and thought amounts to practically nothing, you need first to persuade the *body*." "It is," he says, "crucial for the fate of individuals as well as peoples that culture begin in the *right* place," which is "*not* in the 'soul.'" The right place "is the body, gestures, diet, physicality. *Everything else* follows from this." Knowledge knows the body by the body for the body. Thought is an interpretation of the body. Philosophy translates the body into value judgments. And for Nietzsche, the value judgments organizing modern European civilization were a malicious misunderstanding foisted on humanity by sickly saints.[57]

THE CORPOREAL TURN

From the beginning of theoretical thought in the West down to modern times, philosophy's concept of knowledge has boycotted the body. Obstacle, as Plato called it, nothing but obstacle. Materialism contested this idea, initially with little success, impeded by the rationalism that the first materialists shared with their idealistic antagonists. It was Darwin, writing as a naturalist and not a metaphysician, who finally refuted the idealistic assumption that the highest values are indifferent to the body. Yet after all this time, nearly two centuries since Darwin, we still lack a vocabulary suitable for the evolved, Darwinian body. How do we say "body" and mean mind no less? How do we say "mind" and mean body too?[58]

This is hard to do because the philosophers who invented the difference between mind and body *wanted* a dichotomy, to force this agonizing clarity on the poets and the cult of athletics. Which are you training, mind or body? Which do you value, corporeal pleasure or intellectual virtue? To make these questions troubling requires a compelled choice between body and soul. Little changed in modern times. Descartes wanted the dichotomy between mind and matter to be as sharp and exclusive as can be imagined. For him, a dichotomy between mind and body was a solution, not a problem. The problem was how to get the soul out of physics. Descartes wanted a purely physical physics, which explains everything about bodies in terms of bodies, with no need for the soul or its purposes. Compared with success in that great goal, the mind-body problem was an annoying detail.

A Darwinian body is soulful simply because it is alive. In his book *The Expression of the Emotions in Man and Animals*, Darwin reproduced a line drawing of a cat rubbing against someone's leg. The caption reads: "Cat in an affectionate frame of mind." The cat is affectionate. Indeed, affection is just one of its frames of mind. "Worms," Darwin pointed out elsewhere, "although standing low in the scale of organization, possess some degree of intelligence." He observed their pleasure in eating, their eagerness for certain foods, their sexual passion, and social feelings. Another authority said this about aquatic fan worms: "Touch them, or pass a shadow across [their] filtering crown, and they vanish down their tubes, only emerging, with great caution and very slowly, after several minutes." Their movement is cautious, intelligently so. I think Darwin wanted us to take such language seriously. To censor it or feel the need to sanitize it, to skirt words like "affection" and "caution" with priggish shudder-quotes, or to strive to reduce them to quantifiable movements, thinking that only then will you have distilled what is really going on, is to misunderstand the body, the soul, science, and perhaps even yourself.[59]

The caution of worms and the affection of cats are univocally attributed and are not analogies, equivocations, or pathetic anthropomorphism. Everything we recognize as a mental power, all our intentionality and consciousness, is continuous with powers that probably reach to every level of animate nature. All living bodies, being evolved Darwinian bodies, are to some degree conscious and intelligent, because if something is alive, then it moves, and animate self-movement is the fundamental expression of intelligence. Lately, new work by philosophers attuned to evolutionary biology, cognitive science, and somatic phenomenology has advanced the understanding of this Darwinian body with its Darwinian mind. Let us look at a few examples.

Maxine Sheets-Johnstone is a phenomenologist of living movement. Her argument for the primacy of movement postulates its primacy to mind, to consciousness, and to life. For her, as for Bergson, "alive," "conscious," and "self-moving" are merely verbally different descriptions of the same reality. Animation primarily means responsiveness. Animate movement is a corporeal response to the environment, and such movement is, or can be, a proprioceptively sensed intensive quality that is *felt*. The sense of touch folds back on itself, turning inside to become the proprioceptive sense of a body's own movement. If a creature moves at all, if it is animate and responsive, it needs this qualitative feedback for efficiency. Since anything with such responsiveness seems likely to outcompete anything that lacks it, this inevitable adaptation of life is the beginning of consciousness. "Consciousness," Sheets-Johnstone says, "does not arise *in matter*; it arises in organic forms," and "any form of life that moves itself—any animate form—knows itself to be moving not because there is a *self* in the verbal locution but because there is a kinetic consciousness of some kind, a consciousness subserving movement."[60]

A related theme in Sheets-Johnstone's work is the moving body as the primary source of concepts. "We make sense of our bodies first and foremost," and we make sense of them "in and through movement, in and through *animation*. Moreover, we do so without words. This primordial sense-making is the standard upon which our sense-making of the world unfolds." Our various capacities for movement offer what she calls a semantic template for the development of concepts. Through bodily movements, we become aware of corporeal powers, things we can do (carry, chew, throw, and so on), and this awareness is the beginning of corporeal concepts based on these felt powers of the body: "Animate bodies represent by symbolizing the spatio-kinetic dynamics of their own experiences." Tactility, our feeling for the organism, predisposes us to invent concepts that represent things in terms we know, ultimately from felt knowledge of the body. One case that Sheets-Johnstone works out in detail concerns the evolution she thinks that human ancestors made from feeling their own teeth to inventing a stone tool. Discovering (by conscious feeling) their own teeth and a kinesthetic appreciation of their qualities and powers is, she suggests, the imaginative-cognitive matrix from which stone tools emerged.[61]

Mark Johnson's work takes a different approach to a comparable thesis. Leaning on cognitive science more than phenomenology, Johnson argues that abstract concepts are largely metaphorical and that the basis of the metaphors is usually corporeal, the projection of something that we first recognize from feeling our body. Cognition, or intelligence more broadly, is thus embodied; the imaginative structures of understanding have their origin in the body. We put things into or remove them from containers and thus understand containment. We experience linear and nonlinear paths of movement and thus understand trajectory. We feel what it takes to move a thing and thus understand force and causation. Cognition is not representation; it is action, a response, a strategy, evolved and ecologically situated. Its logic is satisficing—not ideal but adaptive, good enough. And this cognition is social, cooperative, distributed among artifacts and over other agents. People are not homunculi locked in minds with fixed abilities. Mechanisms created by the interaction of biological brains and their environment become proper parts of new cognitive processes. Minds no less than bodies are constantly restructured with new equipment incorporated into thought and action. Really incorporated. The body is not given all at once like a dead lump but is continually subjected to the negotiation of its components, faculties, interfaces, and limitations. We are again reminded of Spinoza: we do not know once and for all what a body can do.[62]

A Darwinian body is not an instrument, as Plato, Aristotle, and their tradition maintained. This body is not an object that we hold at a distance and manipulate by intention. There is no distance between us and our movements. "The ego acts directly on the world," explained body phenomenologist Michel Henry. "It does not act through the intermediary of a body, it does not recur to any means in carrying out its movements, it is itself this body, itself this movement, itself this means. Ego, body, movement, means, are but one and the same thing." This thing is alive, energetic, and willful, is endowed with vitality, and resists instrumental domination. We guide our body only by submitting to it. But guide it we do and can improve it, meliorate it, teach it new tricks.[63]

A Darwinian body is an intelligent body capable of self-improvement. Having such a body creates the opportunity, or really the demand, for the corporeal cultivation that Richard Shusterman calls "somaesthetics," which he explains as the "use of one's body as a locus of sensory-aesthetics appreciation and creative self-fashioning." Our normal spontaneous body sense is often painfully inaccurate and dysfunctional. F. M. Alexander spoke of modern people's "debauched kinesthesia." Somaesthetic theory and practice propose enhancing the use of somatic reflection in body disciplines (dance, martial arts, athletics, juggling), promising to improve performance by putting parts and phases into temporary focus so they can be retrained.[64]

Recent work on the phenomenology of the body advances the proposition that cognitive capacities, including perception and intentional movement, are conditioned by body morphology and dynamics. Clinical research confirms how movement and its perception contribute to the self-organizing development of neuronal structures for motor and cognitive action. According to Shaun Gallagher, a leader in this area of philosophical research, "The very shape of the human body, its lived mechanics, its endogenous processes, and its interactions with the environment" work "in dynamic unity with the human nervous system" to define ineluctable constraints on experience. He refers to the "prenoetic structure" of understanding, which instead of being structured according to the categories of transcendental logic is formed by the ultimately contingent way that human beings are adapted to life on earth.[65]

For example, consider our neurological predisposition to respond to the sight, and especially the visible motion, of other people. I have in mind the so-called mirror neurons. These neurons are active both when an animal moves and when it perceives another make the same movement. The neurons mirror the behavior of the other, as though the observer were making the movement too. Such neurons have been demonstrated in primates and other species, including birds. Of course, *Homo sapiens* has lots of them, generously distributed in the premotor cortex, supplementary motor area, and somatosensory cortex. In monkeys, the same cluster of neurons fires when one performs a noisy action (cracking a peanut) or merely sees another do it or even just hears the noise. In humans, mirror effects can be elicited by merely imagining the action. What we learn in the martial arts about visualization is true and important. It is a preparation for action. By imaginatively visualizing an action in advance, you can move much faster when you actually perform it, because in your brain, no less than in your mind, you have already performed the action several times.[66]

Mirror neurons show action and perception to be interpenetrating phases of each other. Mirror-neuron networks are intact and operating at birth. Infants less than an hour old can imitate facial gestures and hand movements. We learn to move our bodies by the involuntary imitations that ripple through us, unconsciously resonating with the movements of others. Voluntary movement begins in the compulsive replication of another's movement. There is no priority for self-body awareness over perception of the other; the movements of the other trigger an unchosen response that imparts the first lessons in self-awareness. We cannot *not* be affected and respond to the other's movement or fail to discover the other as a compulsive object of imitation. This response to the movement of others is indispensable to acquiring the voluntary control we expect of adults. There is nothing conscious about it, nothing voluntary. We are drawn into voluntary movement like marionettes drawn into action by a puppeteer.[67]

Mirror neurons also show that visual and motor systems interface from birth. We do not *learn* to coordinate what we perceive and how we move. Therefore we must disallow an input-output picture of the relation between perception and action. In that picture, perception is input, nothing but input. Directed, intentional movement is a correlated output, a computational function of input. The difficulty with this way of thinking is that it treats mind as an inner place with a boundary that sets it apart from body, sense, and environment—the inner space where mind computes its motor output from the perceptual input. A Darwinian body cannot work like that. For James Gibson, a psychologist of perception, there is no "visual system" that is anything less than the whole body in the environment to which evolution adapts it. How different can perception and action be? It seems to be a consensus in clinical neurology that the distinction between motor and sensory neurons is arbitrary, or at least not sharp. The neurologist and Nobel laureate Gerald Edelman notes that "there is nothing intrinsically motor about the motor cortex, nor sensory about the sensory cortex." The idea is not new. Roger Sperry, another neurologist and Nobel laureate, had already made the point in 1952:

> Insofar as an organism perceives a given object, it is prepared to respond with reference to it. . . . The structure of the brain, as well as what is known of its physiology, discourages any effort to separate the motor from the sensory and associative processes. To the best of our knowledge there is only a gradual merging and transformation of one into the other, with nothing to suggest where perception might end and motor processes begin.[68]

Parmenides, venerable and awesome, invented a great difference between habit (*ethos*) and intellectual thought (*noema*), depicting habit as a brute force roiling reasonable persuasion. "Let not habit do violence to you upon this empirical way, so that you exercise an unseeing eye and a noisy ear and tongue." Later Socrates complained that artisans do not really understand anything, that their "knowledge" (*techne*) is merely an unthinking habit. Wrong. It is wrong to surmise that there is no understanding. There is merely no conscious, verbal, discursive, rationalized, logical expression of understanding and no need for it. The Socratic argument confuses a lack of verbal, discursively articulated reasons with a lack of knowledge. Plato has Socrates observe that art's *techne*-knowledge remained below the level of discursive consciousness, from which he inferred that it was less lofty, valuable, and pure than the better knowledge of the mind alone. If you cannot say it, describe it, discourse on it, explicate it in a *logos*, then you cannot know or understand, and whatever you *are* capable of doing (the technical work of art) cannot be the highest accomplishment of the best knowledge. What this argument arrogantly overlooks is that consciousness and discursive explication are not a "higher" but merely a different expression of knowledge and often are less effective than reliably productive corporeal performance.[69]

The American pragmatist John Dewey thought it was a mistake for philosophers to listen to Parmenides and oppose habit to intellect. The relevant distinction should be between creative, intelligent habits and less intelligent ones. Instead of trying to set habit aside for something more intuitive or formal, we should attend to its different qualities and learn to identify those that enhance or inhibit habit's usefulness. Habitual actions are spontaneous, performed without the intervention of choice, but they are not performed without focus or an awareness of the interactive context, the object manipulated, conditions of posture, constraint, obstacles, and so on. To act with trained spontaneity is to surrender to the body's ability to discover and select the most suitable form for interaction. We come to feel movements as well timed (or not) and discover movement-generated values—the unsuitable, missed, reached, right, wrong, and so on. According to Paul Ricoeur,

> All the monographs on the acquisition of habits point to this curious relation between the intention which launches out in a specific direction and the response arising from the body and the mind, which always has the air of an improvisation. This is familiar in the case of skaters, pianists, and even aspiring writers. Habit only grows through this type of

germination and inventiveness concealed within it. To acquire a habit does not mean to repeat and consolidate but to invent, to progress.[70]

Are you taking care of your body or your mind? Western rationalism begins with the compulsion to impose this question. It is past time to resist the coercion. Even intellectual virtues like knowledge and wisdom are not indifferent to the powers of the body. Philosophy's corporeal turn may lead to a kind of neo-Pindarianism. The body is an athletic reality, a virtual athlete. Any body of any age, gender, or condition can be trained, its movements enhanced in various dimensions. A body is athletic to the extent that it responds to limits as challenges and is thus less a material *being* than a material process, less an actual, finished body than an always becoming process-body, one that must become what it is and not just wallow in an eternally given essence. A line from Pindar, famously appropriated by Nietzsche, reads, "Become who you are." To become who one is—to *have* to become who one is—is the *questing* that Pindar admired in athletes. This athletic process-body has no permanent essence like "extension" or "passivity." Bodies constantly acquire new potential through art and interaction. To this day, still no one knows all that a body can do.[71]

The body of postmodern materialism never stops changing. Material processes ceaselessly produce new ways to be material. Lines between alive and dead, conscious and unconscious, artificial and natural, and human and nonhuman become fuzzy, as do definitive attributions of agency. This is materialism for a multiverse. Every assemblage, whether of nature or art, convenes material bodies and forces, but there is no homogeneous material that every assemblage inevitably convokes. That means no ultimate material (atoms, impassive *hyle*, dead mass) and no premature closure on the question of what bodies there are or what they can do. But why postmodern materialism at all? Why not drop this metaphysical theme?

The answer comes from an unexpected source. Thinking probably of Democritus, Plato explained that materialists "strenuously affirm that real existence belongs only to that which can be handled and offers resistance to the touch. They define reality as the same thing as body." In his dialogue *Sophist*, Plato has the Stranger ask the obliging Theaetetus what "real" is supposed to mean when materialists say that only the corporeal and tangible is real. Because the tradition has no answer, the Stranger proposes one: "Anything has real being that is so constituted as to possess any sort of power either to affect anything or to be affected, in however small a degree. . . . I am proposing as a mark to distinguish real things that they are nothing but power."[72]

Plato thought that by accepting this explanation materialists would be swallowing a poisoned pill, as it leads to a contradiction they could eliminate only by becoming idealists. The argument is not convincing, though, and begs the question against materialism. Plato believed he already knew what a body can do, and it cannot cause justice or wisdom. Nonetheless, we can use Plato's explanation in the service of materialism, as the Stoics and, later, Spinoza and Nietzsche did, and agree that "body" means not impassive matter but actual power. To be material, to be a body, is to be a power and to act, to act on other bodies. A "material body" is a trajectory more than a lump, constantly transforming in response to environmental interactions and not merely displaced in the homogeneous space of *res extensa*.

Why materialism, then? Because materialism is physicalism, naturalism, the philosophy of reality in the only sense we know, which is the sense we perceive and feel, the reality of apperception and affection. What is common to bodies is their power, not their essence; their affective potential, not their form or actuality. When considering any body, do not ask, What is it in and for itself, its nature or essence? Ask instead how it has evolved its power to interact with other bodies in an environment. What can it do?

IT IS rare to find worthwhile observations on the martial arts in works of Western philosophy, but there is one in the *Thousand Plateaus* of Gilles Deleuze and Félix Guattari. Here is the whole passage:

> The martial arts have always subordinated weapons to speed [*vitesse*], and above all to mental (absolute) speed [*la vitesse mentale (absolue)*]; for this reason, they are also the arts of suspense and immobility [*du suspens et de l'immobilité*]. . . . The martial arts do not adhere to a

code, as an affair of the state, but follow *ways* which are so many paths of the affect; upon these ways, one learns to "unuse" weapons as much as one learns to use them, as if the power and the cultivation of the affect were the true goal of the assemblage, the weapon being only a provisory means. Learning to undo things, and to undo oneself, is proper to the war machine: the "not-doing" of the warrior, the undoing of the subject.[73]

And here is my analysis of several of its points:

• *The martial arts have always subordinated weapons to speed, especially mental (absolute) speed.* It would be better if they had said *timing*. The concern with being fast, or thinking about speed, is a recognized mistake about which martial masters warn. For instance, Chang Naizhou warned: "If you seek speed, you conversely become slow; if you seek keenly, you conversely become dulled." What to a nonpracticing observer may look like speed is often a matter of timing. Speed as such is not a proper goal of martial arts training, although timing is; because if one is not good at timing, it will only be luck, not strength or speed that prevents one from getting hurt. In the words of Miyamoto Musashi, Japan's celebrated samurai, "In martial arts, speed is not the true Way. As far as speed is concerned, the question of fast or slow in anything derives from failure to harmonize with the rhythm." Perhaps Deleuze and Guattari appreciated this point, which may explain their qualification of speed as "mental" and "absolute," a learned allusion to Epicurus. The speed of thought is not really, really fast. It is the absolute velocity of duration, like the instantaneous movement from one musical note to another. In the martial arts, timing is mainly a matter of being able to perform complicated serial movements in one beat, one uninterrupted, interpenetrating measure, whose time is neither fast nor slow but *right*.[74]

• *They are arts of suspense and immobility.* This point is especially apt if we think in terms of timing rather than speed. Greek athletes also worshiped Kairos, the god of the opportune moment, divine timing. Such timing is a matter of suspense and immobility. One has to be good at waiting and holding back, motionless and uncommitted.

• *The martial arts do not adhere to a* code *as an affair of the state but follow* ways, *which are so many paths of the affect.* An "affair of the state" means a legal institution, recognized, legitimate, governed by laws. Operating a motor vehicle is an affair of the state, but playing street hockey is not. The martial arts, Deleuze and Guattari say, are not an affair of the state, which probably was largely true in their premodern (preglobalization) days. In the beginning, the martial arts seem to have been private, organized in families and villages, and only occasionally migrating into the city or even the palace, though always as something esoteric, never as a state ritual. Now, of course, most centers of martial arts instruction are businesses, with all the attendant legalities. But they have not completely lost the ancient quality of private cultivation rather than public display, a way or path of the affect instead of a code-governed affair of state, as Deleuze and Guattari say, a *dao* of intensified affectivity, meaning the capacity both to act and to feel.

• *One learns to "unuse" weapons as much as to use them.* That is, one learns not to need them, not to miss weapons. One knows that empty hands are weapons too, but more than that, one becomes good at not needing weapons or violence of any kind. One realizes that "the power and the cultivation of the affect [is] the true goal of the assemblage, the weapon being only a provisory means." This is the great point on which the Chinese spiritualized their martial arts. Fighting prowess is a by-product of a mastery that is really about the self, the body, the mind, and the way of affects.

• *Learning to undo things, and to undo oneself, is the character of a war machine.* A "war machine" is an assemblage of men, weapons, animals, flags and banners, and so on, capable of prodigious violence, a destructive force almost like one of nature yet intelligently commanded. Wherever there is a state, there is an unassimilable outside that presents itself as such a war machine. These are the nomads. Al-Qaeda is a contemporary example. Nomads are not just outside; they are organized predators, and states are their prey. Nomads emerge in response to states and do not proceed them as an earlier prestate form. For example, the Chinese imperium created the nomads who ravaged its northern borders and twice conquered the empire. A nomadic war machine is a symbiont of civilization, just as rats are symbionts of cities and weeds are symbionts of agriculture. A war machine does not necessarily have battle as its goal. Rather, its object is to make its environing space smooth. That means smoothing unnaturally sharp lines, lines of the sort that only a state can draw, like lines of property. The nomadic Manchus did not have Chinese-style family names passed on from generation to generation. Deleuze and Guattari are saying that nomads are drawn to any such organization, drawn to prey on it and to take satisfaction in overcoming its unnatural rigidity. It is in that sense that they say learning to undo things is proper to a war machine. The nomad's terrible motto is "Make the desert grow."[75]

The Asian martial arts are a nomadic war machine, and the non-action (*wuwei*) these arts teach is a teaching on undoing the self. A philosopher among martial artists described the higher challenge of martial arts training in just this way. "It is a surrendering of control over 'this thing here,' an abandoning also of the illusion of control and a willingness to 'invest in less' that results in mastery." In the words of another long-time practitioner,

> What is sought [in martial arts training] is a state of mind in which the act does not suffer the hindrance of the ego, in which the expression of no-mind [*wuxin*] predominates. This leads to a paradox: in order to carry on combat effectively, you must not think of harming your opponent; you must not think of winning.

Nomads do not think of winning. The fight's the thing. They cannot lose because they have nothing *to* lose, property being an artifact of codes and laws, the stately civilization they relentlessly subvert.[76]

Subjecting violence to a contract has undergone many experiments, for instance, in consensual sexual masochism, in combat sports with their rules, and in politics, in which the social contract *contracts* violence, redistributing it and subjecting it to rules. Violence in martial arts has no contract, which is why training in the martial arts can be dangerous. Although in practice, the contract is the rules and etiquette of the training hall, it is so peripheral to what is being taught that it is constantly in danger of being violated, however unintentionally. Non-contractual violence thus makes the martial arts nomadic, affiliated with war, and it sharply differentiates their violence from that of sport or masochism, which remain playful in a way that the martial arts never are. Unlike the serious use of skills that, say, a football player uses, the serious use of skills practiced in the martial arts is never playful.

THE BODY IN TRAINING

To make sense is to make the body understand. The terms of intelligibility are ultimately corporeal, all good and bad, all sense and nonsense are ultimately qualities of bodies. These have been themes of materialism since Democritus, although soma-centered philosophy is no longer bound to his untenable atomism. Ancient materialism was both an ethos and a metaphysics, with the metaphysics (the materialist theory of nature) supposedly rationalizing the ethos or way of life. The gist of the metaphysics is the idea that body is an ultimate substratum. One sort of entity—body, matter—is common to everything that exists. The corresponding ethos is that if you work on the body, you will work on everything that matters to virtue and happiness. Organize your body for pleasure and you will organize it well and achieve *arete*. The body will guide you with pleasure and pain to the best life for a human being: cheerful happiness and tranquillity. "The criterion of the advantageous and the disadvantageous is enjoyment and the lack of enjoyment," insisted Democritus, known in antiquity as "the laughing philosopher."[77]

Thomas Hobbes was an important transitional figure linking ancient and modern materialism. In his system there are bodies (plural), but no body, singular and substratum, nothing changelessly present throughout even the most turbulent changes. All bodies of whatever scale are moving. To be a body is to be interacting with bodies. There is no body as such, just mere matter, permanently present beneath the rippling surface of nature. The only time that a body like ours is unaffected, imperturbable, or tranquil is when we are dead. Consequently, tranquillity cannot have the value that it had in antiquity. According to Hobbes, "The Felicity of this life consistheth not in the repose of a mind satisfied." There is nothing that upon attaining it, we would want for nothing more: "There is no such *Finis ultimus* (utmost ayme), nor *Summum Bonum* (greatest Good) as is spoken of in the Books of the old Morall Philosophers." The body is always moving; therefore its good must be a quality of motion, not a terminal state like "happiness" or "tranquillity." Hobbes named this kinetic good: "I put for a general inclination of all man kind, a perpetualle and restlesse desire of power after power, that ceaseth onely in Death."[78]

For Hobbes, what made life good was a quality of becoming, a quality of changes. Philosophy, as the art of the good life, thus becomes an art of changing in a way that maximizes pleasure and minimizes pain. The Asian martial arts make a comparable assumption. The goal of practice is an art of moving, not passive stillness. We need movement to be happy. Happiness is nothing *in* life; rather, it is the unfolding or becoming *of* life—not a way of *being* but of *becoming*. Philosophy should be a preparation for enhanced movement instead of death (as Socrates maintained). Hobbes was right to think that nothing is ever really not in motion. It is only a question of scale. But why did he have to oppose tranquillity to change and movement? For Zhuangzi, tranquillity was a *way* of changing and moving: "To be transformed day by day with other things is to be untransformed once and for all." It is a great mistake, commented the Qing-dynasty thinker Wang Fuzhi on that passage, "to think you need to eliminate turmoil to seek tranquillity." Tranquillity is nothing unless it is tranquillity *amid* turmoil, a *becoming* tranquil that never quite displaces turmoil, as the most potent yang never entirely displaces yin. The tranquillity of the wise is not impassable changelessness but is the power (emptiness) to grow through changes. That is an ideal of those who practice the martial arts for ethical self-cultivation rather than self-defense or competition.[79]

Philosophers could have learned some of what the martial arts teach about the body by paying attention to athletics, or indeed to any *techne*, a knowledge of which resists the linguistic, propositional, representational format of Western theory and especially its theories of knowledge. My principal topic in this book is the martial arts traditions beginning in China and variously modified in Korea, Japan, and elsewhere in East Asia before their more recent globalization. That is the sense that most people (in my speech community) understand if you say, for example, that you "practice martial arts," or that you watched a "martial arts movie." I would like to suspend this concentration for a moment in order to consider two practices variously resembling yet clearly distinct from these martial arts. One is Western boxing, and the other is Indian wrestling.

The Sweet Science

Aficionados refer to boxing as the "sweet science." It is also, as Joyce Carol Oates pointed out, "the only sport in which the objective is to cause injury: the brain is the target; the knockout the goal." This sweet science does not distinguish between body and mind because, as Sunzi recognized, the smart way to fight is to fight the mind. Sociologist Loïc Wacquant made an ethnographic study of a boxing gym on Chicago's South Side, where he spent several years enduring a boxer's training and eventually contending in the city's annual Golden Gloves competition. He describes the Woodlawn Boys Club where he trained: "Prominently displayed above the big mirror is a black and white photo of a young, bare-chested colossus, all muscles flexed, a menacing gaze on his face, inscribed with this injunction: '*Select the things that go into your mind!*'"[80]

Wacquant entered the regimen of the club and the tutelage of its trainer, training diligently for several years. Martial arts practitioners will appreciate his account of "the maddeningly slow drift that occurs, from week to week, in the mastery of the moves; in the understanding—most often retrospective and purely gestural—of pugilistic technique; and the modification that transpires in one's relationship to one's body and one's perception of the gym and the activities of which it is the support." One thing his body taught him was to disabuse him of the idea that dispositions can be divided into mental and physical. Eventually he found it impossible to understand the difference. Is courage mental or physical? Is the will that takes one through another day of training psychical or corporeal? Wacquant found the "mutual imbrication" of corporeal and mental to reach such a degree "that even willpower, morale, determination, concentration, and the control of one's emotions change into so many reflexes inscribed within the organism."[81]

To refashion whatever untrained body walks through the door and commits to the training is a formidable task of corporeal remodeling, or what Richard Shusterman calls "melioristic somaesthetics." One instructs the body in the only terms it understands, which are those of movement. Training internalizes a set of dispositions, insepara- bly mental and physical, that eventually "turn the body into a virtual punching machine but," Wacquant adds, "an intelligent and creative machine capable of self-regulation while innovating within a fixed and relative restricted panoply of moves." To strengthen the body, you must strengthen the mind, and vice versa. A mind that sees what is com- ing, recognizes it, and prepares a response is the mind of a stronger body and a better fighter. Boxers have a theory that a fighter will not be knocked out if he sees the punch coming. "For then he suffers no dra- matic lack of communication," as Norman Mailer explains, between body and consciousness:

> The blow may hurt but cannot wipe him out. In contrast, a five punch combination in which every shot lands is certain to stampede any op- ponent into unconsciousness. No matter how light the blows, a jack- pot has been struck. The sudden new loading of the victim's message center is bound to produce that inrush of confusion known as coma.[82]

Wacquant's training taught him something that neurologists and body phenomenologists have discovered too, which is that perception and action are two phases of a single process. Wacquant has a keen sense of their interplay. Learning to box is both learning to move and learning to see: "Every gesture, every posture of the pugilist's body possesses an infinite number of specific properties that are minute and invisible to those who do not have the appropriate categories for percep- tion and appreciation." I like a remark he quotes from a French national trainer: "For a punch to be really thrown effectively, it is unimaginable the number of conditions that have to be met." Wacquant describes his experience with the basic boxing punches. "Far from being 'natural' and self-evident," they "are difficult to execute properly and presup- pose a thorough physical rehabilitation, a genuine remodeling of one's kinetic coordination." In my experience, that is very true. My hapkido teacher takes special pains with punching, more than any other master I have trained with. Anyone who thinks it is a simple thing to throw a powerful and accurate punch or that a punch is made strong by strong arms is suffering from an affliction that Bergson would appreciate: what you cannot do you usually cannot see either.[83]

Wacquant's body taught him that it can acquire knowledge with almost no intervention by consciousness and that it can apply that knowledge without missing conscious thought. Books are pointless, and his trainer dismissed them derisively: "Theoretical mastery is of little help so long as the move is not inscribed within one's bodily schema." You will never understand such books until it is too late and you no longer need them. Training pursues "a comprehension of the body that goes beyond—and comes prior to—full visual and mental cognizance." The body phenomenologist Shaun Gallagher referred to the "prenoetic structuration performed by the body" and required before any understanding, conscious or corporeal, is possible. Wacquant discovered the maxim of martial arts training that identifies mastery with unconscious competence. You approach boxing mastery insofar as you first are able to become conscious of your incompetence and then, with practice, ease back into the unconsciousness of enlarged competence. The body has learned. The crutches of consciousness, with which rationalism wants to hobble the body for the sake of the mind, have no further value. The body expresses its knowledge in the only way it can, by movement (a clever tongue or fingers dancing across a keyboard are special cases of corporeal movement). The trained body is a "spontaneous strategist; it knows, understands, judges, and reacts all at once."[84]

Western boxing is not a martial art in the sense that I use in this book. It is a combative sport, an athletic competition, a game with rules. Martial arts are none of those things. In boxing, the purpose of violence, becoming violent on purpose (within the rules), is required for competitive success and is expected and trained. Wacquant observed the gym's trainer discouraging anyone who had no hope of eventually competing. Many boxers he met were incapable of pursuing their training beyond their mid- to late thirties because they had been hurt too much (the same is often true of dancers). By contrast, the Asian martial arts emphasize lifelong training and consider their practice a contribution to longevity, whether or not it truly is. "As I grow older, I notice that my technique gets stronger," said the aikido grand master Phong

Dang at age sixty-six. An "old Shaolin saying" supposedly advises, "Do not practice now what you will not be able to do better when you are eighty." Many martial arts practitioners train as assiduously as boxers, but it is a different training, more conducive to health. Boxers *learn* violence. In the martial arts, at least those in my experience, this is never done. The training makes no use of violence despite the violent design of the techniques and the expressive violence of demonstration.[85]

Wacquant also found a certain casualness in the ethos of the gym. He was expected to put in his time daily, in a circuit of exercises, punching a bag, shadowboxing at the mirror, calisthenics, and sparing. But he seldom received instruction in what he was trying to learn. Although the trainer and older students of the gym occasionally offered tips and criticism, they were desultory and quite informal. Whatever they said that might have been valuable he mostly had to discover for himself through repetition. "It is only after it has been assimilated by the body in and through endless physical drills and repeated *ad nauseam* that it becomes in turn fully intelligible to the intellect."[86]

Modern martial arts training usually takes a more formal approach to instruction. It may be group instruction, with a teacher leading a class through drills, or one-on-one with an instructor, or a small group of two or three. These smaller groups are the ideal conditions for learning martial arts techniques. The level of detail at which a master can analyze such seemingly simple matters as throwing a punch or kick can hardly be imagined by anyone who imagines that a punch or a kick is a simple thing. Although mastering any of these techniques requires a lot of repetition, the way can be eased by good instruction. Practice becomes more efficient once one becomes conscious of one's incompetence, something that good teachers do in a way that encourages the confidence that with practice one can take one's competence to a higher level. One no longer needs competition to motivate improvement. Rather, one becomes motivated to train and endure because one is made productively aware of one's incompetence and knows what to work on without having to be "instructed" by losing a fight.

When training in the gym, boxing is a craft. The work teaches the value of repetition and discipline. The atmosphere is cooperative. Everybody is alert to the instructional value of everyone else's labor. But competition changes everything. In the ring, boxing is all performance. If, as Wacquant suggested, trainers are not interested in pupils with no hope of competing, then boxing is indeed ultimately about the fight. Without a fight, without competition and an audience, the training loses its point. Martial arts training is not like that. The work is focused on self-improvement, indifferent to any audience except the teacher, and the techniques are too violent for competition. Boxing matches are not scripted and rehearsed as "pro" wrestling is. It is a real match, a real competition, with contestants whose purpose is to be as violent as possible within the rules. If it were not for the fans, the glory, who would do it? The practice of martial arts has no fans and no glory, only the quiet path of somaesthetic cultivation. In the words of the Qing-dynasty master Chang Naizhou, "Those who receive my teachings can on the highest level become enlightened and transcend the mortal realm, and at the very least strengthen their bodies, eliminate illness, and achieve longevity."[87]

A Body of One Color

The practice of the martial arts is an example of what Marcel Mauss called "body techniques" and their associated habitus, meaning social habits, habits that are a function of societies (including the small-scale societies of the training hall or *dōjō*) and vary minimally with individual experience. An ethnographic account of traditional Indian wrestling (*bharatia kushti*) provides an excellent example of such techniques and their habitus. This wrestling is not strictly a martial art, as its techniques have no instrumental martial value suitable to combative use outside the training ground. Yet this wrestling is a discipline that boys and men follow for what, to be brief, we might call spiritual reasons: "The first step of any [wrestling] exercise begins with the question: who am I and what am I put on this earth for? It proceeds along a direct path of regimentation to a subjective experience of self as whole and healthy." The rules apparently resemble Olympic freestyle wrestling, although Indian wrestling is not practiced as a spectacle, and competitions—held, for instance, as fund-raising events for the *akhara*, or training place—do not have the competitive intensity of matches in Western boxing.[88]

Training in this wrestling is a deliberately chosen way of life, combining religion, physical exercise, and diet. A committed wrestler follows rules of daily regimen that set the times of waking, toilet, hygiene, meals, exercise, and training. The wrestlers practice techniques, but they also discuss and write about the relation of moral virtue to physical strength and disciplined abstinence. The values of this habitus are strength, skill, devotion, duty, honesty, humility, and celibacy. The practice ostentatiously crosses professional and especially caste lines: businessmen mixing with teachers, farmers, policemen, and so on. They understand their practice of mutual massage as a critique of caste society. As elite wrestlers, they are too good for the usual rules of purity. Caste differences are an insidious symptom of the illusory divisions afflicting the common mind. The wrestlers' concept of health is yogic. Worldly concerns only divert people from health and self-realization. Accordingly, followers of their Way want to get over them as effectively as they can.[89]

The center of everything in this practice is the *akhara*, "training ground." It is a place carefully set aside, screened by trees, a hidden, sanctified place of calm and clean amid the grimy chaos of India's cities, "where earth is turned into gold." The *akhara* is life as it should be. Everything that is wrong with the world is a departure from something that the men of the *akhara* know to be required for the best life. The soil of the wrestling pit is carefully prepared, refreshed annually, mixed with rose petals and turmeric for healing qualities. A well for drinking and bathing is nearby. A shrine to Lord Hanuman, the divine patron of wrestling, the monkey god, son of the wind, and leader of a monkey army, is ritually saluted on entering and leaving. As a quasi temple, the *akhara* may be served by informal, semiresident priests. According to their ethnographer, the devotions carried out by the men who train there are practical, not mystical, accepted as a phase in the discipline they have embraced.[90]

Everything that takes place in the *akhara* and in the wrestler's whole life is dominated by his guru, who often is from a lineage line with the *akhara*'s founder. His responsibility is to mold disciples into the shape of perfection, "a body of one color." Like the *paidotribus* of the Greek gymnasium, the guru develops a personalized training regime for each wrestler. He sets the day's activities in motion, determines who will wrestle whom, for how long, and supervises the exercises. Beyond this training, he constantly shows disciples the right path to follow. The wrestler must "think upon his guru" and draw strength from this contemplation. Wrestlers are enjoined to always keep his image in mind and make themselves empty vessels to be filled with their guru's wisdom.[91]

One difference between this wrestling and the martial arts of East Asia is that the skill has no external, instrumental value. I suppose that if you were well trained in this wrestling, you would have some enhanced presence and capacity for self-defense, but that would be very tenuous (self-defense against *what?*) and would have nothing to do with the technical details of the wrestling or why men enter this way of life. In the next chapter we will see that this external, instrumental value is characteristic of the Asian martial arts and their contemporary traditions, marking their distinction from dance, sport, and the spiritual athletics of Indian wrestling.

3

POWER AND GRACE

Martial Arts Aesthetics

. . . some distant cousin of beauty, the muse of violence
in all her complexity.
NORMAN MAILER, *THE FIGHT*

Martial arts practice is like sport but not sport and dancelike but not dance. It constantly refers to violence but refuses it a place in the training. The training is athletic, as it is in sport and professional dance, yet the competence that the martial arts teach stands apart from those of sport or dance by means of its external, instrumental value as a weapon. It is precisely this external, instrumental effectiveness, the weapons potential of martial arts, that accounts for the striking beauty of its movements.

There is more than one paradox in that précis of my argument, so the task of this chapter is to unfold them and lighten the air of paradox. Eventually I will develop a systematic contrast among works of fine-arts dance, games of sport, and martial arts practice. To educe the contrast, I first need to observe the similarity of this group, which lies in their athleticism.

ATHLETICS

What makes a movement or series of movements athletic? It would be inadvisable to stipulate precise conditions. Nothing human, nothing historical, no actual practice, has a timeless essence. However, we can sketch athletic movement in a few strokes that highlight its characteristic qualities. For one thing, such movements are trained (possibly self-trained) and practiced; they never come naturally. If an athlete has a gift, it is for learning and self-learning, not spontaneous performance. Athletic movements also exceed normal or average skill and exertion. They are difficult for untrained people to do and exhausting for untrained people, making them fatigued and sore. The movements of typing or sewing are not athletic because of the relatively low expenditure of energy. In addition, athletic movements tend to be explosive rather than manipulative or requiring fine control. Threading a needle is not an athletic movement, whereas even a weight lifter's ponderous motion has an explosive quality. But the explosion is confined to the rule-governed theater of athletic practice. Athletic movement is trained movement, an artifact of training, and does not occur outside a historical economy of training practice.[1]

Athletic training resembles learning a second language. To begin learning, say, how to swim is like beginning to learn Spanish. One is introduced to the movements of a historical practice-community. Athletic movements are even governed by rules, as are those of speech, and these rules are constitutive, as they are in language; they create what they define and do not merely regulate antecedent practice. Athletics, no less than speech, has standards for performance and a practice community competent to judge according to rules, allowing performances to be compared, ranked, and recorded. One thing that obviously differentiates athletics from speech is that athletic movements have no semantic value or linguistic significance, express no proposition, produce no illocutionary effect. What may most distinguish athletic movements from speech acts, however, is that these movements are forceful and efficient and change the world in nonconventional ways.[2]

When the appropriate official states, "I pronounce you husband and wife," that changes the world, creating spouses who did not previously exist (under that description). The effect, though, is institutional, engineered by convention. If a boxer lands a jab, there is nothing conventional about the opponent's distress. When rowers dip their oars in unison and pull, they transmit a real, nonconventional force to their craft's hull. A runner works a track as she would a medium; it receives the runner's exertion and transmits aimed-for effects. These are real effects that do not depend on convention. What is conventional about athletic movement is not its effectiveness (like that of a speech act) but its worth, the point or value of being effective in that way. The value of making an athletic movement is usually its contribution to winning a game, which is a completely conventional effect, no less than apologizing or promising. Only the arbitrary rules of a game explain why a person would struggle to move in the way an athlete does.

We have, then, a profile of athletic movements:

- They are artifacts of training practices, historically conditioned artifacts without an essence.
- They transcend average skills and exertion.
- They are governed by rules, trained and performed under the norms of a practice community.
- They are nonconventionally effective in some medium.

This epitome is no more than the profile of a syndrome, a family of practices, a habitus, or a historical economy of habits. Instances are variations rather than the reiteration of a single form, concept, essence, or idea.

The aesthetic interest of athletic movements lies in their range of qualities. These movements are skilled, achieving their goal without waste or delay. They are graceful, meaning smooth, harmonious, visually fascinating, and avidly watched. They also are achievements of accuracy, willfully arriving at a highly selective target. These qualities occur separately and combine in degrees. Athletic "coordination" is a rhythmic combination of such qualities. The point of a person throwing a discus farther than a discus ever has been thrown before is simply the excellence of it. As Paul Weiss, who practically invented the philosophy of sport, observed, athletic performance "reveals to us the magnitude of what can be done. Illustrating perfection, it gives us a measure for whatever else we do." Such excellence has a perceptual quality that makes it fascinating to watch, exciting, beautiful. Weiss is eloquent (if possibly sexist) about the value of athletic excellence:

There is no need to apologize for or to justify the athlete. It is a great accomplishment to turn a body from a creature of vagrant stimuli, insistent appetites, and poorly focused objectives, into one which is taut and controlled, and directed toward a realizable excellent end. . . . The beauty and grace of his body, his coordination, responsiveness, alertness, efficiency, his devotion and accomplishments, his splendid unity with his equipment, all geared to produce a result at the limit of bodily possibility, set him over against the rest of men.[3]

This much athleticism is shared by sports, professional fine-arts dance, and martial arts practice. I turn next to the differences, beginning with a few words about sport.

SPORT

Sport is the athletic species of the genus *Game*. Chess is a game but not a sport because there is no athletics, no bodily test. I admit to some stipulation in this claim. Chess is sometimes played in tournaments that require quasi-athletic stamina, and it is covered in *Sports Illustrated*. Perhaps it has been turned into a sport. But if so, that happened because a certain way of organizing the play introduced some kind of bodily test. A sports event like a race or basketball game is a competitive exhibition of athletic movement organized under arbitrary rules, and such rules must be accompanied by a historical practice, a habitus, or a tradition of use.

Sports can be called *practices* in the sense that Alistair MacIntyre defines, according to which a practice is a socially established cooperative activity, pursuing values internal to the activity, trying to achieve its standards of excellence. A practice is practically defined by these internal values. They are socially held goods, qualities we enjoy only through others' belief that we possess them. Such goods are practice specific, not group specific; to enjoy them you must be engaged in an appropriate kind of practice and not merely fall into a class or group (like "urban Asian female"). A martial arts black belt is an example of such an internal good. Without the opinion of the master who grants it and the consensus of the training hall where one wears it, it has no more value than any other three meters of bulky black ribbon.[4]

Practices are not the same as institutions, and not all practices are institutionalized. For instance, the practice of street hockey is not institutionalized. Institutions are recognized, established, legitimate ways of pursuing practices and are conditioned by the interests of specific groups who monopolize the practice. Such institutions and their dominant groups sanction and regulate antecedently existing practices. Institutionalization is something that befalls practices, something that happens to them under specific conditions. For example, the connection between sport and money is an effect of how sports practices are currently institutionalized. Money is a completely external good, and the power to earn a lot of money is not an internal good of sports practice.[5]

There are lots of practices. Sports are distinguished by their athleticism and the gratuitousness of their rules. This is the epitome of sport: gratuitous athletic competition. Gratuitousness is as important to games (and therefore to sport) as arbitrariness is to the signs of language. Why should a person use a pole to launch herself over a flimsy barrier to the other side? Why is imparting a certain trajectory to a ball good for some and bad for others? Ultimately there is no reason. Important only is that the feat is difficult and regarded by a practice community as attaining a standard of excellence. That recognition lifts the action out of the instrumental economy of means to ends. The movements become something to work at for their own sake or, more accurately, for the internal goods of their practice. More, though, is required of a sport's practitioners than adherence to constitutive rules. There needs to be a commitment to the ethos of the game. That means the internal values of a sports tradition, which become the compelling reason to accept a sport's gratuitous difficulties and compete under their terms.[6]

SPORT AESTHETICS

The aesthetic qualities of sport are a suggestive source for insight into comparable qualities in the martial arts. Before I get into that, I would like to discuss three preliminary points on the philosophy of aesthetics.

First, aesthetics and art are not the same. Aesthetics is a larger field and only partly overlaps with art or the fine arts. The difference, roughly, is that not every aesthetically valuable quality belongs to something *artificial*, something designed, assembled, and. in that sense, technical, artifactual, artificial, a work of art. Art covers a field of artifacts constructed in the way they are for the sake of their perception. Among such artifacts, I include movements as well as their effects, singing and the song. Aesthetically interesting movement is movement that is aesthetically worthwhile to watch. *Artistic* movement is movement that has this quality *because it has been made that way,* artfully made with its perception in mind. Movement such as that of a running leopard may have an aesthetic quality and be fascinating to watch yet not be artistic or a work of art, that is, not technically made to have, and be perceived to have, an aesthetic quality.[7]

Second, the word "art" covers two different, only partially overlapping, classes. One is fine art, and the other is what the Greeks called *techne*. To say that cooking is an art is not a barbarism. To be an art in the sense of *techne* is to be productive knowledge, as in professional cooking. In this sense, a "work of art" is an effect, an artifact, of technical knowledge. The question that is sometimes raised about whether sport is an art uses "art" in the exalted modern sense that is now the word's primary connotation and the subject matter of art history. In the older sense of "art," from the Latin *ars* (which was their translation of *techne*), an art is an organized technical knowledge that produces effects deemed valuable by its practitioners. Mastery of such an art requires an investment of concentration and a commitment to improvement. *Techne*-arts are foci around which skills cluster. When certain skills are closely integrated and hard to learn, their exercise tends to form an art, making the *techne*-arts into a stock of skill and knowledge cultivated, perfected, and transmitted within a community of practice.[8]

Finally, beauty is not the only aesthetic quality. Others include sublime, picturesque, solemn, melancholy, mysterious, comedic, zany, ridiculous, and cute. In addition are terms of aesthetic evaluation more discerning than simply "I like it"—terms for qualities like presence, proportion, rhythm, harmony, grace, and variety. We should also remember that aesthetic qualities are not invariably pleasant or valuable. Ugliness is an aesthetic quality, but not pleasant or valued. Because "beauty" is an unavoidable term, however, it may be useful to say something about this quality.

It is a commonplace to describe beauty as a sensuous pleasure and relate its value to sensory experience. But beauty is more temporal than it is sensuous, which is why something may appeal to a sense (the taste of chocolate, say), without beauty. Beauty must have a becoming, a continuous series of interpenetrating phases, a beautifully evolving duration. The experience of beauty is temporally extended, a moment with a development, not a fully present, finished, static *now*. This temporality is the basis of the distinction between a reflective feeling like beauty and a sensory feeling like the taste of chocolate. The sensory feeling is full and fully present, given without (much) development, whereas the feeling of beauty is a duration that develops an intensity (when tastes *are* like that, as with some wines, their pleasure approaches beauty). Beauty is sensuous because the senses make us aware of change, conscious of the present as a development of a past. Beauty is a pleasure in the feeling of an enduring present, feeling the becoming of the present, delighted awareness of how it flows, develops, varies, and intensifies with duration.

Beauty is a quality of things, not of the people who perceive them. Hot and cold are qualities we feel in ourselves, but the feeling of beauty is a quality of the thing that affects us. It does more than stir us. We discern something, perceive something, about our own perception of it. Something about the object, its parts and their quality, is appealing, affecting, ardently lingered over. A judgment of beauty does not simply describe a thing, on the model of "The cat is on the mat." Rather, the feeling of beauty is a response to the object. We feelingly perceive it and express (through pleasure and aesthetic judgment) the self-sufficient, endotelic pleasure of the encounter. (*Endotelic* refers to actions that contain their end in their doing, a doing done for the doing of it, without instrumental motivation.)

The feeling of beauty is different from mere preference. The experience of beauty, or any aesthetic quality (even ugliness), demands attention and can be expressed in many ways, marshaling more or less discerning predicates from beauty's semantic family: elegant, intricate, expressive, pretty, charming, attractive, delightful, harmonious, and so on. These judgments are comparative, not absolute. There are degrees and varieties of beauty, not one beauty either fully present or completely absent. Beauty may be exalted, the awesome grandeur of nature, or genius triumphant. Or it may be simple, everyday beauty. Amid all variety, beauty is, at bottom, a matter of looking or sounding right, pleasing the eye or ear.[9]

Why do we like such feelings? What motivates us to explore them? It is difficult to say. Immanuel Kant thought that the feeling hinted at more to us than a natural body. Evolutionary psychologists argue that these responses were adaptive back when our ancestors were becoming human; we now simply inherit them, even though they have lost (or changed) their adaptive value. Others believe that we accidentally discovered these pleasures, which probably are unselected by-products of adaptive (probably neurological) characteristics. What is the right answer? We do not know.[10]

Before considering the aesthetic qualities of athletics, we might spend a moment on qualities of movement in general. Force can be a source of aesthetic qualities through its perception as rhythmic, effortful, or dynamic. Imagine huge waves breaking against a cliff, or a violent storm. I found the following example of beauty in the motion of a motorcycle wheel:

> When it was still, that wheel was merely a contraption of spokes and nuts, of rim and rubber, cobbled together by human hands, improbable as a saxophone. But by spinning, it became a singular jewel, a unity of glittering perfection, fashioned out of higher laws, transformed by wind as the saxophone is when it is played.[11]

The aesthetic interest afforded by motion depends on the conditions and qualities of its perception, which typically is visual. The most pleasing movements are those that are not equivocal, without slippage, and can be grasped at once. Colors are more lambent in motion than at rest. An appealing movement may also have a tactile, proprioceptive valence. A right-handed person can be made uneasy watching a left-handed person perform an energetic movement like pitching a ball.

This feeling is an aesthetic response, despite not being entirely comfortable or pleasing. Movement may also have an auditory quality. Think of watching ballet without music or moving trees without the sound of wind. It is a palpably different, aesthetically different, experience.

Any movement is a vector with force and direction. In animal motion, these forces have their quantity and also a quality, an intensity, and an expressiveness, evoking univocal, Darwinian-body descriptions as sudden, slow, prepared, unprepared, tense, relaxed, strong, weak, hurried, leisurely, affectionate, cautious, and so on. These terms describe expressive qualities of animate movement. The mechanics of animal motion ensure that all or most movements will have some mix of the following perceptually salient qualities:[12]

• *Tension.* Every movement involves effort, and effort requires tension in musculature. We learn to anticipate required effort and can feel, for example, what an athlete has to do.
• *Trajectory.* Every movement creates a path of motion: up, down, linear, curved, jagged, smooth, and so on. Different trajectories have their felt qualities, and audiences feel them along with the performers.
• *Projection.* This is the quality of the release of force. The energy, the force of the movement, may be sustained, slow, controlled, or smooth. It may be percussive, explosive, trembling, nervous, weak, or hovering.
• *Amplitude, or how movements fill space.* Is the movement expansive or constrained, fluid or halting? Aficionados cite the amplitude of gymnastics, performing every movement to its fullest and best, as its preeminent aesthetic quality. To "throw like a girl" is an example of deficient amplitude and also shows that movement can be gendered. What characterizes throwing, hitting, or running "like a girl" is, first, that the whole body is not put into fluid and directed motion, but rather, in swinging and hitting, for example, the motion is concentrated in one body part; and second that the woman's motion tends not to reach, extend, lean, stretch, and follow through in the direction of her intention.[13]
• *Natural speed.* Every muscular exertion has a natural speed related inversely to the work it costs. Compare the movement of fingers over a keyboard with the movement of rowing a boat. It is easy for the

fingers to move fast and no less natural and efficient for the rower to move slowly with greater exertion.

• *Complementary motions.* Muscular movements, especially those involving effort, tend to be preceded and followed by complementary movements, like a preparation and echo. The reason for this so-called adherence of motion may be the difficulty of suddenly interrupting any rhythmic movement. Every muscular movement is a virtual habit, even when performed for the first time. Once a rhythm is established, habit is the name for its tendency to recur. In the martial arts we know these preparatory motions as "tells," corporeal indications that telegraph the coming strike and that we want to bring under control and even exploit as fakes.

Rhythm is more than a perceptible order in movement. It is a tendency, an intensive quality of a series, capable of dominating the flow of movement, and a quality of any movement that is in some way efficient. Efficient movements are rhythmic, and rhythmic movements are efficient, or at least they look as though they are. These qualities go together for a reason. The fixed attachment of muscle to bone requires that most animal movements, and especially those of a biped, be pendular and oscillating. When we factor in the inertia of different limbs, the rhythmic quality of normal animal movement becomes mechanically inevitable.

These movements and their rhythm also must harmonize with the whole economy of life's movements. All the different rhythms of the body (heart, breath, involuntary balance adjustments, and so on) tend to fall into harmony with one another, an effect known as the "entrainment of resonant motions." Each movement resonates through the entire body. As neurologist Charles Sherrington explained, "To take a step is an affair, not of this or that limb solely, but of the total neuromuscular activity of the movement—not least of the head and neck." Chang Naizhou, the eighteenth-century "scholar-boxer," was eloquent on the martial arts value of this whole body coordination:

Dropping to a point hard and rigid, fierce and courageous, invincibly, relies on whole body energy. . . . Feet and hands coordinate, hands and eyes coordinate, eyes and mind coordinate; mind and spirit coordinate, spirit and energy coordinate, energy and body coordinate. There is nothing more marvelous than this.[14]

The whole-body quality of animate movement may explain why almost no two movements, not even highly trained movements, are biomechanically identical. They appear instead to be nonce compilations from different components in different individuals as the occasion demands. The improvisational variety in the movements during a skilled performance correlates with high *invariability* in the *mechanical* movement of any tools or instruments used. If you follow the complementary extension and contraction of a blacksmith's muscle groups and measure either bone stress or patterns of neural stimulation, you will find eccentric variability. Attend instead to the trajectory of the hammer and the changing position of the material on the anvil, and you will see regulated precision action of high mechanical effectiveness. The right conclusion seems to be that skilled action is not built up from prefabricated routines and little resembles a computer program, which also indicts the classical assumption that form or idea governs technical making. Even the most habitual action is a novel improvisation and does not unfold under the guidance of an abstractly represented form.[15]

Herbert Spencer proposed a connection between the gracefulness of movement and its mechanical efficiency. The most graceful motions, he argued, are also the most economical, costing the least effort. Paul Souriau, a nineteenth-century pioneer in the aesthetic theory of movement, called such spurious grace "merely mechanical beauty." He believed that the better beauty of animate movement "cannot be measured by economy alone, that is, by the relationship of the energy expended to the work produced. One must also take into account the actual value of the effort." In other words, quality. Beauty in animate movement is not a quantifiable economy of effort. It is a qualitative, expressive, eloquent effectiveness, an intense, aesthetic quality with no necessary connection to quantifiable economy. What *looks* gracefully effortless may really be strenuous. The aesthetically relevant values are qualitative, expressive, and intensive and cannot be quantified by measurements.[16]

Souriau believed that human movements tend to be aesthetically interesting and beautiful when expressively effortless, despite costing effort. "True kinetic beauty," he stated, "is provided by the evident finality of a movement." "Evident finality" means expressive finality, an intentionality or design quality that is intersubjectively available to an audience. The intentionality of movement is not an inaccessible, private mental fact. To speak of body language is not superstitious, and its expression is much less conscious than consciousness would like. Doing something just for how it looks, *looks different* from movement with a productive or competitive purpose. Doing something with evident adequacy of means *looks different* from actions that are faulty, rough, or halting. We see instrumentality or its absence in movement, and we see adequacy and effectiveness in skilled movement. These qualities tend to make movement fascinating, aesthetically interesting, graceful, and beautiful, but they lack the quantifiable effort that Spencer postulated.[17]

According to Souriau's analysis, this expressive quality requires a combination of physical and psychological ease. Physical ease qualifies movements that conform with personal habit, free of visible effort, or what Souriau calls "noise." "Silent movements seem to happen of their own accord." Another condition of physical ease is convincing firmness at the point of support. He cites the graceless appearance of trudging through mud, sand, or snow: "For a movement to be easy and appear graceful, the point of support of the effect must be firm and look it." We remember Zhuangzi's admonition to breathe down to the heels, and the *Daodejing*: "Those who stand on tiptoe cannot stand firm."[18] Psychological ease comes mostly from freedom in rhythm, not appearing mechanical. Movements are graceful, Souriau maintained, "only when we feel that their rhythm is not imposed," adducing in evidence the gracelessness of tics and seizures. Other sources of expressive ease are freedom from purpose, the movements being visibly (or audibly) playful, and prodigality of effort, the luxurious eloquence of mastery. "In all the arts that give, even indirectly, a feeling of gracefulness in movement, we find the gratuitous feats, the challenges to difficulty, the tours de force that, through a substantial increase in effort, actually erase the impressions of that effort."[19]

For Souriau, an aesthetic, expressive, qualitative difference can be found between play activity and work: "The expenditure of energy may be the same; the difference of purpose alone suffices to modify the impression produced on the spectator."[20] That is not to say the aesthetic quality of playful movement is higher or better than the quality of purposive movement. Movements that are highly instrumental—effective in a technical sense—can be no less aesthetically interesting. My examples would be watching an accomplished potter turn clay or a blacksmith working iron. Glass blowing can be fascinating to watch, and this fascination, this ardent lingering and its memory, is an aesthetic response, whatever name we give it.

The aesthetic qualities of sport are those of animate and human movement generally, though sports events are, like rituals, contrived to intensify the presence of these qualities. Hans Ulrich Gumbrecht invokes these aesthetic qualities to explain sport's popularity:

> The unexpected appearance of a body in space, suddenly taking on a beautiful form that just as quickly and irreversibly dissolves, can be thought of as a kind of epiphany. Such epiphanies are, I believe, the source of the joy we feel when we watch an athletic event, and the mark of the height of our aesthetic response.

There seems to be a consensus regarding the same effect among players and aficionados, as a few examples confirm:

> Bill Russell, basketball coach: "To me, one of the most beautiful things to see is a group of men co-ordinating their efforts toward a common goal—alternately subordinating and asserting themselves to achieve real teamwork in action. . . . Often, in my mind's eye, I stood off and watched that effort. I found it beautiful to watch."

> Arnold Palmer, professional golfer: "What other people may find in poetry or art museums, I find in the flight of a good drive—the white ball sailing up into that blue sky, growing smaller and smaller, then suddenly reaching its apex, curving, falling and finally dropping to the turf to roll some more, just the way I planned it."

Dick Callum, sports journalist, reporting on the George Foreman–Aaron Eastling boxing match (1971): "At that moment Foreman made an odd move, an unusual kind of feint, and his left hand darted out. It was a lightning jab which must have carried a sting, because Eastling's knees softened and Foreman seized him lest he fall. At the end of this round, and in appreciation of that one beautiful punch, the crowd roared its approval."

Umberto Romano, a painter of boxing: "I have been stirred, moved, aroused by the hot sensuous light on human bodies in the ring, by the powerful savagery of two taut, brutal forms in combat, by two violent bodies—at times human, at times animalistic, prancing, pacing, calculating, waiting, waiting for the one great climactic moment, the opening for the punch, that terrific murderous punch—the knockout."[21]

The aesthetic qualities of sport include speed, grace, and elegant lightness, as well as qualities associated with natural beauty, the beauty of the body, its agility and feats of strength and skill, and the expressive qualities of the players and what they do, their courage, endurance, wit, and frailties. Sports may have dramatic qualities, for instance, a tense tennis match or a game between rival teams. Sport reaches its aesthetic summit when a victor narrowly surpasses a worthy opponent. The game becomes a dramatic experience whose intensity climaxes in victory and defeat. Sports even has a sort of intellectual beauty, especially that of a beautiful play; "the sudden, surprising convergence of several athletes' bodies in time and space," as Gumbrecht describes it, an ephemeral duration unfolding unexpectedly and vanishing in the moment it begins to emerge.[22]

Can sports be a fine art in the way that, say, dance is? There indeed are similarities like elegance and grace. Both activate conventions that create a theater for demonstrating skills. How different is a basketball court from a stage? Sports also offer ample opportunity for creative corporeal improvisation. Sports even have a place for disagreeable aesthetic qualities, sports ugliness. Here are two examples from baseball: Marv Throneberry, a player for the 1962 New York Mets, is up, hits, and runs. Between first and second base, he trips over his feet and falls face-first into the dust. A jeering second baseman derisively tagged him out. New York Yankees pitcher Steve Hamilton was an avid chewer of tobacco. One hot afternoon, a batter hits his pitch in a line drive that strikes him midsection, causing him to swallow his plug of tobacco and then vomit his lunch on the mound. The nonplused batter was awarded a base hit.[23]

These are ugly, aversive, unpleasant sights, a weird combination of aversion and compulsive presence characteristic of the ugly. Another example comes from boxing. Mismatches are something of a genre in professional boxing. One of these pitted a young man, unbeaten in thirteen fights, against an overweight forty-year-old who had lost his last fifteen bouts. The older man moved to the center of the ring, crouched, hid his face in his gloves, and then did not move, absorbing body blows from his opponent and occasionally venturing a quick punch. A spectator, the sociologist and amateur boxer whose ethnography of a Chicago gym we examined in the last chapter, deemed the fight "unsightly and sad." The older man was obliged to eat "a dishload of straight punches from both hands." "His face gradually turns purple," deformed by a grimace that gave him "the look of a blubbering urchin." Watching the fight was like watching "a workout on a human punching bag rather than a competitive contest." It is not pretty. Others report similar feelings. "Watching a bad mismatch can make you feel sick. . . . As the combatants labor around the ring, one swinging and the other ducking, you feel complicity in the wrongness of the event." The dislike is an aesthetic response to perceptually aversive qualities in the movement, the ugly in motion.[24]

A game of sport may have aesthetic qualities, it may be aesthetically fascinating to watch, and those things make it *like* a work of art, or like *some* works of art, but not entirely the same as art because the aesthetic qualities of sports are not purposive and are not enough, whereas in art these qualities are both purposive and satisfyingly enough. Of course, "work of art" is a contested concept. But one thing I think is useful to say is that works of art tend to be artifacts and that their aesthetic quality comes by design. Although this is not a definition, it may be a necessary condition. A work of (fine) art is an artifact, which as I explained, I understand broadly to mean any effect of human performance, including actions as well as outcomes, and while many artifacts have various aesthetic qualities, they are works of fine art only to the extent that they have such qualities *by design*. They are made that way. They are artifacts whose design assumes the perception of an audience and takes their response into account.

The movements of sport make no such assumption. Sport is unlike other spectacles, for instance, a circus or a parade. Any beauty in a game is subordinated to competitive victory. Sports demand a commitment to win, and any virtuosity has to be spontaneous and consistent with that commitment. Nonchalant virtuosity that is indifferent to winning loses points, either formally with judges or informally among fans. The beauty of athletic movements and sports events is a dependent beauty, not Kant's free beauty. The main thing is competitive effectiveness, not how the movements look. Any beauty is a by-product that is not designed or intended, and in this respect athletic beauty is more like beauty in nature than in art.[25]

Gymnastics, in which the judges' perception *is* taken into account, is an exception. International rules of judging define a perfect exercise with a maximum rating as "one that is presented with elegance, ease, precision, and in a style and rhythm well adapted to the nature of the aesthetic performance with no faults in execution." The rules also stipulate that "an exercise, although executed without fault, but presented in a rhythm too quick or too slow, or with an ill-proportioned display of force, counts less than a perfect exercise." Elegance, ease, precision, style, rhythm, and proportion all are aesthetic qualities, felt, intensive, and resistant to quantification. Their evaluation calls for sensitive feeling and cannot be impersonally measured. Despite this aestheticism, however, gymnastics and other so-called form-sports remain sports and do not cross the line into performance art.[26]

Gymnastic performers are expected to create an illusion of effortlessness. They should never reveal by countenance or muscle tension an unplanned, inharmonious movement or the least sign of difficulty. Should a slip occur, it must be embraced as a variation and made to flow as if it were by design. To score high, gymnastic movements have to belie any strain. They must *look* effortless, despite the inevitable effort of competitive performance. Gymnastic performances are and have to be *feats*. They *have to be* a strenuous, highly demanding physical performance because the athletic challenge of competitive performance constantly rises.

By contrast, while professional fine-arts dancers are athletic and their graceful motions *may* be strenuous, they do not *have to be* strenuous, not every movement of every dance. This is athleticism without competitive athletics. Add some form of competition, however, as in competitive ballroom dancing or synchronized swimming—an Olympic event that some call competitive dance—and the dance begins to become sportslike and less a performance art. My point is not that in becoming competitive they are no longer dance but that their movements no longer belong to the fine arts. Instead, they gravitate toward sports. Not all dancing is fine art by any means, but synchronized swimming fits into the Olympics in a way that a dance by Martha Graham never will.

The movements of fine-art dance may be described as *endotelic*, meaning, again, actions that contain their end in their doing, a doing done for the doing of it, without instrumental motivation. The dancers are not trying to win something, only to be perceptibly present and worth watching. Dance movements are made to be looked at, but sports movement, however worthwhile it may be to look at, is not *made* to be looked at. Perhaps the game is being played for an audience and, in that sense, is made for watching. But the players' movements are not made for the sake of having some "look" for the audience. They are selected and performed as they are for the paramount goal of winning the game. The *game* may be made for watching, but the movements that comprise its play are made to win.[27]

> EXPRESSIVE INTENTIONALITY
>
> Dance movements look endotelic. The movements *are* endotelic and *look* it, expressing that intentionality.
>
> Sports play looks competitive. The movements *are* competitive and *look* it, expressing that intentionality.

The difference between dance movements and those of sport is a difference in expressive intentionality. The movements of fine-arts dance must look as though they were made for the audience's perception. The movements are made with their perception in mind, but more than that, they look like they are so made, being expressively endotelic, expressing the intention of being movements worth watching. A movement cannot only be intentional; it can express that intentionality, which is not a private mental state but a perceptible, expressive quality of movement. The movements of sport must be performed with a commitment to win and must express this commitment and not depart from it for the sake of spectacle. The expressive intentionality of the movements makes watching sports aesthetically different from watching dance. The movements feel different, look different, and offer different qualities for aesthetic attention. In sports, when the movements are too obviously dancelike, we notice that and see the lapse of commitment to the game. That is why no one takes "pro" wrestling seriously as a sport, regardless of the performers' athleticism. The more evidently that movements are made for look and not in competition, the more likely we are dealing with either a fine art like dance or a spectacle like a circus or a parade.

Even if games of sport are not works of art, the athlete may yet be (like) an artist. A philosopher of sports argues that artists and athletes "share a fundamentally similar stance toward the world." He describes the stance as a playful "responsive openness." "Openness" means a concentrated intentional awareness (of others, equipment, conditions, and so on). "Responsiveness" is responding to opportunities forcefully and well, discerning and responding to the quality the Greeks called *kairos*, the opportune moment. Competitive play demands this responsive openness to a supreme degree. To be a good player is to enter into a kind of contract with other players, judges, and the audience to dedicate oneself to this attitude. Audiences see that dedication, which is an expressive quality of the movement, and are often delighted.[28]

I appreciate the value of responsive openness in sport, and I am sure that many artists have this quality too, but I would be reluctant to say that they all do or that having it is essential to fine art. Perhaps the *good* artists have this quality, but then we have to define what a good artist is. Some prominent modern artists are ostentatiously not "good" in that sense (Marcel Duchamp, Andy Warhol, Tracey Emin) and do not concede the evaluation of their art to the standard of such goodness.

What draws the fans? We should not expect a single answer but can notice a few of the attractions. One notably intellectual fan, Joseph Epstein, longtime editor of the *American Scholar*, says he values the opportunity to watch the practice of craft of a high order. He especially enjoys the absence of fakery, as did fans of ancient Greek athletics, rationalizing the scandalous preference for nakedness. The competitors are totally committed to winning. Sport is the real thing, "fraud-free and fakeproof." Unlike a season's currently popular artist, a player's reputation is earned and cannot be artificially inflated by media representations. Results are a matter of record, and everybody knows where you stand. There are no loopholes. Teams of clever accountants cannot massage the figures, nor is standing decided by lawyers in court. The athlete "is alone out there, naked but for his ability, which counts for everything. Something there is that is elemental about this, and something greatly satisfying."[29]

The expressive intentionality of performance, whether in dance, theater, or sport, is for spectators a visible, audible, even tactile quality. Electromyographic investigation reveals that spectators minutely mimic the movements of a performer, indicating a kind of qualitative participation. The mirror neurons that I mentioned in chapter 2 predict this result. Even the most visual movement has a tactile, proprioceptive dimension. We cannot just look at human movement, as looking already involves responding, imitating. even participating. Spectators become entrained with performers' movements, which then resonate and amplify one another. The thrilling rush of this resonance may account for the less cerebral spectators' pleasure in sports. It may also explain why fights among spectators break out at the same time that fights on the field do; that is, most spectator fights are ignited mimetically by the players' violence.[30]

The spectators of dance also must participate spontaneously (however discreetly), but sports tend to theatrically enhance the entrainment of players and fans. Gumbrecht thinks that boredom disappoints fans more than a loss. Sports events are more intense than political rallies because of the presence of the opposition in the crowd, although all spectators have one thing in common. "Crowds," Gumbrecht says, "long for the moment when their combined physical energy connects with the players' energy and makes the players' energy grow." They are "waiting for that which may occasionally happen but is never guaran-

MARTIAL ARTS AESTHETICS

teed to happen, because it lies beyond the precalculated limits of human performance." The mutually amplified excitement of the unpredictable accounts for the notable difference between spectators of sport and spectators of performance art. Spectators of performance arts are an audience of individual appreciators, while spectators of sports are more intensely entrained and enthusiastically take sides in a zero-sum game. There will never be ballet hooligans.[31]

It has been said that fans experience a game as they experience the world, that is, with emotional commitment. They are not disinterested. They ardently wish for a conventionally constituted fact to become true, namely, that their team will win. To sustain this zeal, sports spectatorship generates a binding power that transcends class and education. "Sports are real life," writes sociologist Randall Collins, "and this makes them engrossing; but real life at its most deliberately and artfully organized and controlled. It is therefore larger than life, conflict in its purified form, better focused and therefore more dramatically satisfying than in ordinary events." That makes games of sport very like a ritual. Collins takes an unflattering view of the fans, describing them as resembling "primitive religious fanatics in the presence of their cult objects." Not all fans are interested in refined aesthetic qualities; they go to the games for something stronger. Games today are not so different from Roman games: competitive violence for popular consumption. Collins thinks the typical attraction of sports events "is the opportunity to take part in moments of collective emotional experience in a conflict motif"—that is, violence—"without most of the dangers and costs of real conflict." Consequently, the pleasure of sport is "the experience of being at a highly successful ritual" and, moreover, a violent one.[32]

MARTIAL ART AESTHETICS

Within the aesthetics of martial arts I include reflections on the perceptual qualities of its movements, or what it feels like to watch them, and their proprioceptive, kinesthetic quality, or what it feels like to perform them. The perceptual qualities are available to spectators, while the proprioceptive qualities performers feel and also express.

Martial Arts, Sports, and Dance

The major difference between martial arts practice and sports is that martial arts have an external, practice-independent value as weapons. In sports, when athletes apply what they have trained in, their effect is determined by a convention: they want to score a goal, win a race, strike a batter out. On the rare occasion when contemporary martial arts practitioners actually apply what they practice their effectiveness proves its nonconventional value as a weapon. The intended effect is a response to violence that is safe for the practitioner and irresistible to a committed assailant. Nothing conventional about that.

Ritual has always had a place in Asian martial arts training. The training hall is a place symbolically set apart, even if it is located, as mine is, in a strip mall. The first thing I do when I come in the door is remove my shoes. In sport, ritual usually belongs to the game but not to the training, whereas in the martial arts it is the reverse. Ceremony is part of martial arts training (for example, bowing in and out of class) but is not part of the actual use of what has been taught. When football players seriously use their long-trained skill, the occasion begins with the playing of the national anthem. When long-trained martial arts techniques are seriously applied (in self-defense, say) the moment is completely without ceremony. Many conventions govern the methods of training in the martial arts, most being flaws deliberately introduced to make the practice safe, for instance, to make attacks unrealistically slow, to pull strikes and kicks just before contact, or to stand a fixed distance apart. A conventionally determined tap will release a joint lock. Sparring has conventions regarding the value of different strikes, the timing of rounds, and the expression of respect for an opponent. For all its conventions, though, the value of martial arts practice is not unconditionally conventional as the ends of sport are.

The purpose for conventions in martial arts training is to prevent injury and express respect. They are not required for the reason that sports require conventions, which is to give purpose to their movements. Sports are differentiated by their rules. The difference between basketball and pole-vaulting is a difference in their constitutive rules. Martial arts are differentiated by their histories and methods of effectiveness.

The difference between wing chun and taiji or aikido and karate are different histories, different lineages, different masters, and centers of practice. Martial arts techniques taught with the help of conventions retain their value and effectiveness without the conventional frame. Sports are not like that. Everything that makes sports *sports* is, in the martial arts, reserved for training and not for the actual use of the competence trained. A football player practices kicking and then seriously kicks in a game. In the martial arts we practice kicking too, but seldom, if ever, do we seriously kick people as we train to. A football player is unlikely to be as effective at incapacitating an assailant with a kick as a well-trained karateka (karate practitioner) would be. The football kick has no nonconventional use, whereas movements taught in the martial arts have an external value as weapons.

External as that value is, the masters agree that the weapons potential is essential to these arts and their training. The Chinese author of the sixteenth-century *Classic of Boxing* states, "In practicing the martial arts, you should imagine that you are striking an actual opponent and not just study superficial techniques." A scholar of karate describes two Japanese masters of the twentieth century:

> For Itosu, karate was an endless and severe tempering of mind and body, one goal of which was to kill or cripple an opponent in an instant. Itosu did not live to see much of the development of karate as a sport. There is little doubt, however, that he would not have approved of it. For him, as for Chibaba, karate practice was worthwhile only if it was directed to the development of the right spirit and technical (that is, combat) effectiveness. Chibaba always stressed karate's potential for lethality.

Even aikido, with its reputation for nonviolence, is unequivocally committed to the weapons potential of its techniques. As the aikido grand master Phong Thong Dang predicted, the art will survive only if "we choose to train with honest intent to apply aikido to a fight. . . . It is only by ensuring its martial application that aikido can remain as a martial art." He enjoins aikido practitioners to "train as if you intend to use aikido one day to protect your life or the life of loved ones. Do not train as if your life is currently threatened, but train as if someday it may be."[33]

The reason why the masters insist on this point is that when training in these arts you have to understand how the techniques function combatively. You have to know, performatively, where the energies go to turn empty-handed movements into effective weapons. Otherwise, the martial art will tend to decline into—dance! An American martial arts practitioner who trained for many years in Taiwan writes that when his *shifu* taught martial arts techniques, "he spent very little time correcting my execution of the movement. However, he made an intense effort to direct the intent of my execution." When the intent is neglected, all that remains is a posture drifting on the current of whim, with nothing to check devolution into a combatively vacuous gesture.[34]

These teachers are not saying that students should think of striking other people when they practice their moves. Rather, they are saying that when practicing, students must strive to understand how the technique is designed for violence. They have to know their weapon, how it works, what makes it strong. To perform a technique well, they have to know where the energies go, how the technique is effective, what kind of effect it is designed to achieve, and how the generation of that effect works combatively and strategically against an opponent. They not only must appreciate these qualities, they must produce them quickly and accurately, even under conditions of stress. To learn these arts well, practice must be alert to the technique's intentionality, how is it designed, the optimal conditions of its use. At the same time, there should be no violent purpose, real or imaginary, and indeed no violence and rarely serious damage.

Unless what you are training for is not sport, that is, not competitive under constitutive rules, you are not training in the Asian martial arts, and it is not uncommon for these martial arts schools to forbid students to enter competition. With competition, a practice that once was a martial art becomes something else, either a sport, like mixed martial arts, or a dance, which is what archery becomes when subordinated to Buddhist enlightenment, as described in *Zen and the Art of Archery*: "By performing the ceremony [shooting the bow] like a religious dance, your spiritual awareness will develop its full force."[35] Here Zen reveals its Confucian face. For Confucians, archery provides a ritual occasion for gentlemen to express humanity. The intelligence that guides the arrow outweighs the force that impales the target. The gentleman touches but does not kill. For Confucians, archery is indeed a religious ceremony, and they explicitly include dance among its parts. The result, however, is not a spiritual martial art. It is a sublimation that relieves the practice of combative worth. The training is emptied of external, instrumental value, and the ineffectual result is sanctified as ritually pure. That is not the way of Chinese or Asian martial arts. You are not training in these arts unless what you are training for is not ritual, not aesthetic, not endotelic, and not any kind of religious dance.

> ### EXPRESSIVE INTENTIONALITY
>
> Dance movements are endotelic and look it.
>
> Sports play is competitive and looks it.
>
> Martial arts look designed for violence. They *are* so designed and *look* it, expressing that design intentionality.

I differentiated sport and dance in terms of expressive intentionality. Dance movements are endotelic and look it. Sport movements are competitive, contesting, and look it. Martial arts movements are weapons, and when they are performed well, they express this design, this violent intentionality, though without any violent purpose on the performer's part. The movements look designed for violence, as indeed they are, visibly expressing that design intentionality.

No martial arts movements are symbolic or merely graceful. None are of merely conventional value. A technique is trained and designed for violence. People who train in the martial arts "are practicing and training in person-to-person violence," according to a law-enforcement officer and highly experienced martial artist. "As a hobby we practice and play at things that are heinous crimes except in very narrow circumstances." That is true not only of those who train in connection with their work as law-enforcement officers or in some other professional capacity. Even the practice of *kata* (forms) is the practice of movements whose design-intentionality is combat and that, when competently performed, visibly express that design, that violent intentionality. Nothing about karate *kata* or Shaolin forms is merely symbolic. The highest standard of their performance must express the violent intentionality designed into the movements. The practitioner must know where the energies go, and that means competence in their use as weapons.[36]

The better one understands these techniques, the more one will appreciate the ingenuity and anatomical sophistication with which they compel the cessation of violence. We can see the design, the instrumentality, the art of the technique, and it is all about violence. But the *purpose* with which movements of such intentionality are practiced in the training hall or in a demonstration is not at all violent. Although violent intentionality is essential to martial arts movements, a violent purpose is repugnant to martial arts practice. Here I am distinguishing between the *intentionality of movements*, which is their design, specified by the description under which they are preferred, selected, and self-evaluated; and the *purpose of action*, which is the purpose for which one produces movements of such intentionality. Usually the purpose for which martial arts movements are executed is demonstration, *kata* performance, or collaboration in training. Another purpose for which those same movements would be effective, however, is self-defense or, for that matter, a mugging or assassination, although these violent purposes never enter traditional training. In teaching techniques of self-defense, for example, we practice movements whose (expressive) intentionality is violent, but we never apply any violence in the training and do not train with a violent purpose.

> **INTENTIONALITY VERSUS PURPOSE**
>
> *The intentionality of movements.* Their design, specified by the description under which the movement is selected.
>
> *The purpose of action.* The purpose for which someone produces movements of such intentionality.

This distinguishes martial arts practice from boxing, to which a violent purpose is crucial. Becoming violent on purpose (within the rules) is required for competitive success in boxing and is deliberately taught. Boxers train for a violent purpose. In traditional Asian martial arts training, that is never done. A paradox of their contemporary practice is that unless one is a law-enforcement officer or chooses to visit places where fights can be expected, one is unlikely ever to move against another person with the athletic violence for which one diligently trains.

Nothing in boxing is closer to martial arts training than the time-honored routine of shadowboxing. Here, of course, the opponent drops out. Shadowboxing has no violent purpose because there is no one to fight. With violence suspended, the boxer concentrates on kinetic form—stance, movement, openings, feints, fakes, footwork, and the like. Many martial arts training halls have a wall of mirrors for the same purpose. But while shadowboxing is one component of a boxer's training, almost everything in martial arts training is shadowlike. The opponent drops out because there is no competition and no real fighting. The other might as well be a shadow. Boxing would not be boxing if one trained only against shadows. Shadowboxing finds its rationale in what it contributes to fighting in the ring, and fighting in the ring requires contestants committed to violence.

Nearly all martial arts techniques are what a dancer would call steps: movements and combinations susceptible to demonstration and repetition. What separates them from dance is the same quality that separates the martial arts from sports: the commitment to an instrumental value external to the practice. A dance step may be mimetic and must be formal, but it is never instrumental, always being endotelic. Mimetic movements refer in some way (for instance, by quotation, simulation, or reenactment) to other movements. Formal movements are arbitrarily precise postures. Martial arts movements are neither mimetic nor merely formal; they are technical, designed and trained for combative effectiveness. Movement in martial arts has a clear aim and direction, and its design, shape, force, and spirit is a weaponed response to violence.[37]

These qualities distinguish the expressive intentionality of martial arts practice from games of sport no less than fine-arts dance, despite their shared athleticism. Movements look different, have a different perceptual quality, and express a different intentionality when they are being practiced as weapons. The difference between dance and martial arts corresponds to a difference in the value of gender for the bodies learning these movements. The sex of a dancer almost always matters and not only because of differences in physique. Whether the movement is performed by a male or a female makes an expressive difference, and the sexuality of the dancer is a normal part of dance. But in the martial arts, this quality disappears because expression is a by-product of technical effectiveness. A correctly performed technique does not change in quality, combative or aesthetic, when performed by a person of either gender.[38]

ALLAN BÄCK, a philosopher, scholar, and master taekwondo practitioner, distinguishes the martial arts from sports in a way different from what I have suggested. To him, the singularity of the martial arts is to have what he calls a double focus, meaning the dual foci of combat skill and meditative movement. Some martial arts practice works on combat skill, like sparring, whereas other aspects of training, such as forms, accentuate the artful and meditative. Bäck thinks that the availability of this aesthetic-meditative goal, which is explicitly noncompetitive, differentiates martial arts practice from sport, which has no alternative to competition, obliging players to put winning above every other consideration.[39]

Dividing the Asian martial arts internally in this way does not seem right to me. Where Bäck sees two foci, I see an incongruous dichotomy. He separates combat skill from artful movement, as if technical effectiveness were one thing and aesthetic quality something else, a different focus. This dichotomy is common in thinking about the relation between technical effectiveness and aesthetic value. We often encounter it in engineering, in the tendency to assume that the engineering design of something like a bridge or an aircraft has a technical goodness that floats free of the work's aesthetic quality. A technically good bridge can still be an eyesore, or as Bäck argues, excellence in combative technique is separable, a distinct focus, from elegant or meditational movement.

I think this assumption is a mistake wherever it is made, in the philosophy of martial arts no less than in technology. The look and feel of technically designed things (their aesthetic, perceptual interface) are ultimately impossible to distinguish from the engineering design quality of the mechanism by which they work (the interface of parts and systems). Techniques and tools do not work, or do not work as well as they could, unless design takes into account both moments, aesthetic and mechanical. They are not really two at all, each blurring into the other. We have no idea how to make something that is merely efficient, a rational instrument indifferent to how it looks or feels. No engineer can design such a thing, and none has ever been built. There is never one best way to make anything technically complex. If all we had to rely on in technology were the economic calculations of means-ends rationality, we would still be waiting for the first stone tool. An abyss separates rationality concerning means or function from the finished artifact. What finishes the work—conditioning its form, shape, parts, and design—is historical sociotechnical practice, including the operation, concerted or solo, of skill, technique, and craft, everything the Greeks called *techne* and the Romans *ars*, centuries before modern rationalism began to insist on distinguishing between beautiful art and efficient technology.[40]

Bäck sees a difference between fighting effectiveness and the artful perfection of martial arts movements: "The most distinctive aspect of the martial arts is that the ability to fight need not be considered the goal of all activity in the martial arts." What is "the ability to fight"? Really fight? Who? Where? If "ability to fight" means ability to score in sparring, I do not believe that sparring is real fighting. In the words of someone who knows the difference, "Sparring is often a chess match of distance and timing. Assault is an overwhelming onslaught. The skills don't transfer." Whatever exactly the ability to fight is, Bäck sees some artfulness to the martial arts that does not translate into combative effectiveness, "something additional to fighting skill alone," an "artistic enjoyment" that can be prized from combative effectiveness and developed for its own sake as a second focus of practice. Here, in the unexpected context of Asian martial arts, we see the rationalist assumption that technical effectiveness has a functional rationality of its own, which only accidentally interacts with the aesthetic quality of artifacts and techniques.[41]

To describe martial arts practice in terms of this dichotomy opens the door to qualities of movement that are not combative, that are merely artful (or meditative). That already has happened in contemporary wushu (what you see performed at the visitors' center at Shaolin

Temple today). Wushu used to be a martial art but now has been transformed into a performance art more like a dance or a circus act. My concept of martial arts makes no provision for movements that are merely artful or meditative. The movements are expressly designed to be martial; their elegant artfulness (when they have it) is the other side of combative effectiveness. A technique is more effective because it is more artfully designed or because its inherited design is more artfully executed. The artfulness comes from enhanced combative effectiveness. It is impossible to learn combative effectiveness without working on what is artful, aesthetic, even meditative, about these arts.

The absence of competition is not the only difference between martial arts practice and sports. There is also the absence of constitutive rules. The techniques taught in sports are typically worthless apart from the constitutive rules of a game. That is not true in martial arts, in which rules function solely to make training safe. The competence being trained does not depend on those rules for its value, as sports competencies usually do. That, and not a separate but equal, noncombative, meditative, spiritual, aesthetic focus, differentiates the martial arts from sports. Who is to say that a sport cannot have this dual focus? No Zen of golf? No moving meditation on the basketball court? Nothing satori-like about those moments called flow? What is true is that there is no tradition of interpreting sports play in that way. But nothing in the movements of the sport would be an insurmountable obstacle, not even the need to place winning ahead of everything. There may be a Zen way to do that, just as there is a Zen way to draw water or shoot an arrow. Who is to say?

I set aside such imponderables and look elsewhere for the difference between martial arts and sports. What differentiates them, beyond the elimination of competition from the martial arts, is the requirement in the martial arts that one train in a competence whose point and value do not depend on formal, artistic, ritual, ceremonial, aesthetic, or spiritual assumptions internal to a martial arts tradition. To attend to what is artful about martial arts techniques means attending to technique, technical details that enhance effectiveness, perfecting the intentionality with which one's body expresses competence, combining combative power with expressively effortless effectiveness (*wuwei*). Any artfulness that a martial arts practitioner chooses to work on, any perfection of form or technique, must enhance combative effectiveness. There is no nice way to say it. To work on what is artful about martial arts movements is to treat them as weapons and to work on their potential for violence. This precludes practice whose point is not combative or that carries the least hint of symbolism, formalism, or gesture.

The importance to the Asian martial arts traditions of the detailed correctness of movements confirms the sportslike quality of the *training*. The level of detail at which techniques can be analyzed seems endless and may be daunting to the novice. The precision required for the maximal effectiveness of many important martial arts techniques is gratuitously high. I say "gratuitous" because it is almost impossible for that precision to be spontaneously produced under conditions of real, not simulated, violence, which always include surprise and fear. And gratuitous because if all you need is street protection, you do not need such exquisite finesse. Yet that finesse can be found in the traditional techniques, as a master will demonstrate.

Martial arts are sportslike only in training and dancelike only in demonstration. In their application, in their actual use, the competence that these arts teach is neither sporting nor expressive. Here, then, is a system of differences to distinguish martial arts, sports, and performance arts like dance:

- A fine art is conventional and symbolic. The fine arts depend on conventions for their imagery and on their imagery for their aesthetic value, which lies in the unity of image and meaning, the aesthetic idea, an imaginary value, not a real effect or physical change.
- The athletic movements of sport are conventional and, under those conventions, really effective. The run, the kick, the tackle, the dive are real physical exchanges and not just symbols or images. The value of such effectiveness, however, depends entirely on conventions.
- Although martial arts training employs conventions, the combative competence that is taught remains effective without them. Being able to do what a football kicker can do in the absence of the conventions

of football has little value, but what is taught in the martial arts is different. The training inculcates instrumental effectiveness as a weapon for purposes external to what is practiced.

Knowing Where the Energies Go

Francis Sparshott, a pioneering philosopher of dance, finds that nothing "is more characteristic of dance than the way it is energized; in learning an exotic dance style, what one has principally to master is how and where the energies go." That is true of the martial arts, too. Training in these techniques is partly about getting the right form, becoming habituated to initially challenging details of posture and movement. But sometimes—or perhaps I should say invariably—small differences of form make large differences in performance. These distinctions are motivated not aesthetically but technically to enhance combative effectiveness. Joint locks are an example. The pain that makes a well-executed joint lock unendurable and compels submission can vary tremendously according to what may seem like slight differences in grip or posture. To master a joint lock entails an exquisite knowledge of where the energies go.[42]

Stillness is a kind of motion and can to be practiced no less than any other. Sometimes it is important to a technique working as designed that a body part, typically a limb, not move while a connected part, typically the torso, moves powerfully. One generates a whipping torque in hapikido's *sudo* (arm) strike precisely by *not* moving the arm while the torso rotates and then releasing the arm at the height of rotational energy in the torso (this principle is ubiquitous in hapkido). This is not something people spontaneously do when lashing out. In fact, impulse runs the opposite way. That is to the technique's advantage, because only trained people move in that way, which makes the strike both powerful and unexpected, hence difficult to evade, but it also means the movement takes a lot of practice.

Martial arts techniques are differentiated by body parts: we practice knee, arm, and hand strikes, head butts, kicks, and so on. The differences among these body parts are not merely formal or mere differences in shape. Legs are heavier than arms, are muscled differently, move differently, have different vulnerabilities, and require different training. A palm is an entirely different weapon from an elbow. The body, too, is not symmetrical; it has left and right sides, upper and lower parts, a front, a back, and flanks. These asymmetries have different values in the martial arts. Diligent training reduces the distinction of left and right. Training also teaches the strategic value of position, for instance moving to an opponent's flank or behind; and puts a different value on moving forward or back, depending, for instance, on the environment (enclosed or open, light or dark), or the threat (knife, bat, other willing attackers). Yet this differentiation of parts is heuristic only and must eventually be left behind for whole-body understanding. When it comes time to move, one does not move an arm or a leg; one moves a whole body. One of the best martial arts technique books I have seen advises,

> You want to move your body as a connected whole, as opposed to moving its parts separately. By timing your movements so that every part of your body starts and stops at the same time, you are able to get your entire body weight into your technique, thus increasing its power many times over.[43]

Space can be Euclidean, a space of position and trajectory; or hodological, a space of near and far; or dynamic, a space of interacting vectors. The spatial consideration in martial arts movement is not only where you are or where in relation to stabilities of the environment; it is also, and primarily, where you are in relation to your opponent. For example, it is more advantageous to be at the opponent's flank and a bit behind rather than facing front on. So one thing we want to practice is how to get to that advantageous place quickly and what to do once we are there. In dance, space is imaginary, with the value of spatial relations among the dancers depending on the spectator's interpretation. The martial arts also have a kind of imaginary space, but only in training, never in serious performance. The practice hall is a kind of theater. Movements on the mat occur in a space of imaginary approaches, responses, affordances, and obstacles, whether in relation to a partner's body or the imagined other of solo *kata* training. One responds to the partner's movement *as if* it were a punch, a jab, or a kick, though in reality it is too slow, ill targeted, and uncommitted to be much like what it represents. This retreat into representation is required for safe training, despite raising a question about how training translates into actual use.

Another spatial aspect of martial arts performance is the articulation of the movement as it is generated and transmitted through the body. A martial arts movement is kinesthetically conveyed; for example, a punch begins in the leg well footed and moves through the torso to the shoulders, arm, and hand. These movements are typically whole-body movements. It matters where all the parts are. A punch is more than a fist or an arm. One must consider how the shoulders and torso move; where the feet are; the position of the legs, the head, the other hand, and so on. Kicking requires a comparable coordination of movements in leg, torso, head, and arms. Body parts that do not usually move (ears, scalp) may be irrelevant, but not always. Ears are certainly a target. Beginners can find it difficult to hold their toes in the way required for barefooted sparring kicks, and that can be worked on. The orientation of the head is important, for instance, a defensive lowering of the chin. A properly executed head butt from about the scalp line is a tremendously powerful strike. Strategic eye movement (for instance, glancing over an opponent's shoulder and feigning recognition) can prepare an opening for a preemptive strike.

Proper parts of actions are themselves actions. When I enter a room, as proper parts of the act I turn the knob, open the door, and cross the threshold. Sparshott believes that a dance has no proper parts, that it is a seamless expressive whole. That seems true of techniques in the martial arts, too. Any analysis into parts is strictly heuristic. Techniques can be broken down for training, but to realize their optimal effectiveness, they must flow in one undivided interval. Rhythm is important to combinations. One rhythm is to strike high, then low, then high. Another is the jab-cross combination, as well as the rhythm of arms and legs in punch-kick combinations, and the intense rhythm of what is sometimes called a *blitz*, delivering multiple strikes as fast as possible. The movements have to be complementary so as not to interfere with one another and to trip one up. I have practiced combinations involving fifteen or more strikes designed to flow into one another in an unstoppable barrage that, with practice, can be performed in one second.[44]

Rhythm is an ambivalent quality in the martial arts because while it is indispensable to smooth flow, it is also something that others notice. It imparts predictability when one should be inscrutable, offering a pattern for an opponent to harmonize with and then use against one. The alternative, which requires art, is to position oneself to be maximally out of synchronization with one's opponent. In the words of a martial arts author, "The martial arts are a deliberate application of disorder. Therefore, they appear disordered and dysrhythmic. The martial artist uses disorder to combat disorder like a physician uses toxins to treat a disease." The same author observed that a distinctive quality of Chinese fighting systems is to "avoid movement endpoints" with "little of the 1–2-3 cadence seen in many non-Chinese boxing systems." The techniques happen in one beat, long or short, one flow without parts.[45]

Because martial arts movements have their own rhythm, music is seldom complementary to training. I have trained in studios where music played in the background, but its value seemed limited to an atmospheric distraction during push-ups. As soon as drills or forms were being practiced, I forgot about the music. After observing a taiji demonstration accompanied by music, Robert W. Smith wrote,

> Music is an externality. Since it has a beat, using it may subordinate taiji to it, making this moving meditation merely a dance. There is an innate rhythm and beat to taiji but it derives from an internal alchemy of breathing, movement, and self rather than externally manufactured melody. Years ago I experimented with music [in taiji class, but] . . . no music was quite so good as that music Taiji itself was producing from deep inside me.[46]

Striking Beauty

Trained and untrained people observing martial arts practice tend to find it fascinating. One of the first responses to the "discovery" of the Chinese martial arts—that is, kung fu—in North America, was the pop song "Kung Fu Fighting," Carl Douglas's one-hit wonder from 1974:

Everybody was kung-fu fighting
Those cats were fast as lightning
In fact, it was a little bit frightening
But they fought with expert timing

The aesthetic intensity of martial arts performance is not that of dance. Dance movements are endotelic, but more, they *look* endotelic. Martial arts movements are practiced under a regime antithetic to dance value, and their aesthetic quality has a different origin. This quality comes from the precision and intensity with which they express their design as weapons, an expressive quality that these movements acquire as a by-product of combative effectiveness.

The aesthetic quality of martial arts movements is partly that of athletics generally, and as with athletics the beauty of these movements is an unintended by-product of design for maximum effectiveness with minimum exertion. Martial arts movements are usually not beautiful or fascinating until one can perform them with combative effectiveness, when they begin to acquire what choreographer Merce Cunningham spoke of as the "eloquence of movement." Proficiency, meaning a high probability of superlatively executed techniques, combines effectiveness with economy and expressive intentionality. Combative effectiveness and aesthetic quality emerge from the same corporeal matrix. The strongest parts of the body are the heaviest and, having the most inertia, also the slowest. To be powerful, movement needs to use these strongest muscles, which are near the body's center of gravity (torso and hips). This energetic requirement also is an aesthetic requisite of expressive grace. Another choreographer labeled this a "kinesiological truth," noting that nearly all human movement "starts in the spine and pelvis, not in the extremities—the legs or arms." The energies of our really and expressively most powerful movements start in the body's center of gravity and flow outward along lines that follow the extremities.[47]

When watching a body in motion the eyes seek a point from which to get the best total view, and the first glance we cast on a moving figure goes to its center of gravity, the point where vision best takes in a changing whole. Typically, especially in advanced martial arts techniques, that somatic center is also the point from which speed, force, and effectiveness radiate. As Robert W. Smith, a lifelong scholar-practitioner of the Chinese martial arts, stated,

> The waist is the foundation of all bodily movement. It is the big axis from which . . . movements derive their celerity, crispness, and power. Only in the flexibility of the waist is there true strength. To fight with arms or legs independently of the waist is the mark of the perpetual beginner.

An aikido grand master made the same point:

> Moving from the center means that action initiates and is generated from the hip area. Your body moves as one with your hip, or your center, leading the way. . . . Your body, moving from the center, moves as a single unit. This allows the utilization of the strength and momentum of your whole body rather than the isolated muscles of the arms. This puts great power into aikido technique with very little effort on your part.

It also accounts for an aesthetic pleasure in the performance of martial arts. The centrifugal force of the body and the pull of gravity collaborate to generate an intense, fluent, precisely directed power that is no less real than expressive—visually eloquent for an audience, exhilaratingly effortless for the performer, and deeply penetrating to the opponent, who is left shaken and debilitated.[48]

A participant observer of somaesthetic qualities in the Asian martial arts distinguishes expressive gestalt qualities from more intimately felt sensory attributes. The gestalt qualities he identifies are, first, psychosomatic integrity, or a corporeal sense of unity in mastering basic movements and the ability to combine and vary them fluidly; and, second, martial grace, or the experience of spontaneous improvisation and flow, characterized by a feeling of effortlessness during training or fighting with a partner. Sensory somasethetic qualities include perceptible variations in corporeal energy—such distinctly felt and no less expressively conveyed consistencies of movement as heavy, light, snapping, sinking, whipping, spiraling, expanding, or shaking—and a kinesthetic sense of the space through which the body moves as gravity and centrifugal force blend in the energetic trajectories of limbs and torso to give palpable shape to the space in which they are completed.[49]

Our movements are inherently articulated simply because we have limbs with joints. The economy of complementary muscles ensures that every move we make consists of proper parts, and their interaction is necessarily resonant and rhythmic. The alternative is spasmodic. Dance intensifies the rhythmic qualities intermittent in all movement. Almost any work people do involves routines, which an efficient worker may perform with elegance. Such movements are dancelike but not dance. In dance, *all* movement (in the conventional frame) is as rhythmic as *some* everyday labor. Although martial arts movements may be dancelike, they are not dance for the same reason that they are not sports, namely, the commitment to combative use as a weapon.[50]

It is not easy to mimic martial arts techniques convincingly. Probably the only way to imitate them well is to practice them for real. It is no coincidence that all the successful martial arts film actors (even the buffoons) were highly proficient martial artists before the movies. This may be the only way to make such movements convincing without actually hurting people. But something in Chinese martial arts history troubles my neat distinction between martial arts and dance. China has a long history of involvement between martial arts and theater. Playing martial roles in a theatrical or operatic troupe was, after the military, the main employment for men with martial arts training, and they predictably sacrificed combative efficiency for cool form. Yet even here, at its most theatrical, with movements made to be looked at, this use of martial arts requires real martial proficiency. One need not be a marksman to play convincingly the role of a cop using a gun. But to play martial roles in the Beijing opera requires a combative mastery of martial arts movements, knowing where the energies go in order to make them effective weapons.[51]

People who think they enjoy watching the Asian martial arts may never have seen any. For instance, watching Olympic taekwondo is not watching martial arts. A U.S. Olympic taekwondo trainer was honest about that: "I don't train martial artists; I train athletes." They are not interested in self-defense or forms but in winning. Watching a kung fu movie also is not watching martial arts because, as in sports, though less conspicuously, conditions have been imposed that change the performance into an imaginary aesthetic mimesis contrived to appeal to spectators without martial arts experience. The fighting in a typical kung fu movie looks authentic only to people who have no experience in these arts. Of course, the whole idea that martial arts performances in cinema should be "authentic" is a Western value of little interest to Asian audiences. For them, the martial arts movie is a variation on the *wuxia* genre mentioned in chapter 1, a literary and now cinematic form of many centuries standing that is amazingly popular throughout East Asia. Asian audiences are less invested in realism than Western audiences are. The imaginative atmospheric fight sequences and portrayal of recognizable characters are more important than martial arts authenticity, whatever that means.[52]

People with more experience in the martial arts will have seen demonstrations featuring *kata* (the Japanese word for "form" or "forms"). There are some fifty karate *kata* and hundreds of kung fu forms, precisely choreographed patterns of movement that are practiced either alone or with a partner. These forms are usually understood as combative sequences of blocking, punching, striking, and kicking, whose value varies from school to school. Forms devised to win competitions emphasize the spectacular, whereas others showcase the school's training syllabus. It may seem obvious that these forms are supposed to have application as a response to attack; that is how karate and kung fu forms were explained to me when I trained in them. The specific interpretations of *kata* often are uncertain, however, and may vary from school to school, master to master, even student to student. Some schools adopt the stance that there is no one correct explanation and even encourage their students to invent applications.

If these forms are necessary for training effective fighting, why is there not more agreement on their use? Lineages of martial arts have been especially careful in passing down *kata* but oddly negligent in passing down an understanding of exactly what is supposed to be happening as one moves through the form. That suggests that the movements are what is important, not the supposed applications. The whole idea of "application" for *kata* may be a modern misunderstanding of the Okinawan tradition, which apparently never had the idea that their moves are a series of strikes and blocks. Such "applications" did not enter karate *kata* instruction until after it was exported to Japan, where karate had to compete for attention with the samurai combative arts.[53]

Karate derives from Shaolin *gongfu*, which Buddhist missionaries brought to Okinawa along with Zen. By our time, Cantonese cinema has so accustomed us to the idea of fighting monks that we disregard the paradox. I noted earlier that fighting is illegal under Buddhist law, as are weapons. Yet fighting monks are not a myth. However the tradition began, the contradiction between violence and Buddhist teaching may have motivated religious virtuosi to try to sublimate these arts to a spiritual vocation. It is as if the Buddhists had to be their own missionaries and spiritualize the demon (violence) that penetrated their temple walls. Nathan Johnson, a high-ranking karate and kung fu teacher and scholar of *kata*, argues that the Chinese monks who invented these forms and passed them on to Okinawa, thence to Japan as karate, were not anticipating their application as blocks and counters to incoming attacks. He thinks the original purpose of karate *kata* was a dynamic or kinetic meditation in which partners try to trap or destabilize each other, as in taiji's "pushing hands," or "sticking hands" routines in wing chun.[54]

Johnson observes that "many of the strange two-handed movements, full stops, turns, and what appear to be blocks" in karate *kata* "make much more sense as seizing, grasping, two-handed grappling, and throwing movements than they do as double blocks against improbable double punch attacks." He thinks the primary point of *kata* is to teach "how to regulate or break and control the unbalancing potential of grips or traps." The photographs in Johnson's book show how the positions and sequences exactingly passed down by Okinawan masters constitute a methodical catalog of the grappling, wrist- and elbow-locking, subduing, and throwing techniques that inevitably emerge from the kinetic potentials of the human body. "The value of the form," he explains, "lies in its formula. It acts as a mnemonic device and serves to train the body and the mind and maintain neural pathways. . . . Forms train posture, stance, body geometry, leverage, independent action of limbs, and refined, economical movement unrelated to feudal battle tactics."[55]

I spent a lot of time practicing forms when I trained in kung fu. I also have trained in some of the karate forms. In China I practiced daily with private lessons twice a week for several months training in one of the contemporary wushu forms. For the last several years, however, forms have dropped out of my training, as they are not used in the Korean hapkido that I currently train in. Johnson's theory may explain why. Chinese martial arts seeped into Korea as early as the third century C.E., some five hundred years before Chan Buddhism and Shaolin's experiment with a Zen spiritualization of martial arts. This spiritualized version of the Chinese martial arts is what was transmitted (with Zen) to Okinawa and eventually to Japan as karate. I am not suggesting that modern hapkido dates from that ancient period. Rather, the Koreans were able to sample the Chinese martial arts before their modification under Zen and built their own traditions (of which hapkido is a relatively modern evolution) on this older foundation. Forms were not as crucial to these earlier currents of Chinese martial arts as they became for Shaolin Buddhists, who made the practice of forms fundamental to their spiritualization of fighting arts.[56]

. . . And Then Another Thousand Times

Probably anyone with martial arts training has heard about the value of a thousand repetitions, or the adage that it is not ten thousand techniques but one technique practiced ten thousand times that makes a formidable fighter. Chang Naizhou admonished students of his art: "To make [the technique] dynamic, efficacious, and lively, it must be done approximately a thousand times before it is well practiced. If it is not well practiced, do it another thousand times." Everybody knows practice makes perfect, but a mystery lurks in this platitude. It seems obvious that repetition is the way to learn somatic techniques. You watch a teacher's movement and imitate it with movement of your own. Then you see your own repetitions, feel them proprioceptively, perceive the quality of your own movement, and fine-tune it. Repetition thus begins with perception. You must first repeat what you only *see* the teacher do before you can repeat your own repetition and begin to practice. But it is difficult to see movements that you cannot perform. How little you really see of the teacher's movement becomes evident when you try to repeat it. You think you see the movement, but your body understands little or nothing and can do only what it already knows. Training therefore has to work on perception no less than movement, which prove to be two interpenetrating phases in the evolution of skill.[57]

The teacher performs a technique. Students observe attentively and then try it themselves. Their first perception is obscure, and the first effort to reproduce what they think they saw is weak. The technique may therefore be divided into serial movements that can be practiced separately. The series will look jerky until the student feels out where the energies go, the kinetic melody that orchestrates motions into one beat. "The true effect of repetition," says Henri Bergson, "is to decompose, and then to recompose, and thus appeal to the intelligence of the body." To appeal to body intelligence, one must use intelligent means, consciously, experimentally, imaginatively moving the body, and attentively watching movements correctly made. One becomes conscious of small bodily adjustments never before attended to. Each new attempt, Bergson observed, "separates movements which were interpenetrating" and "[calls] the attention of the body to a new detail which had passed unperceived." Repetition thus "bids the body discriminate and classify; it teaches what is the essential; it points out, one after another, within the total movement, the lines that mark off [the movement's] internal structure. In this sense a movement is learnt when the body has been made to understand it."[58]

The fruit of repetition is accomplished habit. Parmenides badly misled posterity with his invidious dichotomy of habit and intellect. "Habit" is one word but not one thing, and it is not opposed to intelligence or thought. Some habits are more intelligent than others. Thoughtfulness can be a habit. Some habits make us more obtuse, others more skillful. Some habits degenerate into mechanical routine, and others increase attention. There are habits of sensitivity, of discernment, even habits of habit adjustment, which is another word for "imagination," the creative recalibration of habits. Repetition is as much about judging and reforming habits as about forming them. The repetitions may be exhausting, but they are not monotonous and even can be a kind of practice in autonomy, doing for yourself, finding for yourself, making the technique your own.

You do it over, go back to the start, begin again, and gradually make discoveries. To an audience it may seem mindless, but practitioners know that from the inside, repetition is reprise, invention, discovery, and expansion of content. None of that will happen, however, until you begin to *imagine* that it already has and remember that image until it swells into actual competence. Asian martial arts speak strongly to our somatic imagination because imagination is stimulated by the difficult and incomplete. When students new to these arts watch techniques being performed, they see that they are unexpected, unwonted, not ordinary everyday movements. They may doubt whether they can perform them, though they may be keen to try. They also see them incompletely, puzzlingly—how did the hand turn? Where are the feet? Is the elbow tucked in or out? We want to see them again, think we get it, try again, and thus commence exploratory repetition under the guidance of somatic imagination.

Repetition is the only way to initiate the productive interplay between what you can already do and what you are beginning to imagine doing. The more perfused with imagination your repetitions are, the more effective they will be in training. What is imaginative about repetition is anticipation. We become aware of the rhythmic potentials of the movement, which are available for adjustment and variation. The better imagined they are, the more flexible and farseeing the anticipation will be. Spectators will not see the richness of repetition, the minute metamorphoses that accompany the gradual emergence of rhythm, and the enlarged anticipation that introduces variations of tempo into what to an audience (though not a vigilant teacher) may look like the same thing over and over. Repetition begins to become endotelic. At first we do it because we have to. We set a quota and stop. But eventually we find we are repeating it just to repeat it, to do it again, find it again, feel it again. Musicians know this as the Isaac Stern rule: The better your technique is, the longer you will be able to rehearse without boredom. When practice is organized around a fixed goal, people tend to meet it and stop. More challenging practice is open-ended and makes a stronger call on imagination as competence advances into unknown territory.[59]

There is no substitute for repetition. Thinking, talking, theory will never yield performance. To teach actual performance, not discursive commentary, one has to address the body more immediately than talking can. Martial arts teachers in the Japanese tradition tend to demonstrate only, tolerating no explanation. "The student must 'steal' the knowledge," an aikido grand master explained, "meaning learn from his or her own practice and exercise. . . . True knowing is taken, not given." Aikido founder Ueshiba Morihei had an unforgettable way of imparting this lesson: should a student have the temerity to ask a question, the impassive master would throw him to the floor.[60]

Training arouses a new somatic consciousness. One becomes aware of innumerable details of position and movement never before noticed. This enhanced consciousness is not a goal but only a phase and by-product of the development that eventually returns to unconsciousness in the body's heightened performative capacity. A nice appreciation of this point can be found in the samurai Munenori's *Book of Family Traditions on the Art of War*:

> When the effects of exercise build up unawares and practice accumulates, thoughts of wishing to quickly develop skill disappear quietly, and whatever you do, you spontaneously become free from conscious thoughts. At the time, you do not even know yourself: when your body, feet, and hands act without your doing anything in your mind, you make no misses, ten times out of ten.[61]

People who train in the martial arts like the idea of four levels of competence: unconscious incompetence (the everyday norm), conscious incompetence (beginning training), conscious competence (acquiring skill), and, finally, unconscious competence. That is the itinerary of mastery in the martial arts as it is in every art or *techne*. The four-levels theory comes from American psychology of the 1950s, but the conception of mastery as the maturation of unconscious competence has deep roots in the Asian martial arts. Here is Munenori again:

> When what you have studied leaves your mind entirely, and practice also disappears, then, when you perform whatever art you are engaged in, you accomplish the techniques easily without being inhibited by concern over what you have learned, and yet without deviating

from what you have learned. This is spontaneously conforming to learning without being consciously aware of doing so. The science of the art
of war can be understood through this.

When you have succeeded in learning, when everything you learned
disappears from your conscious mind and you become innocent, this
is the spirit of perfecting things. . . . You are detached from your learning yet do not deviate from your learning. . . . The learning is for the
purpose of reaching this state. Once you have learned this successfully,
learning disappears. . . . Forgetting learning, relinquishing mind, harmonizing without any self-conscious knowledge thereof, is the ultimate
consummation of the Way.[62]

The Chinese word for "unconscious competence" is *wuxin*, "no mind"
(*mushin* in Japanese). The less action depends on consciousness, the
more masterful, the more perfect, the knowledge will be. Only then
is movement *ziran* (from itself, spontaneous) and *wuwei* (effortlessly
efficacious).

The eloquence of movement is the eloquence of unconscious
competence, when the body unfolds its movement without conscious
effort. As a process with a temporal course, any movement requires
what neurologist Aleksandr Luria described as "a continuous chain of
interchanging impulses." In the formative stage, as one learns the movement, this chain "consist[s] of a series of isolated impulses," but with
the development of skill, "the individual impulses are synthesized and
combined into integral kinesthetic structures." Luria calls them kinetic
melodies, "when a single impulse is sufficient to activate a complete
dynamic stereotype of automatically [unfolding] elements."[63]

The eloquence of movement is the improvisational eloquence of
these kinetic melodies. The beginning of the melody becomes sufficient
to call forth the entire performance with circumstantially appropriate
improvisation. These kinetic melodies form the repertory of our basic actions, the basic intentional parts of everything we do—walking,
speaking, reaching, throwing, and so on. Performing these melodies is
not a brain event and not a computation but is a muscular whole-body
event. The part movements are no longer a series (as they may have
been when we were learning the melody), but indivisible phases of one

extended movement. Once set in motion, the corporeal energy of the resonant part-movements ripples through the whole body, allowing us to perform the technique in one beat. Speed, being fast or faster, is not the point. The point is one beat, one interpenetrating duration without parts, whether performed slowly or with speed.

This eloquence of movement is the training goal in the martial arts, as well as the source of all its qualities, aesthetic and combative. Movements without expressive eloquence, which look unbalanced, jerky, or mechanical, also are incapable of generating the power for which the technique is designed. The ungainly aesthetic appearance and the disappointing combative effectiveness of a beginner's movements are two sides of the same thing. Several movements are performed in a series as if each were a beat of its own, and they are strung together without becoming indivisible phases of one interval. Intensity and strength come with eloquence, when the many part movements become an elegantly improvised riff on a kinetic melody designed for weaponed potential.

The value of composing movements into a continuous duration explains the Asian martial arts' fascination with circles and spirals. The principle of hapkido, for instance, is *hwa won yue*, "harmony of circular flow." Circular and spiral movements are at once delightful to watch or perform and hold the greatest combative potential. "One needs very little movement from the center of a circle to generate great speed and power on the outside circumference," says a martial master. "Every movement in correct boxing takes circles," says another. "If you are attacked on a straight line and you resist with a straight line defense, the stronger force will prevail. But if the incoming force is neutralized by circularity, it is a simple matter to defeat an opponent, regardless [of] how strong." The principle does, of course, have a Chinese pedigree, for instance, in the writing of Chang Naizhou: "To study this *dao*, first draw a big circle, gradually drawing smaller and smaller, until at completion there are circles, yet no visible circles. They are purely as ideas known, naturally leaving no trace."[64]

For an audience, the aesthetic quality of circular movement comes from its powerful appeal to perception, which delights in curved motion's visibly flowing continuity and change. Curved lines and circular or spiral motions are delightful, Bergson pointed out, because even though a curved line "changes its direction at every moment, every new direction is indicated in the preceding one." That is what Merce Cunningham called eloquence, the unfolding of a kinetic melody. "Thus," Bergson added, "the perception of ease in motion passes over into the pleasure of mastering the flow of time and holding the future in the present."[65]

The manifestations of martial arts skill are agility, which is the precision control of the body's power, and eloquent improvisation on the kinetic melodies of a tradition's technical repertory. The skill that grows under training is that of a body becoming artifactual (or more artifactual than it was). Any art progresses in depth and complexity by the successive discovery of ways in which its materials can be arranged and exploited to advance the ends of the art. In the martial arts, the line between students (however senior) and masters is the line between those who are still learning what the tradition knows and those who are inventing techniques and enriching traditions. This is still happening in the Asian martial arts. I have personal experience of techniques that were invented and perfected by the hapkido grand master who taught them to me. These are techniques not found beyond the circle of his students. They share a technical quality with the wheel and the clothes button. They are simple, efficient, and logical, but only after you see them. If you have not seen them, then you won't see them and won't know what hit you.

IF ALL ONE KNEW about the Asian martial arts came from watching kung fu movies, or just from having heard about them, these arts might seem seeped in violence. They are indeed combat arts and train real effectiveness, not symbols, gestures, or aesthetic ideas. They were born in war, and they always have something of war's violence about them, however sublimated. Martial arts techniques and skills are designed to destroy an opponent's ability to fight, and practitioners constantly think about violent effects and how to intensify them. Yet violence is not an internal good of martial arts and is completely external to the practice. Although we constantly refer to it, we refuse it a place in the training.

Having eliminated the dread of actual violence from the training environment, one can concentrate on the martial art's kinetic essence and how corporeal violence works, including techniques to amplify or neutralize it. One practices improvising on the art's kinetic melodies. As the improvisation becomes skilled and unconsciously competent, the eloquence and pleasure with which the movements are performed and viewed rises too, as does their weaponed potential. It is the suspension of a violent purpose that allows the expressive qualities of martial arts movements to come to the fore.

Movement tends to become aesthetically interesting as it becomes fluid, flowing, efficient, visibly energetic, and seemingly effortless, the design qualities of Asian martial arts techniques. Training becomes a theater of skilled movement for the agent and an audience of teachers and fellow students. What they observe is not the darkly fascinating beauty of violence, as it is in boxing. It is a violent essence or violent kinetic form that, in not being violently actualized (having no actual purpose of violence) can be calmly contemplated by both performer and audience. But if you add real use, in combat or self-defense, the beauty disappears into the chaos of violence.

4

WHAT A BODY CAN DO

Martial Arts Ethics

No one ought to wait to be struck, unless he is a fool.
ALBERICO GENTILI, *DE JURE BELLI LIBRI TRES*

The techniques that the Asian martial arts teach are weapons. There is no other way to put it, which means that training in these arts is training in the use of weapons. They are special weapons, of course, and ineffective against many other weapons or against various threats. But what weapon is not specialized in some way and ineffectual in certain situations? People who train in martial arts might never actually use these weapons, just as many people who own a gun never fire it in self-defense. But they might, and unless they have prepared themselves, they might be disagreeably surprised by the consequences, even (especially) if they successfully defend themselves against assault.

For instance, the law will not always hold them completely innocent, however righteous they may feel. They may be asked to justify the level of their violence. Was a predictably lethal or permanently disabling technique really called for? Did your training not enable you to use something less dangerous to your attacker? Why were you fighting in the first place? Why did you not submit, give the attacker what he wanted, or run away? Moreover, facing the law, the police, and the courts is only one of the foreseeable if not always well-considered implications of a violent altercation. The movies—often the only source for what modern people think they know about violence—give a seriously misleading picture of its aftermath, especially for the one who wins the fight.

Precisely because there is no actual violence in martial arts training, because we surround our practice with conventions and rituals to keep violence at bay, it is easy to overlook what it really would be like to use the techniques we have learned on another person with full force and commitment. Students may have an inaccurate, even simplistic, understanding of the whole range of consequences—emotional no less than physical, legal, and financial—of the potential violence they are learning. Even seasoned practitioners may be grievously distraught by the unexpected aftermath of using on another person the art that they have struggled to master. It therefore behooves thoughtful practitioners to consider the complicated topic of violence, to appreciate the place of their training in the economy of violence, and to prepare themselves for the event of what, if they are fortunate, they should never have to experience.

Besides the question of violence, another ethical question is simply why learn martial arts at all, especially now when (though people tend to doubt this) interpersonal violence, particularly the sort against which martial arts might be effective, has never been more unlikely? What is the training for? What is the ethical value of our practice?

DREAD VIOLENCE

People writing about violence like to compare it to an elephant. Sometimes they invoke the story about the blind men investigating an elephant. One of them feels a tusk, another a leg, and so on, each reporting a completely different animal. Others make a different allusion. Violence is the elephant in the room, the big, obvious thing we refuse to acknowledge, as sex supposedly was for Victorians. Indeed, after sex, violence must be the most mystified facet of social existence. Of course we want to ask what exactly "violence" is. Formal definitions are not as valuable as some tend to believe. A complicated topic like violence can be approached more usefully than by struggling over a definition.[1]

Here is a question to start with. Presumably violence is a harm. If I am successfully violent against another, and this violence is intentional and not in any way staged or bound by a rule, then I have harmed the other. But is violence merely one harm among many, or is it a quality of all harms, perhaps even what makes harms harmful? Bear in mind the full range of harms, which besides obvious violence include predatory lending, regressive taxation, environmental destruction, the desecration of a heritage site, a racist slur, a homophobic stare, a sexist joke. I don't think these harms are acts of violence because they lack the willful domination of one body by another, which seems characteristic of violence. Violence is assault, physical, body on body, with the intent to destroy the other's will.

Some people think that physical assault like that is merely "subjective" violence, besides which is the "objective" violence of, for instance, capitalism and hate speech. I do not think we need this dichotomy, though, and I do not want to separate violence from a violent subject. Violence is profoundly subjective. It happens to a person, and another person does it. Cases of supposedly not subjective, impersonal, "objective" violence seem to me to belong to the category of *harms*, which takes in greater variety than violence and is the genus of its species. Violence is harming in a specific way.[2]

We also should distinguish between violence and cruelty. To be cruel is to make others suffer for their fateful accidents, like where they were born, what they love or fear, or even how their species evolved, and the suffering to which they are fatefully susceptible. Cruelty is the manipulation of these accidents to cause suffering and is vicious but often, even usually, not violent. I may do something, say, not come home one night, which I know will distress my spouse. Or I may say something, perhaps even something true, knowing that it will embarrass another. It is the words, the proposition, its truth or publicity that hurts. I did not hurt her in the sense of physical assault. The event hurt her. I made the event happen, and the event hurt her. That is cruelty, which is a way of harming others while avoiding violence, not a way of partaking in it.

Violence is body on body, with or without a weapon, but with arrogant disregard for the other's will, with the intent of destroying that will, either temporarily or permanently. There is no incorporeal violence and no violence against the dead. Ancient Greeks were connoisseurs of violence, their Olympic *pankration* making our "extreme fighting" look genteel. All those rules! Yet these same violence-loving people abhorred and strictly punished violence in civic life. They saw it as an intolerable hubris, an offense against the whole city, indeed, against the very idea of civil, civic life, a sentiment Pindar expresses well:

> Honor, father Zeus, . . .
> the man who has found excellence with his fist,
> grant him the favor of a respected reputation
> among fellow citizens and strangers.
> When he walks straight on the path
> hostile to insolent violence (*hubris*), you
> clearly illuminate the ways which the upright minds of his ancestors
>   used.[3]

The great Athenian lawyer Demosthenes explained the reprehensible hubris of violent crime: "The law-giver considered every deed one commits with violence to be a public wrong and directed also against those unconcerned with the affair. . . . For he thought that one who commits hubris wrongs the city, and not only his victim." Only tyrants resort to violence, and any violent crime is a small tyranny. As Isocrates, another Athenian orator, pointed out, "Hubris ravages all of our interests, and many houses have been destroyed by it, many cities overthrown. . . . We ourselves have already twice seen our democracy dissolved . . . [by] those who commit acts of outrage (*hubrizein*) against citizens." Felonious violence is not just body on body, for the violence of the athletes is noble. The soul of violence is in the will. Violence is malevolent, arrogant, anarchic, tyrannical. Not bestial, no regression to amoral animality, but selfish and willful as only people can be.[4]

Some people believe that there is violence in merely using symbols, speaking a language, or going through the rituals of everyday life, bypassing a violent will. Pierre Bourdieu, a leader of this persuasion, defines symbolic violence as a "gentle, hidden form which violence takes when overt violence is impossible." Symbolic violence is a violence that people carry out merely by "paying due respect to forms." This means action or discourse whose mere form, regardless of content, endows it with prima facie morality, yet whose content is, in effect, an open and hurtful expression of a wish that if presented in any other way would be unacceptable. Put the words in the mouth of a robed man whom people call magistrate and anything he says, provided the form is right, becomes a sacred object. His words and their effect cause the impersonal symbolic violence implied by labels like "criminal" and "delinquent." This is not a violence limited to bad laws or bad legal systems. According to this argument, the mere form of the law is an instrument of violence, no less than the sword with which law has long been identified. Law is not an alternative to violence, as the Greeks supposed, but merely transposes violence to the economy of symbols, where it is ideologically mystified and rendered invisible.[5]

Symbolic violence is the violence (if it is violence) of intolerance and hate before these spill over into the outright physical violence of assault. Symbolic violence is the violence of a word or a look even when battery is unlikely. It also is the anonymous violence of class differences, economic circumstances, and other types of structural violence. It even is the violence of knowledge when applied to define, disable, and discipline minority populations (for example, homosexuals or dissidents). A further supposedly impersonal, symbolic violence occurs when people on society's lower rungs suffer increased rates of death and disability compared with the people above, harms that seem like violence structurally produced by the operation of a class system. Such are the claims of those who disagree with the insistent subjectivity that I impart to violence. I already have suggested how I view these inflationary efforts. Everything described as symbolic violence is a harm of one kind or another, but not violent in what seems to me the most important use of the term. These are harms but not violence because they lack the intentional, subjective destruction of another's will, which is a harm sufficiently distinct to merit discriminating it from generic harms by the word "violence." A joke or stare may be a precursor to violence if it communicates a credible threat, but the look or word is then a *threat* of violence, not its actuality on an incorporeal plane of symbols.

One of the myths that mystify violence is that for some people (and for most men under some circumstances), violence comes easily. You lose your temper and become homicidal. Anyone can be pushed to it; some need little pushing at all. Mass media representations of violence confirm the myth, as do scholars who rationalize it with a popular theory of human nature. According to this theory, human beings (or perhaps just men) are by nature violent and become civilized only under the repressive force of culture and its institutions, especially religion and law. The original animal violence occasionally breaks through, however: symbolically in dreams and religion, and physically in real, if ritualized, acts of violence, like scapegoats, human sacrifice, capital punishment, and war.

In a classic statement of this myth, Sigmund Freud defined "civiliza-tion" (*Kultur*) as "the whole sum of the achievements and the regula-tions which distinguish our lives from those of our animal ancestors and which serve two purposes—namely to protect men against nature and to adjust their mutual relations." He believed that these achieve-ments require a resented renunciation that makes all of us somewhat hostile to civilization and its demands: "Men are not gentle creatures who want to be loved, and who at the most can defend themselves if they are attacked." On the contrary. They are creatures "among whose instinctual endowments is to be reckoned a powerful share of aggres-siveness." There can be no culture, no civilization, no recognizably human existence until this primordial propensity for violence is sub-limated or stifled. That is the contribution of morality, which Freud called "a therapeutic attempt . . . to achieve, by means of a command of the super-ego, . . . [control of] the constitutional inclination of hu-man beings to be aggressive toward one another." This "constitutional inclination to be aggressive toward one another" is an original, natural, instinctive violence, only partially tamed by culture, and ready to flow down any available channel.[6]

Another theory of original violence comes from evolutionary psy-chology, which explains human violence (or at least the most common sort, that of men in their twenties) as a naturally selected characteristic of the males in many species to struggle among themselves for repro-ductive dominance. This explanation is unlikely, however, because the greatest *quantity* of violence takes place between people of nonrepro-ductive age and is evenly spread between males and females. This is the violence of children, who have far more violence in their tender lives than an average adult experiences from day to day. Although the violence of children may seem to take us back to Freud and original violence, I suggest instead that we ask one of those elephant questions nobody is asking. Is violence ever easy?[7]

Not even children find violence easy, and they are, of course, childishly incompetent at it. What makes them susceptible to violence is that they are susceptible to falling into the kinds of interactions that predictably will elicit violence from others. Violence is not a mere effect of a villain's background, whether evolutionary or sociological. The background of violent people never explains their violence. That is another myth, that violence is, as they say, socially constructed, that people are made to be violent, made so by their background, racism, or poverty, or perhaps just the reproductive advantage of randomly violent ancestors. None of the many studies of the background variables of violent individuals have found any credible evidence of their effect. Background conditions never predict violence. Any way you cut it, most people (including most discriminated people, most poor people, most victims of former abuse, and so on) are not violent. Violence is something most people *dread*.[8]

An alternative to theories of instinctual enmity explains violence as an emergent quality of interactions. Even though there may be no violent individuals, there are violent situations, meaning situations whose contours shape the emotions of people who step into them and dependably lead to violence. Features of present situations, not something that occurred in the past of the people who meet there, determine whether violence happens and write its script. I am describing the sociologist Randall Collins's "ritual interaction" theory of violence. As a theory, it seems as well based in evolutionary thought as the idea of people's barely repressed animal violence. Something truly singular about human evolution is our capacity for sharing a focus of attention, which is the foundation of nearly all our social life, from language to violence. Comparative research across all the primates confirms the singularity of the human infant's capacity to share an object of attention with another. Infants begin to share attention from the age of nine months, when many joint attention behaviors emerge together, including pointing for the other and a pointing gaze. Normal development requires abundant opportunities for infants to engage in intentional back-and-forths with others, learning to read and imitate their beliefs, desires, and emotions. This continuous reciprocal signaling is not found in apes, but the experience is crucial to learning how to convey intent and respond to signaled intent rather than wait for action.[9]

For us humans, a truly natural feature of our evolved, instinctive psychology is to home in on the other in any interaction. What is our common focus, reference, or object, and how do we feel about it? The common object is also a common affect. We cannot converge on the same object without a similitude of emotion, as it will not mean the same thing to us. Here is a banal example of our evolved disposition to become momentarily entrained in the other's rhythm: "Once, during a job interview, I found myself reproducing, involuntarily and without any delay, the movements made by the director of personnel: I was compelled to mime his crossed legs and interlaced fingers, and thus expressed my interest in the position and eventual willingness to co-operate."[10]

A second example shows how predatory street violence exploits the tendency to become entrained on a mutual reference. A man has had to stop his car at a self-serve gas station in a unsafe neighborhood late at night. As he is filling his tank, a young man approaches from out of the darkness and asks him for the time:

> I looked him in the eye and said, "What's up, buddy?" as though I expected an answer. There was silence. Then I said, "I ain't got no watch, man." Experience on the streets had taught me that one ruse muggers use is to ask an intended victim a question that distracts him, getting him to drop his guard and setting him up for the mugging. In a stickup or a mugging, timing is crucial. My body language, my tone of voice, and my words, all taken together in that instant, may have thrown him off, possibly averting an attempted stickup.

The younger man did not care about the time. But he wanted the other to think, wrongly, that they had a mutual object and to prepare to share his feeling about it. In other words, as this writer states, you drop your guard. Then the predator moves, fast and violently. But refusing the question, questioning the question, expressing no inclination to assume a mutual reference, withers tendrils of shared emotion and turns back the ruse. Now the young man is the one who is caught by surprise, who momentarily freezes, just as he expected the other to do.[11]

The emotional energy of any interaction, violent or not, varies with the degree that people become entrained in one another's emotions and bodily rhythms, captured by an object of mutual attention. Confrontational tension results when this entrainment turns antagonistic. The object that you thought was a common focus is gone, and the affect that you thought you shared turns out to be unrequited. All but very few of us dread such a scenario, which makes violence difficult, not easy. What Collins calls "the dirty little secret of violence" is that this dread usually "makes fighting incompetent when it happens, and produces much more gesture than real fight." Joy in the moment of combat "is almost nonexistent." Apprehension is the prevalent emotion, and we can understand why. As the evolutionary psychologist Steven Pinker observes, "If you attack one of your own kind, your adversary may be as strong and pugnacious as you are, and armed with the same weapons and defenses. The likelihood that, in attacking a member of your own species, you will get hurt is a powerful selection pressure that disfavors indiscriminate pouncing or lashing out."[12]

Another strategic consideration is that any move toward violence gives others the overriding goal of hurting you first. Initiating violence is therefore to be carefully considered. Of course, nobody does the calculation. We do not need to. Instead of conscious calculation, we have the more reliably inhibiting emotion of dread. The calculation merely confirms the adaptive potential of the affect for animals as intensely social as our evolutionary ancestors were. These ancestors were animals, but not bears or cats. They were primates, social mammals living in groups. The extraordinary demands of human neonatal neurological development are so urgent, so necessary for a recognizably human adult, that we *must* be born to get along. In this respect, we are for good and all what Nietzsche called "herd animals." The idea of the fight-or-flight response to danger applies only to cross-species encounters.

Among members of the same species, the options include posturing and submission. The first response of a baboon or rooster to aggression from its own kind is to go through a series of intimidating but harmless posturing. Should posturing prove ineffectual and a fight break out, it almost never results in death. Piranhas do not bite one another; they fight with their tails.

With few exceptions, people, even seasoned perpetrators, are tense and fearful when violence is imminent. Trepidation makes most violence incompetent. This does not mean violent people are not dangerous, just that their violence is not well controlled, and they are apprehensive, even frightened. Martial arts practitioners are told (or should be) that their skill level drops by at least half under conditions of real violence. Competent violence is rare, and even competent violence (underworld hit men, for instance) is never without fear, requiring sometimes elaborate rituals to control.

The ease with which a person falls into aggressive bluster (for example, machismo) should not be confused with the ease of violence. Interviews with muggers show that their chief concerns are selecting a weak victim and managing their own fear. To be successfully violent, one has to be good at upsetting a victim's rhythms, establishing situational dominance, and destroying the other's will. Such persons' violence works not because they control it so well but because of their skill in selecting and manipulating others to play the role of a victim.[13]

VIOLENCE ROUGHLY divides into status violence and predatory violence. A predator's calculated violence is not a contest or a fight. Human predators usually follow one of two strategies: either a sudden, brutal ambush or the use of charm to get close and then attack with overwhelming force. The goal may be something tangible, like your wallet, or, with a serial rapist or killer, the goal may be the attack itself. Predators assail from the greatest advantage they can muster. If a predator cannot surprise you, he will not attack, which makes self-defense against predatory violence hard to train for.

Violence for status is usually some variation on what a martial arts author calls the "Monkey Dance," his term for the male ritual combat to establish dominance. Men can find themselves uncontrollably falling into its ancient rhythms: "You do not play it. It plays you." The ritual has recognizable steps that may differ to some degree in different cultures. This author, Rory Miller, describes his local litany: eye contact, hard stare, verbal challenge, close the distance, finger poke or two-handed push to chest, dominant-hand roundhouse punch. That is the scenario in a lot of martial arts training, yet it pertains to only one form of violence, and not necessarily the most likely or dangerous one. It is important to be able to distinguish between predator and status violence, because what may be effective in one situation may be a dangerous mistake in another. For instance, whereas submissive body language may circumvent a status attack, the same behavior can be dangerous because retreating in the face of bluster is itself a trigger for attack. Submissive comportment also may make one look weak, which entices predators. What might allow you to back out of a bluster-ridden monkey dance could instead precipitate a predatory assault.[14]

People seem always to have been violent; we can find plenty of evidence for it in humanity's evolutionary ancestors. Cautious authorities agree on consumption cannibalism in both *Homo antecessor*, a proto-*sapiens* ancestor from about 780,000 years ago, and the Neanderthals, as well as in early members of our own species. Organized large-scale violence—in other words, warfare—has a documented history reaching back at least ten thousand years and probably much further. We should not assume that these earliest wars were less violent than war among civilized societies, although we do live on the other side of a quiet revolution in military technology. The technology about which we hear so much—nuclear and biological weapons, unmanned drones, cyberattacks, and so on—overshadow what one well-placed expert calls "a technological revolution on the battlefield, a revolution that represents total superiority in close combat." The details are interesting and not well known.[15]

More than a century of study of frontline combat confirms that most soldiers (some 85 percent) never fire their weapons. They do not run, hide, or panic; rather, they do other things: fetch ammunition, carry messages, tend to the fallen. They simply will not target and fire their weapon to kill the enemy. Military psychologist Dave Grossman thinks (as does sociologist Randall Collins) that this apparently robust fact confirms a dread of killing as an evolved default condition. Supposedly, some 2 percent of the male population, if pushed or given a legitimate reason, will kill without regret. But most people (and most men) dread the prospect of killing, and if they do kill, they suffer a long time for it. Grossman deems close-range violence the universal human phobia. It is uncommonly misleading common knowledge that what men fear in combat is death. Of course, they fear death, just as they fear disfigurement. The most dreadful experience, though, is killing others up close. The leading cause of psychiatric casualties on the battlefield is violent confrontation: "Looking another human being in the eye, making an independent decision to kill him, and watching as he dies due to your action combine to form the single most basic, important, primal and potentially traumatic occurrence of war."[16]

That may explain why posttraumatic stress disorder is rare and mild in response to natural disasters or automobile accidents. To bring it on takes interpersonal aggression, which we evidently process in a completely different way. The stress of combat debilitates more soldiers than does direct, hostile action. Psychiatric casualties outnumbered fatalities in World Wars I and II and the Korean War. Those who do not kill on the battlefield (the majority) seldom experience psychiatric casualty for the same reason that bombing cities is not a good strategy. In World War II, the Allies, who innovated this strategy, assumed that bombing cities would produce psychiatric casualties sufficient to compel their leaders to submit. Studies by the United States after the war showed that it does not work, that bombing cities makes the victims even more determined in their struggle and produces few psychiatric casualties. The strategy works only when combined with the credible threat of invasion and interpersonal violence: "The *potential* of close-up, inescapable, *inter*personal hatred and aggression is more effective and has greater impact on the morale of the soldier than the *presence* of inescapable, *im*personal death and destruction."[17]

The mechanically easiest way to kill a person is to thrust a thumb through the eye and as deeply into the brain as one can reach and then violently rip the thumb back out. Some martial arts schools teach this with pieces of ripe fruit in place of the eye. Grossman could not find a single documented use of this technique in the history of combat; most people find it unbearable even to contemplate. Only a little less horrible is the thought of driving a long, sharp steel blade deep into another's body and watching him die. The history of warfare is a history of increasingly more effective ways to overcome this repugnance to killing. Violence becomes much easier with distance, any kind of distance. The space of violence is non-Euclidian: Besides cultural distance, in racial and ethnic differences, there is moral distance, the conviction of the vigilante or avenger; social distance, an inculcated sense of superiority; and even the distance created by a mechanical buffer, like night-vision instruments or thermal imaging. Military technology for distance is as old as dehumanizing names for an enemy. But it has not made men more likely to kill up close, at handgun, bayonet, or thumb-in-eyeball range.[18]

This limitation, however, has finally succumbed to technology. Now, with the proper training, anyone can become a killer. After World War II, the U.S. Army, acting on what was known about low front-line firing rates, looked for a solution and found it in the theories of learning associated with Ivan Pavlov and B. F. Skinner, classical and operant conditioning, respectively. A psychologically more sophisticated training regime overcomes people's dread and makes killing an automatic response. Battlefield killing is now rehearsed, visualized, and conditioned, using realistic scenarios with immediate feedback and pleasant reinforcement. This scientifically engineered approach to defeating instinctually inhibited violence is what Grossman referred to as the "new, different ingredient in killing in modern combat" and "a technological revolution on the battlefield."[19]

These methods were abundantly confirmed in Vietnam, with the rate jumping to around 90 percent of combat soldiers firing their weapons. It is truly a technological revolution when software engineering so dramatically alters the rate at which soldiers fire, from 15 to 90 percent! Adding this advantage to all their others, one wonders why the war in Vietnam ended so ignominiously for the United States. The soldiers learned to fire their guns automatically, but they did not learn, or conveniently unlearned, how to aim them, and the high rate of fire achieved in Vietnam did not translate into a high kill rate. In fact, kill numbers have probably never been more asymmetrical: fifty thousand rounds fired for every one confirmed enemy kill. Firing those noisy guns was not just a trained reflex; it was a way of posturing, and posturing is a way of avoiding violence.[20]

REPRESENTATIONS OF VIOLENCE

Experience with killing and death used to be more common in the days when most people still lived in the countryside, raised livestock, and died without hospitals and mortuaries. Violence, too, is less conspicuous than it was in the past. Now it is channeled into prisons and other secluded institutions, into mean streets that most people do not visit, or into distant wars. Consequently, as if to compensate for people's lack of experience with violence, its depiction in cinema has never been more graphic. One theory is that the violence of popular cinema reaffirms the reality of violence that is otherwise carefully concealed in the orderly world of modern society. It seems equally possible, however, that the long-standing decline in real violence, which has been a worldwide historical trend for several centuries, encourages cinema to exploit the evident pleasure that people take in its representation. According to psychologist Stephen Pinker, this pleasure shows that people crave information about the conduct of violence: "In evolutionary history, violence was not so improbable that people could afford not to understand how it works." Grossman observes that human beings "are biologically primed to seek survival data, and violence is the ultimate survival data." What, he asks, is "the one event on the playground guaranteed to draw every child like a magnet? A fight. Children fight to see a fight because if there is violence in their environment, they must witness it so they can adapt to it as quickly as possible."[21]

For most of human history, any violence that one observed was real violence, a real fight, maybe real killing. But when mundane violence retreats and cinema steps in, the reality principle gives way to the pleasure principle, and artful representations replace personal experience. What we used to learn about violence we learned by experiencing it for ourselves, whether as witness, victim, agent, or accomplice. Now we learn what we think we know about violence from cinematic renditions unhinged from reality and tending toward the fantastic, often with no way for modern audiences to tell the difference.

Our ancestors also used to see a lot more spectacular, staged violence, the violence of bear baiting, a bullfight, or a criminal execution. Such violence is theatrical, mediated, but not unreal; these spectacles are horribly violent attacks with lethal intent and effect. But the fact that such violence occurs at all is highly contrived, and everyone knows it. By contrast, cinematic violence is not really violent at all (no one is really hurt), but it does not appear contrived, at least not to people with little experience of violence. Gladiatorial games offered Roman audiences real violence, a staged fight, and not a representation. No cunning mimesis gave the audience an illusion of violence; it was really happening before their eyes. By contrast, cinematic violence seems realistic, and because modern audiences typically have little experience of violence, nothing contradicts the representations that film invents. We accept them and think we know what violence looks like.

If you accept these representations, then you can believe that ordinary men can throw off the inhibitions of a lifetime and kill without guilt. According to Grossman, though, the psychologist of combat, "the men who have killed, and who will talk about it, tell a different tale." We may think that cinematic violence is too realistic. For sociologist Randall Collins, "Nothing could be further from the truth." The conventions for portraying violence almost always miss its important dynamics, which are to start from dread on all sides, to consist mostly of bluster, and for the fighting to be incompetent, to be more ugly than entertaining. Most fights are short and take place in the presence of others who are expected to stop them. Most aggressors are tense and fearful. The smiling villain is a myth, according to Collins, a narrative device to indicate the unreality of the depiction and facilitate the entertainment.[22]

The fighters in a kung fu movie look pretty, even though real fighters do not look like bodybuilders. Boxers do not look like bodybuilders, and real fights often take place in darkness or amid smoke, noise, confusion, and the smell of fear. Cinematic fights are paced for drama, though not because the rhythm of a fight is like that. A cinema fight ends when the director thinks the audience's excitement will have peaked. These carefully scripted fights also cater to the audience's idea of fairness. The fight is close all the way to the end, and the victory is narrow, which is unrealistic. "In a lethal fight," says a man who has had many, "one party has the advantage or gets it as soon as possible and presses it to the quick, brutal end. It's fast. There is very little drama."[23]

Although martial arts movies are notorious for their violence, anyone who has had much training knows that the fights in these movies usually are ridiculous. Probably the most ridiculous thing about them is their duration. If those martial artists were as proficient as they are represented to be, the fights would be finished in seconds, with ugly casualties. What these films typically depict, therefore, is not martial arts but a kind of performance art with a genealogical relationship to martial arts. This performance art is its own creature, organized by principles alien to those of the martial arts it supposedly imitates.[24]

VIOLENCE AND POWER

That violence can be a way to control people seems obvious. When it is successful, violence overrides the other's will, makes the violator the master and forces compliance, at least for the moment. Is violence only an instrument of control, or is power over others (political or otherwise) always violent or at least accompanied by the threat of violence? It is possible to harm people without using violence. Is it also possible to rule them, to attain authority and exercise political power, without violence?

Mao Zedong believed that political power came from the barrel of a gun. Political authority is an endless fight, the fight to seize it, to hold it, to enlarge it. Machiavelli and Hobbes might have agreed with this realpolitik, but in our time, Hannah Arendt reckoned the assumption to be deeply mistaken. In her view, the political power to decide and control collective action—call that legitimate authority or political power—arises from uncoerced consensus, not from the barrel of a gun. Uncoerced consensus requires agreement and cooperation. Political power is the *conatus* of a political community, its power to persist and act in coalition. That is polis power, Jean-Jacques Rousseau's general will. Such power is the opposite of violence and does not arise from violence. Authority, legitimate political power, is the peace that violence violates. Such power requires a concurring community, the concord of allies. Violence is the action of individuals or confederated individuals; it is seditious, coercive, and impossible without a mechanical advantage, because violence is violence against the power of a political community to persist. The majority, the general will, is, by definition, against you and will not comply without a credible threat, which requires a war machine. Recall Demosthenes: "Every deed one commits with violence [is] a public wrong . . . [and] wrongs the city."[25]

Violence against a community (for instance, by an oppressed minority) may be rational and justified. It can achieve its goal, and the goal may be just. It cannot, however, be legitimate, because legitimacy (authority) depends on how the community came into existence. Might does not make right for the same reason that yesterday is not tomorrow. Any right must refer to the past, the constitution, the law, tradition, or the like. Violence cannot do that, as it is too warlike. An episode of violence is a momentary war when civil relations are suspended if not entirely swept away. It may achieve its goal, but political goals attained through violence tend to be short-run components in a wider strategy. Long-term goals are too exposed to unpredictable circumstances to be reliably promoted with violence. Violence can destroy authority, but it is incapable of renewing political relations.

For Arendt, as for the Greeks, violence is anarchic, interrupting and subverting the polis. This view of power and violence is attractive to friends of democracy, but it diminishes the coercion of modern states, democratic or otherwise. The Western experience of democracy is Arendt's implicit context. Although modern Western history includes the rise of its democracies, this is also the history of the growth of state power and national sovereignty, which have introduced novelties into the exercise of power that the Athenians, and even modern democracy's founding fathers, did not anticipate. The tendency in Western thought since the Middle Ages is to conceptualize political power on a juridical model: to have power is to lay down the law, to command obedience by majesty, authority, and ultimately by what Max Weber called a "monopoly on violence." For all our differences from medieval Europe, we still tend to think in these archaic terms when we think about authority, legitimacy, and political power. Hence Michel Foucault's mordant comment that "in political thought and analysis we still have not cut off the head of the king."[26]

Foucault thinks we need an alternative to the model of sovereignty for thinking about the power that makes acts and relationships political. "I don't believe there can be a society without relations of power," he maintained, explaining that he meant all the ways "by which individuals try to conduct, to determine the behavior of others." He does not entirely disagree with Arendt. To speak of power is to speak of an authority that necessarily arises with political society. Yet this power is not a will, not even a collective will, and is not limited to the instruments of will against will, such as the law and the force of arms. The power that makes acts and relationships political is the whole open-ended ensemble of means by which people try to govern or reliably conduct others' choices. Violence can have that effect and is certainly an instrument of power. But so, too, is knowledge, like biomedical science, statistics, or psychiatry. We need an understanding of power that can recognize it in a monopoly on knowledge no less than in a monopoly on violence.[27] As Foucault explained, "In effect, what defines a relationship of power is that it is a mode of action that does not act directly or immediately upon others [as violence does]. Instead, it acts upon their actions: an action upon an action, on existing actions or on those which may arise in the present or the future." Viewed in this way, he continued, power is less matter of violence, "a confrontation between two adversaries," and more a matter "of *government.*" That is not simply another word for "state" but names something we now take for granted that states do a lot of: governing, meaning "to act upon the possibilities of action of other people. To govern, in this sense, is to structure the possible field of actions of others." States do that, as do parents, lovers, colleagues, everyone. It is the *conatus* of social existence, its power to persist. A state is a monopoly on government before it is a monopoly on violence. The power that makes actions and relationships political—the power of government or the power to govern others—is the power to modify how people symbolize and interpret their options, the liberties they anticipate, repudiate, exercise, or are denied.[28]

Modern governmental agencies exercise their legitimate power not solely by contract but also through the dignity of knowledge and the norm of rationality. The government of modern conduct is different from what it was before the age of scientific and democratic revolution. It is organized at sites neither strictly juridical nor economic (hospitals, schools, bureaucracies) and works by means more subtle than commands backed up by threat and ideological mystification. We have made a place in our politics for the productive work of advertising and media, for the therapist and psychiatrist, the statistician, the pharmacologist, and the molecular biologist. Knowledge (of norms, averages, chances) and the technology that both produces and applies this knowledge reveal their capacity for the political effects of government.

Violence is effective for government because it is feared, and knowledge is effective because it is rational. As the positivist philosopher Auguste Comte put it, "Knowledge . . . enforces resignation. . . . No one is so foolish as knowingly to place himself in opposition to the nature of things." Foucault's argument is that the appeal to rationality can be no less coercive than violence. Modern management has discovered how to coerce and govern without the threat of violence. It is one thing to destroy another's will, which is what violence does (and what its threat threatens). It is something else to arrange a situation so that another has to choose and can be expected to rationally select what accommodates a different and contrary interest. That is manipulation, coercion, power without violence.[29]

Foucault is known for his concept of the political anatomy of the body. The body can be analyzed for efficiency and, with careful training, be made into a reliable machine—reliable both mechanically and politically. A well-disciplined body, like a Prussian infantryman or one of Henry Ford's factory workers, is at once more effective (for the defined task) and more "docile," that is, incapable of using that effectiveness for subjectively preferred ends or, what is more, incapable of subjectively preferring ends contrary to the regime that trained him. It may not occur to him to want what his masters do not want him to want.[30]

While Asian martial arts training is a protracted discipline of the body, it is not a discipline in Foucault's sense, so we cannot compare a trained martial arts body with the docile body of an infantryman or

WHAT A BODY CAN DO

a factory worker. Asian medical tradition eschews anatomical analysis. Chinese bodies do not have well-defined organs or compartmentalized pathogens. A Chinese body is a flux. The acupuncture man has no muscles. Organs are not anatomically conceived as machines with functions; instead, they are the lakes and streams of *qi* in an interior landscape. *Fu* (stomach, intestines, bladder) are hollow depots; solid viscera are *zang*, caches of refined *qi* that do not allow it to escape. The corporeal analytics of Asian martial arts concentrate on the *qi* flowing within such circuits. When clinical methods of quantitative biomechanical analysis are employed, however, the martial arts prove recalcitrant to assessment.[31]

The point of martial arts training is not to conform the body to a task but to make it responsive, eloquent, and as hard to hold as a stream of water. The summit of this training is not a mechanically flawless technique but the development of improvisatorially effective ways of moving. If you prevail against incoming violence, it is unlikely to be due to the precision of your technique. Instead, it will be the contextual, tactical effectiveness of how you move, ways of moving that you learn by practicing techniques but that are not limited to technical movements. Training is more like planting seeds and tending sprouts than like encoding a stereotyped routine to replay with more or less fidelity. One practices techniques to get beyond techniques, to respond to incoming violence in the way that a jazz musician responds to a musical opening, intending, however, to maximize disharmony rather than harmony. The hallmark of Chinese martial art techniques (*jue*) is that once they are released, they are maximally out of proportion and out of synchronization with the opponent, more like mad jazz than mechanical playback.[32]

Asian martial arts are not arts of power; they are not designed to govern others or bend them to one's will. What one practices is not how to exercise violent power over others but how to resist such violence when others offer it. When another offers violence we cannot not respond, because no response is still a response. How, then, should we respond? That is an ethical question that requires an ethical answer. The ethos of these arts is not violence but a disempowering response to it. These are arts of answering violence, teaching competence and the confidence in it instead of docility. Accordingly, these arts are profoundly subjective, being ethical arts for a subject who is and wants to remain autonomous. They are arts of liberty, nomadic arts dedicated to preserving subjective choice from the onslaught of a domineering will.

WAR AND VIOLENCE

Even if power cannot be maintained by violence, it can use violence as a tactic as long as the target (a minority, say, or a neighbor) is carefully selected and credibly demonized. We know that people can be enthusiastic about war, making politically easy the decision to attack others. The word "war" comes from the Old German *werran* (to bring into confusion). This legacy is appropriate because besides chaos being the soul of war, the very topic of war is confusing even to think about.

For example, some jurists reserve the word "war" (*bellum*) for acts by states and sovereigns, whereas others understand war as a conflict that may arise between individuals as often as between sovereign states. On the first account, hostility among individuals is never war; it is assault, homicide, piracy, or other such crimes. This was Roman law as explained by Cicero and codified by Justinian. War must be formally declared, and only sovereigns have the legal means to do that. We saw something comparable in the Confucian tradition: a reluctance to describe as *wu* (martial, military) anything that is not ordained by Heaven and subordinated to *wen* civility. The rest is just criminal violence. The thesis that only sovereigns can make war was prestigiously transmitted to European law by the thirteenth-century pope Innocent IV: "War, properly speaking, can only be declared by a prince who does not have a superior." The other view regards war and personal violence as continuous, one quality differing only in intensity, for example in this comment by the sixteenth-century jurist Hugo Grotius: "War is the state of those contending by force, viewed simply as such." "Where juridical means fail, war begins." This also is Clausewitz's strategic realism: "War is nothing but a duel on a larger scale. . . . A picture of it as a whole can be formed by imaging a pair of wrestlers."[33]

Is law the lord of war, so that without law, war is impossible? That would imply some legality for war, that a war can be lawful, perhaps even just. According to Saint Ambrose, "Justice is binding even in war."

This thought inaugurates the long tradition of so-called just-war theory. According to the canonical explanation by Saint Thomas Aquinas, a just war is one fought to defend a presumptively innocent party against an impending or ongoing attack, with the aim of establishing a lasting peace. He specified the criteria for such a war: right authority, right intention, just cause. The idea is distinctly medieval and Christian, not Greek. Thucydides had the Athenians say to their intended victims, "Calculations of interest have made you take up the cry of justice [against our pending attack]—a consideration which no one ever yet brought forward to hinder his ambition when he had a chance of gaining anything by might. . . . Right, as the world goes, is only in question between equals in power, while the strong do what they can and the weak suffer what they must."[34]

If we side with the realists, war is the violence that erupts when the law is preempted and civilization is unavailing. Where there is war, there is no law, and where there is law, there is no war. War's enmity is neither legal nor illegal; instead, the theory eliminates differences of legality or justice under the conditions of war. Both sides are just, or at least neither is unjust. According to the legal concept of "military necessity," all parties to war are justified in using whatever violence they believe will advance their victory. A jurist of this persuasion explained that "in general, it may be true in nearly every kind of dispute that neither of the two disputants is unjust." "War," another added, "should be considered just on either side. . . . No nation can assume for itself the functions of a judge, and consequently cannot pronounce upon the justice of the war." Some even find the idea of "just war" absurd; for instance, Hobbes: "There be in war no law the breech whereof is injury"; and Samuel von Puffendorf: "It is permissible to use whatever means I think will best prevail against such a person, who, by the injury done me, has made it impossible for me to do him an injury." The thinking again climaxes with Clausewitz: "If one side uses force without compunction, undeterred by the bloodshed it involves, while the other side refrains, the first will gain the upper hand. . . . To introduce the principle of moderation into the theory of war itself would always lead to logical absurdity."[35]

Is "war" merely another name for violence, or is it a special kind of violence? Is war sanctioned by law and amenable to its norms, or is it a condition in which norms are cast aside? There is authority for deciding either way. A complementary confusion surrounds the law of self-defense. Everybody (well, nearly) agrees that there is lawful self-defense. The twelfth-century Gratian maintained that both lay people and clerics are permitted to hit back, making the distinctions we have come to expect, for instance, between the defense of a person and the defense of property. The defense should be moderate, although if moderation is exceeded but not on purpose, there is no liability. Western law is especially sensitive to the difference between self-defense and revenge, which is never lawful. There must be a reasonable presumption that the attacker intends to continue attacking, and the defense must be performed "on the spot" (*incontinenti*). The least delay makes "self-defense" into a revenge attack, which Western law refuses to sanction. (The Chinese, we remember, ruled differently, recognizing a duty to enact revenge [*da fuchou*].)

Gratian allowed preemptive defense: "Force may be resisted before it strikes." Perhaps the most spirited statement on lawful self-defense, which also confirms the legality of preemptive attack, is by Alberico Gentili, a jurist in the sixteenth century: "We ought not to wait for violence to be offered us, if it is safer to meet it half way. . . . Those who desire to live without danger ought to meet impending evils and anticipate them. One ought not to delay. . . . No one ought to wait to be struck, unless he is a fool." Agreement is not uniform, however, and occasional fanaticism is predictable: For Saint Augustine, "The law is not just which allows a traveler to kill a robber in order to avoid being killed by him. Nor is the law just which allows any man or woman, if able, to slay a violent rapist before the rape is committed."[36]

Saint Thomas Aquinas's theory of double effect cast new light on the whole question of self-defense. Acts have many effects, not all of which are intended, while the morality of an act depends on the intention. An act of self-defense may have a double effect: saving one's life and killing the attacker, making one and the same act an allowable self-defense and an unintentional killing. Daniel Webster, writing as the U.S. secretary of state, offered an influential modern interpretation of the expectations appropriate to lawful self-defense. The conditions he required are necessity, proportionality, and discrimination. You *had* to do it, had to do it *with that intensity*, and had to do it to precisely *that individual*. In addition, as is seldom mentioned in the older sources, one is expected to show that admonition or remonstrance "was impracticable or would have been unavailing."[37]

Some authorities see self-defense as a product of law, something for law to create, like a binding contract. Others see self-defense as a response to the violent preemption of law. It is not a ritual declaration or legal form but the violent purpose to destroy another's will that instigates a state of war. Destroy the commanding will—that is the mission of every violent assault, on the battlefield no less than at home. If it comes down to self-defense, law and civilization have left you in the lurch. What do you do when law is unavailing? Philosophically, you are at war. The wars of states and princes merely enlarge and orchestrate this private war that breaks out whenever individuals fall into violence. Authorities speak for this interpretation too:

> There is one sort of war which can be declared by any private person, so that in defense or recovery of his property on the spot he can gather people and justly fight against the other.

> Any person, even a private citizen, may declare and wage defensive war. . . . any person may wage war without another person's authority, not only for self-defense but also for the defense of their property and goods.

> If an attack by violence is made on one's body, endangering life, and no other way of escape is open, then war is permissible, even though it involve the slaying of the assailant.[38]

Is war a state created by law, or does it arise when there is no law? Is self-defense a lawful action or an exigent action in lieu of law? Can war be just, or does it suspend justice? One side assumes that violence is something law regulates. Law rules, even in war. The other side frankly acknowledges that law cannot consistently regulate violence; there are gaps; war is violence outside the law. Any real use of martial arts training would be warlike, extralegal, what criminologists call self-help. A good citizen would not train in the martial arts. A good citizen would say that violence is detestable and that law alone should rule. Civilian training in the martial arts seems implicitly to side with the view that law does not rule so magisterially that a person is wrong to worry about war in the gaps.

The Asian martial arts do not belong to the state or the state's law. Historically they rose on the margins of legality, and for most of their history they have been practiced in the gaps where law does not reach. That is what Deleuze and Guattari meant when they described the martial arts as a war machine. A war machine is an assemblage—an army, its weapons, or an individual warrior are all "war machines." Such machines work to make their space smooth, meaning to breech and destroy the unnaturally sharp lines that law and the state draw and enforce. A war machine moves with a nomad's indifference to the lines that legality struggles to define and maintain. Such a machine arises on the outside, among nomads, functionally defined as any agency operating where state power is uncertain. The Asian martial arts and the bodies trained under their tutelage are such machines, or at least they used to be. In China this war machine was domesticated and co-opted by the empire, though never completely. Today the Asian martial arts have been co-opted by capitalism, though also not completely. To be resourceful in lieu of law, and tranquil even where law does not rule, is the martial arts way of being able to take care of yourself.[39]

TERRIBLE BEAUTY

Violence has been thought to have an aesthetic quality and enigmatic appeal. An example is the sheer spectacle of war, "the fascination that manifestations of power and magnitude hold," a "weird but genuine beauty in the sight of massed men and weapons in combat." One soldier reminisces about this military sublime, recounting a battle in Afghanistan in 2002:

> For almost 18 long, blood-soaked hours, it was often hand-to-hand fighting with knives, pistols, and rifle butts. That terrible night, the Rangers were supported by USAF C-130 Specter gunships that, according

to an Aussie SAS commando on a nearby knob, lit up the hills around them. "It was bloody amazing, the most beautiful—yet fearsome—sight I'd ever seen," he said.

That unsentimental sentiment may be related to another dark attraction, the sensuous delight in destruction:

> When soldiers step over the line that separates self defense from fighting for its own sake, as it is so easy for them to do, they experience something that stirs deep chords in their being. The soldier-killer is learning to serve a different deity, and his concern is with death and not life, destruction and not construction.[40]

These terrible moments of sublime violence have persuaded some people that a world without violence would be diminished. Is violence something we could overcome, as we have overcome human sacrifice and (almost) slavery? Would the elimination of violence be no less an advance of civilization? Ethnographers and anthropologists, scientific observers of human diversity, regard such a future as unlikely. Violence may decline, but it probably would never become a thing of the past. "Ethnography and history give ample evidence that violence in its endless manifestations is part and parcel of human experience," says one. This thought is usually received as sad but true, despite the opposite view, that violence adds to life, serves and enhances it. A future without violence would be regression, not progress. For instance, according to Simone de Beauvoir, "Violence is the authentic proof of each one's loyalty to himself, to his passions, to his own will." A world without violence would be a world without authenticity.[41]

Violence is evil to those who see in it nothing but suffering and see suffering as something that is wrong with the world and should be alleviated wherever possible. Nietzsche identified this attitude with Christian sacred pity and Plato's rationalism. Many religious traditions link violence and suffering to sacrifice and exaltation. Some people even argue that rationality and consciousness require violence to jolt them into operation. Violence breaks the ego out of isolation, convinces the ego that it is not the whole world. We discover our vulnerability in another's violence, a power external, not me but like me, that overrides my will. "Violence educates me to the inescapable reality of others," asserts a philosopher of this persuasion. "I finally begin to view myself as being only one particular self among other selves." I admit to doubt about this argument, which seems to presuppose a kind of original solitude for ego or self. The natal disposition for shared attention that I mentioned earlier looks like spontaneous sociality. It may be true, though, that if not for violence, we would never discover the value of peace. "For I can find common ground with that other only insofar as both of us can endure the mortal danger of the struggle and can thus think independently of a blind attachment to our particular selves."[42]

Some people think that violence is necessary to transcend the ordinary and realize higher values worthy of suffering. Instead of overcoming violence, we should overcome our revulsion to it. Violence is not a reversion to prehuman brutality. It is among the most human things we do and not without what Yeats called "a terrible beauty." Another writer offers this description of the sublimity of violence:

> The advent of violence, more specifically its sight, somehow shatters reality, splitting it open and providing access to a different dimension of being. Moreover, there is a sense that this opening, for all the horror and fear it causes, has the potential to transform those willing to expose themselves to it.

Such thinking may be a rationalization for survivors but is unlikely to edify a victim. Perhaps only in myth is violence sublime, as the history of victims suggests otherwise.[43]

Usually nothing remotely beautiful comes from violence. René Girard devoted a lifetime to studying the supposed redeeming value of violence. He argued that the Bible saved Western civilization from sacred violence. Jesus was not a sacrificial atonement. The Gospels present him as innocent of crime and wrongly killed, and what happened to Job also is explicitly unmerited. For Girard, the whole Bible is a progressive unmasking of sacrificial violence and a repudiation of its mystical effectiveness. Those transcendent values, the terrible beauties of violence, depend on what Girard called the "*false* transcendence of a

WHAT A BODY CAN DO

victim, who is made sacred because of the unanimous verdict of guilt."
This false transcendence—inventing it, believing in it, consenting to its
violence—legitimates the scapegoat ritual and conceals the innocence
of the victim. By relentlessly questioning this idolatrous presumption,
Judeo-Christianity has slowly made the scapegoat an unreliable ritual.
Isn't that moral progress?[44]

Although transcendence sounds wonderful, it is just another way of
saying "deviant," wandering outside the norms. The motive of transcendence is a serious, if not mainstream, sociological explanation of crime.
The mainstream theory is economic materialism, according to which
the motive for underclass criminality is destitution. Why are violent
criminals disproportionately from the underclass? Because the violent
criminal is just as rational as anybody else and wants the same things
we all do but is constrained by poverty, racism, and so on and is obliged
to pursue deviant means to reasonable goals. Criminologist Jack Katz
dismissed this theory as bourgeois sentimentality: "If we look at per-
sistent criminals, we see a life of action in which materialism is by no
means the god. Instead, material goods are treated more like offerings
to be burnt, quickly, lest retention become sacrilege." Common criminal aims "are specifically unconventional: to go beyond the established
moral definitions of the situation as it visibly obtains"—that is, beyond
the conditions into which criminals are existentially thrown. Katz thinks
we should not forget that morally unattractive as crime may be, "there
is a genuine experiential creativity in it as well," which accounts for its
"authentic attractions," of which the most compelling is that of "overcoming a personal challenge to moral—not to material—existence."[45]

Imagine that you are caught in a situation inexorably humiliating,
which is a common pattern in homicide: the violence erupts in situations that endanger what people momentarily regard as sacred, for
example, marital fidelity, filial respect, or property. A typical homicide
is unpremeditated, a quick rage indifferent to legal consequences, self-
righteous, undertaken in defense of a sacred value. The killer feels compelled to respond to a fundamental challenge to worth, which may be
intensified by the presence of an audience. The most common precipi-
tating incidents of nonpredatory homicide are "trivial" ones like jos-
tling, cursing, or insulting; annoying behavior; comments interpreted

as attacks on integrity; a failure to discharge obligations or comply with commands; ignoring another, boasting, or causing another's loss. The aggressor is likely not to be the deviant but the one who attempts to restore normality. In most aggressive encounters, the provocation for the first attack is an alleged (even theatrically contrived) violation of a rule.[46]

I won't take it! You can't do that! Over my dead body! These words, spoken in anger, are precursors to homicide. They also express a willing transcendence, the refusal to be reasonable, that is, prudent, practical, calculating, materialistic. The Greeks were right. Hubris, not economic rationality, fuels felonious violence. Katz regards criminal deviance as "not merely a reaction against something negative in a person's background, but a reaching for exquisite possibilities," even to the point of self-destruction. Consider, for example, the robberies committed by hard stickup men, so-called professionals in armed robbery, ready to back their intentions with remorseless violence. These men are not the rational pros that sentimental sociology makes them out to be: "In virtually all robberies, the offender discovers, fantasizes, or manufactures an angle of moral superiority over the intended victim. The stickup man knows that dominance requires a more sophisticated competence than the application of brute force alone." When such men kill, it is seldom either panic or a rational concern for leaving witnesses. Instead, it is "a commitment to the transcendence of a hard will."[47]

A different connection between violence and transcendence appears in the warrior culture of the Cheyenne, a Native American people of the Great Plains whose techniques of spiritual violence made them dreaded warriors. Their preparation for battle began with the warriors counting themselves among the dead, saying farewell to their relatives, dressing for their funeral, and singing their death songs. They ritually consigned themselves to death and apparently were surprised if they happened to survive. This practice has a subtle psychology: It is dreadful to confront someone prepared to kill you, but it is worse when you can see the other's complete absence of fear, and that is what you get when warriors are spiritually oblivious to death. Having already accepted death, their expressive indifference to violence becomes a weapon in its own right, causing psychological terror.

First in the Cheyenne order of battle come the "suicide boys," usually unarmed. They are seeking death because they have experienced
some loss of face or are grieving over a lost relative. These young men
throw themselves on their foes in an effort to tear them apart with their
bare hands. In the eyes of the enemy, forced to kill these unarmed boys,
the indifference to their death both by the boys and the men who send
them over is terrifying evidence of the opposition's fiendish intensity.
Next come the "dog rope men," who fix themselves to the ground with
a cord tied to a stake, from which position they sing their death songs,
taunt the enemy, and fight to their death with lances, clubs, and bow
and arrow. These dire preliminaries eventually break into a cavalry assault concentrated on a single point in the enemy line and the remorseless pursuit of those who attempt to escape. The sublime violence and
ritual self-destruction of these tactics made the Cheyenne the dominant
military power of the western plains.[48]

Terrible beauty, indeed. What seems right in the idea of violent
beauty is that the only way to create something worth dying for is to
die violently for it. To die *for* something is necessarily to die a violent
death. If some things are worth dying for, it is because others have died
violently for them, and if there is no violence, then nothing is worth
dying for. But violence, the real thing, is never beautiful except in the
selective memory of those who benefit from it. "A military victory is not
a thing of beauty," said the *Daodejing*. "To beautify victory is to delight
in the slaughter of human beings. One who delights in the slaughter of
human beings will not realize his ambitions in the world."[49]

ETHICS AND ARTS OF VIOLENCE

The Asian martial arts may seem seeped in violence, an apprentice-
ship for violence, teaching a violent response to violence. Although this
impression is not completely wrong, it is seriously incomplete. Martial
arts techniques are designed for compulsory compliance, destroying an
opponent's will to fight. The kinetics of violence—how it works, what
makes one response strong and another weak—sets the technical problems of these arts. While training, we constantly think about how to
intensify our violence—what would make the strike harder, the kick

quicker? Nevertheless, violence is not an internal good of these martial arts and, as an end or purpose, is completely external to their practice. We constantly refer to violence but refuse to give it a place in our training. This internal externalization of violence is the chief difference between the practice of martial arts and boxing. Violence in boxing is not external but is subjected to rules and made an internal good of the sport. If you are a boxer or a fan, the quality of unrelenting precision violence is highly valuable, an internal good of boxing.

Boxing and other combat sports are both more and less violent than the martial arts. They are more violent because their purpose is real violence. The competition demands it. The contestants have to want to win, and in combat sports like boxing, that means intending to destroy another's will by means of violence. Yet in a way, these sports are less violent because the rules confine the violence, whereas the martial arts are based on the assumption that when these techniques seriously come into action, the rules will have disappeared. One fights with total commitment, respecting nothing except the outcome, which should be as disproportional as possible. Certain relatively simple martial arts techniques are predictably lethal, assuming, of course, that you are not surprised, do not freeze, and can make the technique work on a fast-moving person who means to hurt you. That is a lot of assumptions.

From a martial arts perspective, the problem of violence is what to do when it becomes imminent. It does not matter who the threat is or how he got to be that way. Before there is a victim—in the interval when victimization is still virtual and indeterminate—what resources might an unarmed person prepare? The only thing that really prepares one for violence, however, is experience with violence, and there is no violence in martial arts practice. It is an open question just how prepared even well-trained martial artists are for the violence they might encounter in prison. Martial arts training uses imaginary violence, violent intentionality without a violent purpose. In self-defense, you need that purpose. You have to turn it on, quickly, or become a victim. Yet precisely that—turning on the violent purpose—is seldom taught in the martial arts. How could it be? How can you practice a violent purpose without acting violently? Who would want to train with you? Boxers, of course, are routinely violent with each other, but in a context of rules and usually with protective gear. If you want to practice a violent purpose, to practice attacking another person as hard and fast as you can, boxing would be more appropriate than traditional training in the Asian martial arts.

Scientists of the street concur that a potential perpetrator's first consideration is selecting the right victim. Predators appreciate the element of surprise, which, as one of these sociologists observed, makes the potential assailant "not always identifiable as such; at most times and in most circumstances, he is part of the cultural woodwork, revealing himself only at the opportune moment." Interviews with violent felons reveal how they target victims by their body language: slumped walk, passive behavior, lack of awareness. When cues indicate that a potential victim might fight back, they prefer to walk away.[50]

For people seriously concerned about street self-defense, Marc "Animal" MacYoung, an erstwhile gangbanger and highly regarded self-defense professional, recommends developing what he calls a trigger, meaning a conditioned response to known danger signals, the body language antecedent to assault. The samurai Munenori called this trigger the "first sword of combat." MacYoung says that developing a trigger "means any time someone tries to offer you physical violence, you immediately land on him with whatever level of violence is appropriate to end it." He says that "once you enter this level of thinking, ninety percent of all the trouble that was out there before will choose to pass you by." There is, he says, "something about people who have triggers that makes the average trouble hunters instinctively look elsewhere for their fun and games. Knowing how to spot this is a matter of life and death to them . . . your preparedness will be sensed by the other player." Grossman regards this effect as "the great paradox of combat: If you are truly prepared to kill someone, you are less likely to have to do it. That person will look into your eyes and see the steely determination to kill him, and be less eager to attack and more likely to surrender."[51]

People inexperienced with violence may look at a man's girth or muscle definition in assessing a threat. Experienced people look at how someone moves. A suitable presence can preempt whatever tendency there may be in an environment to violence, but it is a presence that comes as a by-product of training and is not easily imitated. Dedicated martial arts training tends to minimize the likelihood of an occasion when one would have to use the competence that one has learned. One learns to avoid violence by not acting like a victim. Scientists of the mean streets agree:

> If your habits of presence—how you walk, how you scan, what you do with positioning and your hands—are good, the bad guy quietly moves on, never even coming to your attention. . . . Everything happen[s] in the threat's own head. He sees a witness or a poor target choice and he moves on.[52]

That is an effectiveness the Chinese art of war admires. The pinnacle of strategy is to evade a fight. The value of a non-augmenting neutralization of another's violence is something that people who study martial arts should consider. We think about how we can outassail an assailant and less about how to respond to his lawyer in court. Two longtime martial arts teachers who also work around violence as law-enforcement and security officers call this omission "one of the biggest disconnects of martial arts training." The more you train, the more you should think about exactly what you are training to do. At an advanced level, the violence of martial arts techniques is extraordinary. In training, since we never actually apply these techniques with a violent purpose, we can easily overlook what it would be like to use them on another person with full force and commitment. We need to think about that, however, because after self-defense from assault comes self-defense from *lawyers*.[53]

In the eyes of the law (in North America and, I think, European countries, Australia, and so on), any blow "delivered powerfully and deliberately to a vital part of the body" may be construed as deadly force "so long as it can be shown that it was struck with the intention, or predictable likelihood, of killing." Deadly force is thus a technical concept with a legal definition. To justify that level of force requires a fairly sophisticated assessment on your part. When this topic arises among martial arts practitioners, one often hears the inane rejoinder: "Better to be judged by twelve than carried by six!" It is not that simple. And if you think carefully about exactly what "being tried by twelve" for aggravated assault or homicide actually entails, you may ardently wish to avoid the choice altogether.[54]

A plea of self-defense is called an "affirmative defense" at law, meaning that you admit to a crime (assault, homicide) but assert necessity. The prosecutor therefore does not have to establish that a crime was committed because you already have admitted as much. Instead you, the defendant, must prove preclusion: there was no reasonable alternative. It is not enough to say, "I felt my life was in danger, and acted in self-defense." The lawyers will want to know precisely why you felt that danger. What exactly was said, or seen, or done? Why were you unable to leave? Why did the danger you felt require deadly force and not something more moderate? If the lawyers know that you have had martial arts training, they may wonder whether you did not have the use of a lower and (as they are trying to prove) more appropriate level of force. And if the lawyers decide that you exceeded their idea of reasonable force, you, and not your assailant, will "be tried by twelve."[55]

So while it is fine to perfect techniques and learn self-defense, it also is good never, ever actually to use these arts against another person. The best way to ensure that outcome is with the body language that is a by-product of martial arts training. The way to become an unappealing victim is by diligently practicing a martial art that you will never use.

"ETHICS" AND "MORALS" are two words that derive from the same one Greek word *ethos*, meaning people's habitual, characteristic, usual, normatively normal ways. *Ethos*, from which our "ethics" comes, is, in Latin, *mores*, from which we get "morals." Although they should be interchangeable, a real difference in practice is nicely designated by these terms. Morality concerns how a person's action stands in the light of group norms. Morality is the common norm we accept (or not) as the price of being part of a group and enjoying its protection. There is no reliable connection between being moral in this sense and happiness or a good life. To be moral is to be inoffensive, ensuring toleration by others and mutual protection. We still have the problem of what Greeks called *arete*, excellence, living the best life a person can. Morality is about getting along with others, and ethics is about flourishing, excellence, happiness. For Greeks, ethical philosophy concerned the principles, maxims, and understanding necessary to make life consistently tranquil, which was the philosophers' idea of happiness.

A moral question that violence raises is whether there could ever be a duty of violence, that is, circumstances in which morality required violence. Provided that certain conditions are met, self-defense can be a moral as well as a legal use of violence, I can morally justify violently destroying another's will when that will is going to destroy my own *right now*. Pacifism, principled nonviolence, is supererogatory, saintly but not a duty. Is one ever *required* to be violent, though? For instance, is there a duty to violence in self-defense or the defense of dependents? Probably not, since violence is a means to something else, and nonviolent alternatives make unlikely a categorical *duty* to be violent. Violence might be required to perform a duty (protecting a child, say), but no one would be criticized for finding a nonviolent way to do what has to be done. Yet even self-defense has its moral critics. I mentioned Saint Augustine, "the law [is not] just which allows any man or woman, if able, to slay a violent rapist before the rape is committed." Such saintly fanaticism is all too rational. Injustice is illusory. Real injustice is impossible because God exists and God is good. So do not soil yourself to save a victim. It makes you as criminally God-hating as the criminal.[56]

A different question concerns the *ethos* or ethics of violence, living ethically in a world that includes violence. Can ethical habits neutralize the potential of violence to trouble our life? It seems implicit in the practice of martial arts that violence is not an aberration, not a mark against nature or human nature. That is not to say that violence is good, just that it is a fact of life. Instead of judging its right to exist, martial arts remove its existence as a problem. The relation of these arts to violence is ethical rather than moral. They neither glorify violence nor denounce it; instead, they assist the individual to respond and adapt to it without abject submission.

I mentioned Spinoza as a precursor of the corporeal turn in philosophy. In the *Ethics* he wrote, "One who has a body capable of a great many things has a mind whose greater part is eternal." Usually body and mind are conceived in quasi-moral terms: one of them is agent, the other passively receptive; one dominates, the other submits.

Either the mind dominates the body, the moral ideal, or the body dominates the mind, the disorder Plato despised in the democratic mob. Spinoza overturns this moral model. The only way to act on the body is to act on the mind, and vice versa. To measure the mind, measure what the body can do. The joy of the body is the happiness of the mind. The soul of the soul is the body.[57]

Spinoza chided those who are "persuaded that the body now moves, now is at rest, solely from the mind's command, and that it does a great many things which depend only on the mind's will and its art of thinking." This belief, the nucleus of metaphysical idealism ever since Plato, assumes that making the body intelligent and intentional requires something completely different from the body. The objection to such thinking is that we do not know in advance or once and for all what a body can do: "We do not know *what the body can do*, or what can be deduced from the consideration of its nature alone." Idealists say that a mere body cannot have purpose or thought. These powers come to the body from elsewhere, a higher nature subject to higher principles than the body. No, Spinoza insisted. Nobody knows that. No one has determined what all a body can do: "Experience has not yet taught anyone what the body can do from the laws of [body] alone. . . . The body itself, simply from the laws of its own nature, can do many things which its mind wonders at."[58]

We learn more every year about what bodies can do, the powers that lie in the depths of matter, which grows more complex rather than simpler the closer we look. "What a body can do" means its capacity to be affected. Such affections are either active affections or actions, or passive affections or passions, including feelings, emotions, and moods. Ethical life is a selective proportion between these two psychosomatic conditions, maximizing a capacity for action and minimizing the helpless, passive affection from which we suffer. The problem of ethical life arises because people tend to acquire bad habits induced by irrational superstition. From superstitious notions and the fear and hatred they engender, we develop the bad habit of inhibiting our own capacity for activity, cutting ourselves off from what we can do. Such inhibition cannot fail to be painful. That pain is the felt, somatic core of all the sad, negative emotions that depress people.

To be active, to conduct one's life lucidly, encountering ever fewer obstacles and eventually consistent joy—that for Spinoza was ethical excellence, human flourishing, the good life. "That individual will be called *good* (or free, or rational, or strong)," says Deleuze, commenting on Spinoza,

> who strives, insofar as he is capable, to organize his encounters, to join with whatever agrees with his nature, to combine his relations with relations that are comparable with his, and thereby to increase his power. . . . That individual will be called *bad,* or servile, or weak, or foolish, who lives haphazardly, who is content to undergo the effects of his encounters, but wails and accuses every time the effect undergone does not agree with him and reveals his own impotence.[59]

Suggesting that people do everything they can do may sound alarming. One imagines moral disasters, like evil people growing even more uninhibited and violent and everybody selfishly doing all they can get away with. The answer to this misgiving is that "what one can do"—meaning the range of action in which one is truly active and not a pathetic victim of forces one merely feels but does not control—is conditioned by what one understands, what one knows, the lucidity of one's choices. A moral monster like Adolf Hitler was passively dominated by irrational fears, blind hatreds, and credulous superstitions that precluded happiness and eventually destroyed him. For Spinoza, evil is the result of a mind trapped by its own imagination and not autonomously active, doing what it can do, being the cause of its own affections, rather than living life as a hostage to fortune.

Nietzsche developed Spinoza's thought in an original way with his thesis concerning master and slave values. Spinoza's idea of an ethically good life has more recently (if unknowingly) been advocated by the philosopher and economist Amartya Sen, with his "capability-approach" to assessing advantage. The usual approach in economics tries to reduce people's advantages to a common quality like pleasure or money, which can be measured. Sen is a leader in criticizing such models. In contrast, he believes that individual advantages should be judged "by a person's capability to do things he or she has reason to value."[60]

That is exactly Spinoza's idea. Any realistic choice that a person faces involves selecting among incommensurable goods, or things with incommensurable aspects. To ask which alternative gives the most pleasure or promises the greatest profit is of little value for understanding human behavior. Choice requires us (and the social scientists who want to model our behavior) to reason about relative importance and not merely estimate a homogeneous quantity and make an obvious decision to maximize. To assess our advantage, we have to think about the purposes that matter to us and how a given choice will affect the capabilities that these purposes require. In Spinoza's terms, Sen is saying that a relatively advantaged life is one in which a person is capable of doing all that he or she can do. Maximizing activity, Sen's capability, and minimizing passive suffering—only that balance of valued intensities promises joy.

From a Spinozist point of view, the ethical question for martial arts practice is whether the training makes one more active, less passive, more joyous, less depressed. Suppose you are attacked. You cannot *not* respond, for freezing and doing nothing is a response, probably the one your assailant expects. The ethical question is whether this fraught occasion might be invested with some scope for autonomy or self-determination. Is it possible to cultivate habits (an ethos) that would give you some choice about what happens in such a situation? How could you respond actively rather than merely enduring your assailant's violence? Martial arts practice teaches techniques capable of making a violent encounter agree with you (or disagree less), despite the other's hostile intention. The other has the purpose of violence, but art renders one active in relation to such encounters, able to merge with them and turn them into an occasion of activity rather than abject suffering.

The ideal martial arts response to violence is not to endure it as a pacifist would, or to turn the other cheek as a Christian would, or to destroy it with an overwhelming counterforce as Conan the Barbarian would. The ideal is a response that, while active, nevertheless does not augment violence, redirecting the energy of an assault without adding to it. That is a specialty of the Asian martial arts, notably aikido. It is not easy to do and takes years of training, but it is possible to eliminate strikes and rely on nothing except how an opponent tries to attack. By simply not being available to intercept his energy, no matter how he tries to throw himself at you—creating new, never intended trajectories for his body, which it is compelled to follow by no force save his own—the attack is spent on the aggressor, who is disabled without any additional violence over what he himself initiated. Such a response is (or should be) an ideal of martial arts mastery. In a pinch, one may have to settle for a parry, punch, and kick, but that only means one has further to go in the martial arts, which are endless anyway.

Spinoza regarded scientific knowledge as the key to avoiding passive suffering and maintaining activity, a classic thesis of philosophical rationalism. The more you know about nature, the better you will be at turning every occasion into joyful activity. For Spinoza, "knowledge" means a scientific knowledge of causes, an explicit, theoretical (mathematical) understanding of the mechanism that makes the effect inevitable. This raises a problem, however. You could never have such knowledge of the singular causes of violence; I mean the singular moment when violence actually occurs. No virtual victim can know so much about the violence that is about to befall him. Even Spinoza escaped an assassin's blade by sheer luck.

The actuality of violence, in your face *now*, is dreadful and always surprising. Indeed, if it does not shock you, it is not violence. Even if you see it coming, it shocks you. Violence lurks where science does not shine, pouring through gaps where the law is unavailing. It always strikes where you do not know. Consequently, calculating, mechanical knowledge is not adequate to make you active in relation to violence. You need something more flexible, an art, not a theory. Unfortunately, Spinoza remained true to his rationalist tradition and considered scientific theory to be the best and highest knowledge, with the technical knowledge of art scarcely meriting the name knowledge at all.

WHY NOW?

The ubiquitous historical decline of violence in all its usual forms, from personal assault to warfare, is well documented. People tend to disbelieve the claim at first, but the evidence is quite convincing and not disputed by experts. There has never been less violence in the world, more peace for more people, than at the beginning of the twenty-first century. The trend is interesting because it implies that whatever causes violence, it is not a perennial urge like hunger, sex, or the need to sleep. Of course, we want to know the reason for the decline. There matters become controversial, but I need not get into that. The point is, it seems like an odd time for a martial arts revival. Never have so many people in so many places been practicing so many Asian combat arts at so high a level. Why now, when the likelihood of a personal run-in with violence, especially the variety against which these arts are effective, has never been lower?[61]

Common claims for the value of martial arts training include

- The benefit of physical exercise, promoting health and enhancing endurance.
- The development of learning skills, including learning about one's body and how to move efficiently and elegantly.
- The beneficial effects of discipline and committed practice.
- The growth of self-understanding.
- Practice in the use of an intuitive response, and a special kind of concentration, *wuxin*, no mind.
- The practical value of self-defense.[62]

We should not suppose these (and other) purposes are in competition, as if one were more authentic than the rest. There appears to be no single value for which the Asian martial arts are currently practiced. Someone might think that a practice with nothing every participant values and makes the reason for engagement has lost its soul or reason for being. What is absent from contemporary Asian martial arts practice is only the singularity of a soul. Rather than a master purpose or raison d'être, there is a rhizomatic network of martial arts practice, extending to almost every city around the world, sharing descent from common ancestors and a creative, living relation to Asian, and ultimately Chinese, traditions.

Fitness is probably the most objective effect of training, which typically includes aerobic and strength exercises. Over time people experience enhanced flexibility, agility, and endurance, with a relatively low risk of injury. As Jean-Jacques Rousseau, a sickly self-observer, wrote, "The weaker the body, the more it commands [the soul]." Discounting the hint of mind-body dualism, his observation has merit. The effects on motility and posture produced by regular exercise (dance, martial arts, Pilates, and the like) influence how one feels about one's body.[63]

Research confirms that neuromuscular coordination, strength, endurance, balance, and agility contribute to a sense of competence and satisfaction with one's body, and these are predictable results of regular exercise. The changes in muscle tone enhance alertness; one is more aware of the environment and less preoccupied by aches and pains. In contrast—and this is Rousseau's case—the loss of muscle tone correlates with a rising awareness of one's own body and a depressed body image. The popular martial arts literature routinely claims the superiority of its practice for such healthful benefits. Only recently has clinical research begun to examine this claim, and the results are so far inconclusive, the health benefits of martial arts training being difficult to disentangle from those associated with any form of aerobic and strength exercise.[64]

A common assumption is that martial arts training is primarily about self-defense. Of course, it can be, yet it is not unusual for even highly trained martial artists to have no experience of real-world violence. As Grand Master Phong Dang, sixth-dan aikido, sixth-dan taekwondo, fifth-dan judo, eighth-dan Vietnamese Shaolin kung fu, twice inducted into the World Martial Arts Hall of Fame admits, "I have been practicing martial arts for a total of about forty-three years, but I've never had to apply techniques on anybody." Loren Christensen describes a champion karateka: "He can put his fist or his foot wherever he wants and there isn't much his opponent can do about it." Yet "he has doubts as to how well he would do in a real fight, a blood-letting, knock down drag out. 'I can play tournament tag,' he says. 'But if I had to fight for real, I don't know how I would do.'" As these remarks suggest, self-defense is actually a smaller part of martial arts practice than nonpractitioners may assume and is an unlikely candidate for explaining a renaissance of the Asian martial arts.[65]

The topic of self-defense merits a few more words. Training for self-defense has to be training for surprise, the surprising shock of unexpected violent assault. That is difficult to do safely. It is not to parody metaphysics that I distinguish between the essence of violence and its existence. The essence of violence is its design, its mechanism, or intentionality. How is the violence produced? With what weapon, by what mechanism, for what target, with what effect? This is what we in the martial arts study and practice. But the same training may leave one unprepared for the existence of violence, the actuality of it unexpectedly in one's face.

Rory Miller is a master jujitsu practitioner, a jail guard, a SWAT-team commander, and a man with ample experience in both the martial arts and real-world violence. He observes that "most people don't recognize the sheer chaos of survival fighting or the effects that the stress hormones dumped into your bloodstream will have." The flash flood of hormones unleashed by shock or the sudden awareness of threat predictably causes a loss of peripheral and depth vision, auditory exclusion, and degraded motor skill and coordination, as well as obsessive thoughts and counterproductive behavioral looping, when one hysterically repeats ineffectual movements. The prospect of acutely degraded skill is food for thought for the martial artist. Under conditions of real threat, trained law-enforcement officers firing their service handgun from no more than six feet away completely miss their target 62 percent of the time, a figure that rises to 83 percent at ten to twenty feet away. It is unlikely that empty-hand martial arts techniques would fare better.[66]

A realistic self-defense scenario would begin with a successful assault—real violence, and not a mere simulation—for only that would produce the corporeal effects that one then attempts to master. Bearing in mind that a predator will not attack unless he believes he can surprise you, in a realistic self-defense scenario you probably already would have been injured before you become aware of the assault. In such circumstances, people have a tendency to freeze. No training can truly be a preparation for self-defense unless it teaches one to beat this freeze. The U.S. Army got its soldiers to fire their weapons by ingraining in them a conditioned response, a trigger. Practice it endlessly, make it a reflex: See the threat, fire the weapon. In this way, one bypasses consciousness and beats the freeze. The samurai called that trigger the "first sword of combat." Miller astutely observes that it takes at least one heartbeat for the hormonal effects of startle and fear to kick in, which is ample time to initiate a trained response. What is perhaps most important is that such a response will surprise the attacker and provoke *his* hormonal reaction. All his stealth and pumped-up confidence are premised on his immediate domination of the situation. Now he is in a fight, and that definitely was not the plan.

To make this strategy work, one must be capable of acting decisively, without hesitation. That is easy to say and both hard to do and hard to train, especially when it may mean acting preemptively. When violence is imminent and you have the chance to avoid becoming a victim, a preemptive strike may be the most effective defense, "but," Miller cautions, it "takes great skill to use and justify." The first attack usually gets in and does damage, shocking and slowing a would-be assailant and opening the way for finishing strikes. Training in self-defense has to train to do that, because if any mistakes are made here, everything one knows about the essence of violence (all the techniques of martial arts) will be unavailing. However, as Miller said, a preemptive strike, especially when successful, can be difficult to justify later on, when it may look to witnesses as if you started the fight.

Despite the difficulty of realistic training for self-defense, martial arts do make one aware of an expanded range of options and also provide opportunities to practice them. That may instill a kind of confidence that is not necessarily misplaced. The training teaches walking, standing, breathing, and posture in ways that amplify the body language of competence. This is practice in not looking like a victim, which may be the most useful thing one can learn for self-defense: "Without speaking, [the trained body] says that this is a person committed to a discipline. And passers-by 'hear' and respect this. Here is someone who has no fear and that sustains him." In the words of a female karateka,

A good black belt female is mentally tough. No sexual harassment. No put-downs. No bad relationships. No crap. . . . A female black belt is very unlikely to be a target of male violence. She sends out the signal, "Don't mess with me"—not appealing to a would-be attacker.[67]

Violent predators want a victim, not a fight. Fights are chaotic, hard to control, and dangerous on multiple levels to seasoned criminals, who usually lack pensions and health insurance. Such people scan their environment for victims and know what they look like. If you never look like a victim, your self-defense problem will go away. The Chinese art of war reserves its highest praise for the commander who never has to fight. He apparently does nothing, yet obstacles are neutralized by his presence. "We practice fighting," Robert W. Smith said of the Asian martial arts, "so that we don't have to fight. If there is a secret in these arts, it is that."[68]

Another value of martial arts practice is the challenging context it offers for enjoyable work on the self. It demands commitment to a program of retraining in things as elementary as breathing and walking. The kinetics of habitual movement has to be reassembled on a consistent, efficient pattern. One discovers the body one never knew, its capacities and vulnerabilities, and how it responds to rehabilitation. In the words of one practitioner,

> The study of a traditional martial art provides a framework in which to situate one's continual development as a human being. The emphasis on striving for perfection of both mind and body make the dojo an ideal place to continue to re-create ourselves by going beyond our current understanding and abilities.

Martial arts are not arts practiced by martial subjects; rather, the encounter with these arts formulates subjectivity. It does not presuppose a competent subject but an incompetent, not yet finished subject, which training complements and, provisionally and partially, completes. "You work until your body aches," says a longtime aikidoka,

> and your mind is bursting, you share a sense of communitas with other aikidoka—in your dojo and beyond, you avoid being late to the mat and would not contemplate leaving early. You do all this because of your commitment to others, your understanding of your practice in terms of your own personal development, and also because of the ritual formalities that envelop the space and time of your bodily practice.

The gradual but palpably cumulative result is a pleasing sense of competence that is at once mental and physical and is valued if only because modern environments fragment people's experience and promote unawareness of embodiment, making competent corporeal integration increasingly rare.[69]

Martial arts can form part of a religious practice, especially Zen Buddhism, as it apparently once did at the Shaolin Temple. Considering Japanese military values or samurai culture as integral to the Asian martial arts would be a mistake. Not counting sumo, which is hardly a martial art, no Japanese martial art acquired its current form until the twentieth century. The samurai image is especially inappropriate to the Chinese martial arts, and Zen began in China. Thanks to the kung fu movies, the idea of Shaolin martial arts as an almost mystically powerful system of fighting is ingrained in the minds of millions of people. Teachers of these arts find the image pernicious. In the words of one, the cinematic myth is "an outright impediment to developing the very teachings that the Shaolin art was devised to convey." This teacher argues that the martial arts tradition created at Shaolin Temple was not designed to defeat anything but one's own fear and delusion, teaching corporeal lessons in letting go and not contending. The martial arts training there became continuous with meditation, teaching a dispassionate Buddhist calm under pressure, and the transcendence of fear and insecurity. Fighting prowess is a by-product of self-mastery.[70]

Whether this approach to martial arts training was really the thought and practice of the ancient Shaolin Buddhists, I do not know. I do know that the Shaolin Temple exists, as I have visited it twice; crumbling frescos depicting monks training fighting techniques appear authentically ancient; and records of fighting Shaolin monks are not in dispute by scholars. Be that as it may, some martial arts schools today claim an authentic Shaolin heritage and practice a Chan or Zen Buddhism that includes martial arts training. A document from such a group illuminates this martial arts ethos. *The Shaolin Grandmasters' Text* purports to have been composed or overseen by the last escaping masters of the Shaolin Temple. Deserting their war-torn monastery, they made their way to the United States, where they quietly re-created the Chan Buddhism of the Shaolin Temple, including the martial arts:

"The authors of this text are members of the Order of Shaolin Ch'an, originally established in 520 C.E. The masters who provided the material for this volume were remnants of a once and large and peaceful tile in the grand mosaic of China."[71]

Martial skill, they say,

> is not the primary goal of Shaolin *gongfu*. Just as sculptors reveal the form hidden in a block of granite with hammer and chisel, we employ martial arts to unveil and realize our original Buddha-natures. Shaolin practice forms and engage in combat to chip away at the ego until nothing is left of it.

They explain their martial arts practice using the Buddhist concept of skillful means. The practice of these martial arts has been found to work for Buddhist enlightenment, and they are practiced religiously because they work, without any dogmatic claim to understand why they should work or to deny that other ways might work as well: "Our specific martial arts training methods stem from our pragmatism—we have found that self-defense and combat training offer an expedient and excellent means of teaching Buddhist lessons." For example, they say that the practice of martial arts "acts as an expedient device to teach the student *wuxin* [no mind], as does forms training" and that "meditative martial arts practice pacifies the grasping nature of the unsettled mind."[72]

To make this narrative one's own presupposes a commitment to Buddhism, which funds the spiritualization of martial training. One trains in this *gongfu* for the same reason that one meditates, repairs to a monastery, or studies Zen masters: for enlightenment, salvation, nirvana. I respect this approach to martial arts but do not share it, because I do not want to make that commitment to Buddhism and do not believe that the authenticity of Asian martial arts practice depends on it. So what about me? I started training not knowing anything about martial arts. I had never seen a martial arts movie (although I remember watching the *Kung Fu* television series when I was a child), and had no interest in Chinese philosophy or Zen. Instead, I was looking for variation in my personal fitness routine, an alternative to running. One January morning, I telephoned a couple of studios, visited one, took a first lesson, and never looked back. I have had to change what I practice because of various accidents and opportunities. A sabbatical year in China provided the opportunity for training there, an experience I repeated some years later when I studied wing chun in Hong Kong, and training continues to occupy several hours of my week. I started with an interest in fitness, but that is not what motivated my eventual commitment. So having asked everybody else, I ask myself, Why?

Part of my answer has to be fascination, both aesthetic and intellectual, with the techniques, combined with the gradual discovery that I could perform them and not merely appreciate them theoretically. Training became a philosophical experiment in discovering what my body can do. Currently I train in hapkido, a technique-heavy art with an extensive gallery of joint locks, plus exquisitely technical training in punching and kicking. It is all very interesting to me: interesting to learn from the master, interesting to practice and see improvement, and interesting to teach to beginners. These arts are endless. You can begin at any age and train to any age and never touch bottom. My teacher invokes a Korean proverb about rice getting sweeter the longer you chew. There is always more to unfold, more challenge, more to practice, more to appreciate and understand. A satisfying piece of luck got me to the point that I can enjoy such things. The longer I practice, the more the practice becomes a commitment. Martial arts *techniques* are not endotelic, dancelike moves. They are technical instruments, weapons in fact. But the *practice* of training them can be endotelic, done for the sake of doing it, a source of its own rewards. The more one trains, the better one gets, and the more one can learn and also teach. The training becomes ever more interesting and satisfying and involves me with others from widely different walks of life whom I might otherwise never meet, sharing no more than love of the art and respect for our teacher.

EPILOGUE

Martial Arts and Philosophy

The day will come when you will not know
what you have understood.
BAGUA MASTER GONG BAOZHAI

An aesthetic paradox of Asian martial arts is that something so warlike in conception should be beautiful to watch and joyful to perform. While designed for violence and visibly expressing that functionality, the martial arts are not practiced with a violent purpose and do no harm (although they certainly could). By suspending the dread of violence, the practice creates a theater in which to contemplate movements combining artful design with eloquent efficacy. But if you remove the training conventions and introduce unfeigned violence (as in boxing), the aesthetic serenity will vanish into the sometimes irrepressibly fascinating chaos of violence.

Hence an ethical paradox: Training in the martial arts is training in weapons avowed to violence, which is usually illegal and immoral except in a narrow range of special circumstances. How can something so respectfully trained, so ethically serious, so philosophical in conception, so elegant in demonstration, so challenging to master, and so exhilarating to perform, with so venerable a tradition, be vested in the vile purpose of violence? The answer is that these martial arts are not vested in violence. They are vested in life and address the ethical problem of a response to violence. We train *for* it without *training* in it. It is internal to Asian martial arts practice that violence is external to the training. Doubly external. Violence is excluded from training, yet the training has external value as a weapon.

Martial arts training is (or was) an ethical response to the problem of living in a violent world, although these arts do not require such a world to make sense of their practice. That is why self-defense is not as all-important as it may appear to outsiders or beginners. The probability of assault today is nothing like what it was on the byways of medieval China. Most modern citizens, including those who train in the martial arts, do not need to learn techniques against violent attack, and even if they did need them, if they had an urgent practical need for instruction in real world self-defense, traditional training in one of the Asian martial arts would not be the way to go.

What makes the mastery of the martial arts a congenial challenge, rewarding to accomplish, is also what gives ethical significance to its postmodern practice. This significance lies in the aesthetics of existence and what Michel Foucault called "techniques of the self." The Confucians called it "self-cultivation" (*xiu shen*). The good of philosophy was traditionally also this work on the self until that ethical value was eliminated with the arrival of scholasticism and professionalism. The *art* of the martial arts is a *techne*, a productive, effective, technical knowledge. It is narrowly technical in training techniques apposite to this or that presentment of violence, and more broadly productive as an ethical work on the self. An ethical question to those who practice these arts is, what do you perceive, feel, appreciate, know, or enjoy that you would not without the experience of training?[1]

Every aficionado will have a different answer. What do you perceive, feel, or appreciate? It could be something about yourself, how you respond to challenge, how your body learns, and how it can change. You know your capacity for commitment, endurance, and discipline. You know something uncommon about how violence works, about how bodies respond to forces, about vital vulnerabilities and positions of weakness and strength. You learn to recognize opportunities to learn, which can make you a better teacher. You learn to read another's body, to smile at bluster, to laugh at yourself, and to always try again. Maybe you have become a better dancer. That could be good for anyone. Philosophers also may find something in these arts, which brings me to a last paradox. The exercise of martial arts is corporeal and violent, generating nondiscursive force rather than symbols or discourse. So how can it express knowledge without a proposition that is true?

Accomplishment in martial arts is the accomplishment of a corporeal knowledge, a body that knows what to do. Western philosophy tends to discount such knowledge as secondary, philosophically insignificant, never the main thing in epistemology. Socrates taught philosophers that technicians do not really *know* anything, not in the most prestigious sense of "know." *Techne* knowledge is unthinking habit, more machinelike or beastlike than suits a scientist. That was not Socrates's best argument, however. Using the same evidence we could come to the opposite conclusion in favor of *techne*. Socrates's interrogations do not prove that technicians have no true knowledge; they prove that their obviously valuable knowledge does not take the form of a true theory. Why should it? The itinerary of technical mastery passes only briefly through an explicit phase on the way from incompetence to an unconscious competence expressed in masterful performance. A philosopher alert to the indispensable value of *techne* to civilization could decide that consciousness and reasons are epistemic options and that truth is just one of many values realized in the accomplishment of knowledge.

The rationalism that classical philosophers favor favors conscious, verbal, explicit, formal, discursive, theoretically articulated knowledge. Plato concocted a concept of "knowledge of truth" (*episteme*) and commended it to philosophers as the most godlike science. Everything else is contemptibly petty if not fraudulent. The entire history of human experience with the arts, technics, and technology speaks against this point of view, or would if it were allowed to speak at all. Linguistic consciousness and discursive reasons are on the same level as other expressions of knowledge, including art and technology, and are not a higher grade of knowledge than other reliably productive corporeal effects. The specious distinction between theory and practice reduces to an indifferent difference between a clever tongue and clever hands. The same brain oversees both. Knowledge qualifies a somatic performance, not a mental representation. You can have discursive reasons and lack performative knowledge; you can have technical mastery and lack discursive reasons; but you cannot have consistently superlative performance and lack knowledge, because that is what knowing is—superlative artifactual performance.[2]

The martial arts that began in China now belong to the world. The same can be said of the philosophical traditions that began in ancient Greece, matured in modern Europe, and are now adapting to a multicentered global civilization. The Asian martial arts do not essentially belong to any ethnicity, and philosophical thought is not essentially Western. Both are mongrels and free to mingle, except they do not, or at least they have not so far. Students of the martial arts who seek concepts for their practice have turned to Asian thought, especially Daoism and Zen, which offer an abundance of ideas. They have avoided Western philosophy for obvious geographical and linguistic reasons and because, at least until recently, this philosophy has been adverse to collaboration and really had nothing to say.

Despite the legend that Plato was a wrestler, our canonical philosophers are not interested in anything so corporeal as combat arts. They cannot imagine that such arts express authentic knowledge no less than geometry does. There is no truth in such arts, or noetic virtue. We have seen the long-standing animus between philosophy and athletics, a one-sided polemic almost as old as philosophy itself, running parallel with the old enmity against poetry and rhetoric. The first philosophers invented the insidious idea of intellectual virtue, a virtue of pure mind. They insisted that we are split into a divine part that is incorporeal and a beastly body, compelling people to make an agonizing choice that no one had to make before, whether to prefer the good of the mind or that of the body. Ever since then, Western philosophy has neglected athletics and shunned corporeal excellence, acknowledging no value in achievements of the body except for their enhancement of the mind.

The Socratic compulsion to make knowledge conscious, or define it by feats of consciousness like definition, justification, or proof, subverts the corporeal value of *techne*-knowledge in favor of something (reason, concepts, logic) that supposedly does not rely on the body at all. That is a problem with epistemology. Its principles tend to ensure that knowledge is purely mental, all a matter of mental things in the right order—the right justification for the right proposition, rightly deduced with the right logical form. Philosophy should turn away from thinking that isolates mind and body or distinguishes pure form and material content, which is an avatar of the same dualism. We have nothing to think with that is not an evolved power of the organism, no "pure" knowledge or "pure" thought or consciousness. There is no separated psyche to embody, no sequestered soma to enliven with soul, only the contingently evolved Darwinian body, whose ruthlessly abstracted mental and physical qualities are completely continuous. Whatever we mean by words like "cognition," "intellect," "reason," and "knowledge" must be a corporeal power of an evolved, adapted body. This body is not an animated form but a singular survivor, more given to cunning than contemplation.

Philosophy could enhance vitality rather than be a preparation for death, as Socrates wanted. It might unite the healthy need for viability in change with clarity concerning the resources we have to achieve it. It might attack the obstacles—conceptual, political, cultural, emotional— to somatic imagination and the harmonies it harbors. Spinoza insisted that we do not know what a body can do, and we still do not, especially in regard to our own body. We cannot know in advance what we are capable of or the extent of our power. The only way to find out is to try and become active. Make the experiment. Nietzsche added that we do not know what humanity can do. "There are a thousand paths that have never yet been walked; a thousand healths and hidden islands of life. Human being and human earth are still unexhausted and undiscovered." This is how they will remain, hidden in gloom, unless we forsake subordination to the sad knowledge of institutions premised on fear and recognize the passion for certainty as a displacement of anxious distress in the face of the nameless and trackless.[3]

It is sad. It is sick. Western philosophy, like the Hippocratic medicine that inspired it, has traditionally conceived health in terms of balance. To be healthy is to be in balance, a prelude to happiness defined as impassive tranquillity. But life is a constant state of conflict, which is the normal condition of health even at the cellular level. Any organism, any organ, any cell struggles to maintain its boundaries, the margin between inside and outside, against environmental challenge. A living body is a crucible of conflict. Its ability to overcome resistance and harmonize contesting tendencies is a measure of both health and power, two words for the same somatic reality.

When life is strife, health is a funded, capable need to go beyond the normal or ordinary, a joyful achievement undiminished by impermanence, and a kind of happiness consistent with change. In chapter 2, I referred to a Daoist thought that tranquillity is not an alternative to change, as ancient philosophy assumes, but a particular way of changing. It is a mistake to think that you need to eliminate turmoil to obtain tranquillity, which has no value unless it is tranquillity amid turmoil, a "becoming tranquil" that never entirely displaces the tumultuous agitation that is synonymous with being alive. The tranquillity of the wise is not impassive changelessness but the competence to greet change with gratitude.

Without discord, there is no harmony, which is another word for a gracious, artful, synergistic response to change. According to a Confucian teaching, harmony (*he*) is not uniformity (*tong*). It is not the elimination of differences; it is their integration into a more capacious constellation. It is like making soup: you mix water, vinegar, pickle, salt, plums, and fish or meat, harmonizing the ingredients, "balancing the various flavors, strengthening the taste of whatever is lacking, and moderating the taste of whatever is excessive." Such harmony, it is said, "gives birth to things, while uniformity does not have issue. Harmony yields plentiful growth and things return to it." Harmony is creative, giving birth to unexampled things, surpassing the pieces that comprise them, amplified by concretion in an unprecedented rapport.[4]

The preeminent power engendering ever widening circles of harmony across the spectrum of life is imagination, which we must not misunderstand as romantically mystified mentation. Imagination is as material as metabolism, as somatic as any power of a Darwinian body. The cash value of "imagination" is the facility to integrate novelty with familiarity and to reweave the inherited fabric of experience in an unanticipated, more ample, life-enhancing way. Everyday life affords abundant opportunities for exercising the imagination, yet it is easy to become complacent and resist or evade the challenge of change. "Never ceasing for an instant," wrote Guo Xiang, commenting on the *Zhuangzi*, "we find ourselves constantly thrown suddenly into newness.

There is no moment when all things between heaven and earth are not moving along. The world is ever new but believes itself to be old."⁵

Art is the antidote to the hazard of not paying attention. From our experience with art, from the entertaining exertion that art invites and requites—playfully practicing our capacity to question assumptions, linger on unexpected possibilities, and greet complexity, even strangeness without anxiety—we receive our best training in imagination. I mean art in all forms and regardless of the mode of engagement, whether as artist or audience. Imagination makes these a pair with a common bond. Imagination is needed to create art and to enjoy and learn from it. The visual, plastic arts, music, and literature exercise the imagination no less than do technical challenges to skill and craft, or the corporeal arts I have discussed, the modern traditions of Asian martial arts.⁶

Before we know what our body can do, we have to try, and before we can try, we have to imagine the movement, even if the image is obscure and indeterminate, as it must be when the effort is authentically venturesome. Unwonted movements must be integrated with what we already know we can do, which requires, in part, imagining doing them, forming a virtual image of corporeal integration, which funds the practice it takes to actualize the image in augmented competence. An agile imagination surmounts bodily challenges, enlarging our repertory of basic actions and enhancing the somatic resources we draw on in every tangible encounter.

Tranquillity greets change with gratitude. Longevity absorbs change and does not evade it. Training in the martial arts produces, as product and by-product, psychosomatic competencies that lend themselves to these attainments. Unlike dance or sport, these arts affirm and afford lifelong learning. Even if you eventually quit, the training, the learning, the potential for becoming more and better is endless. The experience resonates with everything it touches, changing how you think and act, perceive and feel. The beginning of power, knowing what your body can do, is the imagination of power, daring the experiment, and, only in that way, becoming more consistently who you are.

CHINESE–ENGLISH GLOSSARY

Every Chinese term or expression used in *Striking Beauty* is given here in Chinese characters, alphabetically according to the *pinyin* spelling.

BAGUA 八卦   the eight trigrams of the *Yijing*; also the name of a martial art
BAOPUZI 《抱朴子》   *The Master Who Embraces Simplicity*
BINGFA 兵法   military methods, art of war
BU ZHAN 不戰   no fighting
BU ZHENG 不爭   do not contend
CHAN 禪   meditation (in Japanese, Zen)
DA FUCHOU 大復仇   glorifying revenge
DANTIAN 丹田   energy center, "elixir field," "sea of *qi*"
DAO 道   way, path
DAODEJING 《道德經》   (also *Laozi*) *Classic of the Way and Its Virtue*
DAOJIA 道家   Daoist, Daoism
DAOYIN 導引   guided stretching
DAOYIN TU 《導引圖》   *Guiding and Stretching Diagram*
DE 德   power, virtue
DIQI 地氣   terrestrial *qi*
DONG JING 懂筋   interpreting energy
FANGSHI 方士   master of formulas, shaman
FENGSHUI 風水   geomancy
FU 腹   stomach, intestines, bladder
GONGFU 功夫   skill, practice, "kung fu"
GUI 詭   deception

GUOSHU 國術　national arts

HE 和　harmony, harmonious

HOU FA XIAN ZHI 後發先至　last to shoot, first to reach

HOU REN FA, XIAN REN ZHI 后人發，先人至　set out after and arrive before

HOUXI 喉息　throat breathing

HOU ZHI YI FA, XIAN ZHI YI ZHI 后之以發，先之以至　behind in making a move, ahead in striking home

HUAINANZI 《淮南子》　*Master of Huainan*

HUA QUAN 花拳　flowery boxing

JIAN 劍　double-edged sword

JIANGHU 江湖　rivers and lakes, Chinese underworld

JING 靜　stillness

JINGWU MENG 精武門　Essence of Martial Arts Association

JI SHAN 積善　accumulating goodness

JUE 訣　martial art technique

JUELI 角力　wrestling

KAI ZHI YI LI 開之以利　tempts you to take advantage

LAOZI 老子　old master, old child; another name for the *Daodejing*

LI 禮　rites, ceremonies; ritual propriety

LIJI 《禮記》　*Record of Rites*

MINGJING 明經　Illuminated Classics examination degree

NEIDAN 內丹　inner alchemy

NEIYE 《內業》　*Inward Training*

PAI 派　martial arts style

PEIYANG ZHONGQI 《培養中氣》　*Nourishing Central Energy*

QI 氣　breath, vital energy, Greek *pneuma*

QI 奇　unorthodox, strange, mysterious

QIGONG 氣功　breath (or *qi*) cultivation

QUAN 拳　boxing, empty-hand combat

QUAN BIAN 權變　weighing changes

QUAN TAO 拳套　martial arts practice routines

REN 仁　benevolence, humanity

RU 儒　scholar, Confucian

RUQUANSHI 儒拳師　scholar-boxer

SHEN 神　spirit

SHENMING 神明　divine insight

SHEN WAI SHEN 身外身　body within (or outside) the body

SHI 勢　strategic potential

SHIFU 師傅　martial arts master and teacher

SHOUBO 手搏　empty-hand combat

SHU 術　arts, techniques

SHUN CHING VING TSUN GUOSHU HUI 淳正詠春國術會　Pure and Righteous Wing Chun National Arts Association

SUNZI BINGFA 《孫子兵法》　Sunzi's *Art of War*

TAIJI 太極　supreme ultimate

TAIJIQUAN 太極拳　taiji martial art
TAIPING 太平　ideal world
TAIQING DAO 太清道　Way of Great Clarity
TAIXI 胎息　embryonic respiration
TIAN 天　heaven/nature
TIANQI 天氣　celestial *qi*
TIAOXI 調息　harmonizing the breath
TIXI 體系　martial arts system
TONG 同　sameness, uniformity
TUI SHOU 推手　taiji pushing-hands exercise
WAIDAN 外丹　external alchemy
WEI WU WEI 為無為　do not-doing
WEN 文　spiritual, civil, civilization, culture
WENDE 文德　scholarly virtue
WEN ZHI WU GONG 文治武功　use military to get, use culture to keep
WU 舞　dance
WU 武　military, combative
WU 無　nothing, not
WUGONG 武功　martial arts
WU QIN ZHI XI 五禽之戲　frolics of the five animals
WUSHI 無事　no activity
WUSHU 武術　martial arts
WUWEI 無為　non-action, not-doing
WUXIA 武俠　martial arts adventure stories
WUXIN 無心　no mind (in Japanese, *mushin*)
WUYI 武藝　martial arts
XIA 俠　chivalrous spirit
XIAN 仙　immortal
XIANTAI 仙胎　immortal embryo
XIANÜ 俠女　*wuxia* martial-arts story heroine
XIASHI 俠士　freelance martial artist
XIA YI 俠義　protecting the weak
XIE 邪　wayward
XIU SHEN 修身　self-cultivation
XÜ 虛　empty
XÜ SHI 虛奇　empty and full, *Sunzi bingfa*, chapter 6
YANGSHENG 養生　nourishing life
YI 義　righteous
YI BING 義兵　just war
YIJING 《易經》　*Classic of Changes*
YIJINJING 《易筋經》　*Change Muscles Classic*
YINSHU 《引書》　*Stretching Book*
YIN YANG 陰陽　shady/bright, cold/hot, female/male, soft/hard, and the like
YONG 勇　courage
YONGQUAN 湧泉　bubbling-well acupuncture point

YOU 有　being, existence

YOU ZHI YI LI 誘之以利　tempt with advantages

YUAN 圓　circularity

YUAN 源　flow

YUSHI 羽士　bird-men, masters of wings

YUYU 預御　advance defense

ZANG 臟　solid viscera, cache

ZHENG 正　upright

ZHENREN 真人　genuine person

ZHENYOU 真有　true existence

ZHENZHI 真知　genuine knowledge

ZHONGXI 踵息　heel breathing

ZHONGYONG 《中庸》　*Maintaining Perfect Balance*

ZHUANGZI 《莊子》　*Master Zhuang*

ZIRAN 自然　spontaneous, natural, so of itself

ZUOWANG 坐忘　sitting in oblivion, sitting and forgetting

NOTES

PREFACE

1. Sabrina Qiong Yu describes transnational kung fu stardom as "Chinese cinema's most widely acknowledged contribution to world cinema" (*Jet Li: Chinese Masculinity and Transnational Film Stardom* [Edinburgh: Edinburgh University Press, 2012], 10). See also Paul Bowman, *Beyond Bruce Lee: Chasing the Dragon Through Film, Philosophy and Popular Culture* (London: Wallflower Press, 2013). On the globalization of Asian martial arts, see John C. Cox, "Traditional Asian Martial Arts Training," *Quest* 45 (1993): 366–88; John J. Donohue, *Warrior Dreams: The Martial Arts and the American Imagination* (Westport, Conn.: Bergin & Garvey, 1994); Gary J. Krug, "At the Feet of the Master: Three Stages in the Appropriation of Okinawan Karate," *Critical Studies: Critical Methodologies* 1, no. 4 (2001): 395–410; and D. S. Farrer and John Whalen-Bridge, eds., *Martial Arts as Embodied Knowledge: Asian Traditions in a Transnational World* (Albany: State University of New York Press, 2011).

2. Work by professional philosophers writing in English on the martial arts includes Allan Bäck, "The Way to Virtue in Sport," *Journal of the Philosophy of Sport* 36, no. 2 (2009): 217–37; Allan Bäck, with Daeshik Kim, "Towards a Western Philosophy of Eastern Martial Arts," *Journal of the Philosophy of Sport* 6, no. 1 (1979): 19–28, and "Pacifism and the Eastern Martial Arts," *Philosophy East and West* 32, no. 2 (1982): 177–86; and Graham Priest and Damon Young, eds., *Martial Arts and Philosophy: Beating and Nothingness* (Chicago: Open Court, 2010), and *Philosophy and the Martial Arts: Engagement* (New York: Routledge, 2014).

1. THE *DAO* OF ASIAN MARTIAL ARTS

1. Aron Boretz, *Gods, Ghosts, and Gangsters: Ritual Violence, Martial Arts, and Masculinity on the Margins of Chinese Society* (Honolulu: University of Hawai'i Press, 2011), 2. A valuable contribution to the understanding of martial arts lore and tradition is Meir Shahar, *Shaolin Monastery: History, Religion, and the Chinese Martial Arts* (Honolulu: University of Hawai'i Press, 2008). On Indian martial arts, see Donn F. Draeger and Robert W. Smith, *Asian Fighting Arts* (Tokyo: Kodansha International, 1969), 141–54; and Joseph S. Alter, *The Wrestler's Body: Identity and Ideology in Northern India* (Berkeley: University of California Press, 1992). On Mesopotamia and Greece, see Michael B. Poliakoff, *Combat Sports in the Ancient World: Competition, Violence, and Culture* (New Haven, Conn.: Yale University Press, 1982); and E. Yamauchi, "Athletics in the Ancient Near East," in *Life and Culture in the Ancient Near East*, ed. R. E. Averbeck, W. M. Chavalas, and D. Weisberg (Bethesda, Md.: CDL Press, 2003), 491–500.

2. Confucius, *Analects, with Selections from Traditional Commentaries*, trans. Edward Slingerland (Indianapolis: Hackett, 2003), 3.7. Subsequent references are cited in the text, with the abbreviation A.

3. "Yang Family Forty Chapters," in Douglas Wile, *Lost T'ai-chi Classics from the Late Ch'ing Dynasty* (Albany: State University of New York Press, 1996), 70, 86–87.

4. The whole idea of Chinese "philosophy" is controversial. For an introduction to the controversies, see Carine Defoort, "Is There Such a Thing as Chinese Philosophy?" *Philosophy East and West* 51 (2001): 393–413; and Tang Yijie, "Constructing 'Chinese Philosophy' in Sino-European Cultural Exchange," in *New Interdisciplinary Perspectives in Chinese Philosophy*, ed. Karyn L. Lai (Oxford: Blackwell, 2007), 33–42. I explain my approach to the use of Chinese material in philosophy in *Vanishing into Things: Knowledge in Chinese Tradition* (Cambridge, Mass.: Harvard University Press, 2015).

5. Peter A. Lorge, *Chinese Martial Arts: From Antiquity to the Twenty-First Century* (Cambridge: Cambridge University Press, 2011), 10, 46.

6. I draw from John R. McRae, *The Northern School and the Formation of Early Ch'an Buddhism* (Honolulu: University of Hawai'i Press, 1986); Bernard Faure, *The Will to Orthodoxy: A Critical Genealogy of Northern Chan Buddhism*, trans. Phyllis Brooks (Stanford, Calif.: Stanford University Press, 1997); and Mario Poceski, *Ordinary Mind as the Way: The Hongzhou School and the Growth of Chan Buddhism* (Oxford: Oxford University Press, 2007).

7. Nikolas Broy, "Martial Monks in Medieval Chinese Buddhism," *Journal of Chinese Religions* 40 (2012): 45–89. See also Yue Xu, "Buddhism and the Justification of War with Focus on Chinese Buddhist History," in *Buddhism and Violence: Militarism and Buddhism in Modern Asia*, ed. Vladimir Tikhonov and Terkel Brekke (New York: Routledge, 2013), 194–208. A legend makes Gautama Buddha a champion archer. Some Tibetan monks still practice archery, despite the canonical ban on weapons. Tibet even has a tradition of a special category of fighting

monks known as *dapdop*, recruited from among the less intellectually talented novices, given distinctive hair styles and personal ornaments, and trained for fighting. See Frits Staal, "Indian Bodies," in *Self as Body in Asian Theory and Practice*, ed. Thomas P. Kasulis, with Roger T. Ames and Wimal Dissanayake (Albany: State University of New York Press, 1993), 87–88.

8. The *Treatise on Military Affairs* and *Exposition of the Original Shaolin Staff Method* are cited from Shahar, *Shaolin Monastery*, 77, 62, I also draw from Shahar, *Shaolin Monastery*, 137, 147, 149; Douglas Wile, "Taijiquan and Daoism," *Journal of Asian Martial Arts* 16, no. 4 (2007): 10; and Stanley E. Hemming, "Academic Encounters with the Chinese Martial Arts," *China Review International* 6, no. 2 (1999): 324–25.

9. "The Breakthrough Sermon," in *The Zen Teaching of Bodhidharma*, trans. Red Pine (San Francisco: North Point Press, 1989), 97; *Heart Sutra*, in *Zen Sourcebook*, ed. Stephen Addiss (Indianapolis: Hackett, 2008), 5; Takuan Soho, "The Mysterious Record of Immovable Wisdom," in *The Unfettered Mind: Writings from a Zen Master to a Master Swordsman*, trans. William Scott Wilson (Tokyo: Kodansha International, 1986), 26.

10. Takuan Soho, "Mysterious Record," 26–27, 32, 24.

11. Yagyu Munenori, *The Book of Family Traditions on the Art of War*, in Miyamoto Musashi, *The Book of Five Rings*, trans. Thomas Cleary (Boston: Shambhala, 2003), 158, 157.

12. Internal references indicate that the later chapters of the *Sunzi* were compiled in the early third century B.C.E. and that the book itself was probably begun in the fourth century. With no immediate predecessors, the *Sunzi* defined the basic issues and concepts of the genre, and subsequent contributions worked within its terms with no rethinking of the fundamentals. See Mark Edward Lewis, "Writings on Warfare Found in Ancient Chinese Tombs," *Sino-Platonic Papers* 158 (2005): 1–15. I expand on my interpretation of the *Sunzi* and its tradition in "War as a Problem of Knowledge," *Philosophy East and West* 65, no. 1 (2015).

13. Sun Tzu, *Master Sun's Art of War*, trans. Philip J. Ivanhoe (Indianapolis: Hackett, 2011), chaps. 6, 3.

14. Arthur Waldron, foreword to *The Art of War: Sun Zi's Military Methods*, trans. Victor H. Mair (New York: Columbia University Press, 2007), xix, xv; *Wuzi*, in *The Seven Military Classics of Ancient China*, ed. and trans. Ralph D. Sawyer (New York: Basic Books, 1993), 220. An example of these scenarios in Sunzi's *Art of War* is in chapter 11.

15. Sun Tzu, *Master Sun's Art of War*, chap. 3; Rory Miller, *Facing Violence: Preparing for the Unexpected* (Wolfeboro, N.H.: YMAA Publication Center, 2011), 104, 159.

16. Sun Tzu, *Master Sun's Art of War*, chap. 6.

17. Shi Zimei and Yu Qian, quoted in Alastair Iain Johnston, *Cultural Realism: Strategic Culture and Grand Strategy in Chinese History* (Princeton, N.J.: Princeton University Press, 1995), 151, 212.

18. Rory Miller, *Meditations on Violence: A Comparison of Martial Arts Training and Real World Violence* (Boston: YMAA Publication Center, 2008), 147;

Michael L. Raposa, *Meditation and the Martial Arts* (Charlottesville: University of Virginia Press, 2003), 59; Musashi, *Book of Five Rings*, 89–90.

19. Sun Tzu, *Master Sun's Art of War*, chaps. 11, 5.

20. Roger Ames, *Confucian Role Ethics: A Vocabulary* (Honolulu: University of Hawai'i Press, 2011), 157; Li I-ye, "Essentials of the Practice of Form and Push Hands," in *The Essence of T'ai Chi Ch'uan: The Literary Tradition*, ed. and trans. Benjamin Pang-Jeng Lo, Martin Inn, Robert Amacher, and Susan Foe (Berkeley, Calif.: Blue Snake Books, 1979), 82. On the concept of strategic potential (*shi*) in the Chinese military philosophy, see François Jullien, *The Propensity of Things: Toward a History of Efficacy in China*, trans. Janet Lloyd (New York: Zone Books, 1999).

21. Loren W. Christensen and Wim Demeere, *Timing in the Fighting Arts: Your Guide to Winning in the Ring and Surviving on the Street* (Santa Fe, N.M.: Turtle Press, 2004), 264–267.

22. On the modern appropriation of Daoism in martial arts literature, see Dominic LaRochelle, "The Daoist Origins of Chinese Martial Arts in *Taiji Quan* Manuals Published in the West," *Journal of Chinese Martial Arts* (2013), http://cmajournal.com (accessed February 2014).

23. Subsequent references to the *Zhuangzi* are cited in the text with the abbreviations G: A. C. Graham, *Chuang-Tzu: The Inner Chapters* (Indianapolis: Hackett, 2001); K: *Zhuangzi*, trans. Paul Kjellberg, in *Readings in Classical Chinese Philosophy*, ed. Philip J. Ivanhoe and Bryan W. Van Norden (Indianapolis: Hackett, 2001); and Z: *Zhuangzi: The Essential Writings, with Selections from Traditional Commentaries*, trans. Brook Ziporyn (Indianapolis: Hackett, 2009).

24. The first record of the expression *zuowang* ("sitting and forgetting" or "sitting in oblivion") is in *Zhuangzi*, chap. 6. See Livia Kohn, *Sitting in Oblivion: The Heart of Daoist Meditation* (Dunedin, Fla.: Three Pines Press, 2010); and Liu An, *The Huainanzi*, ed. and trans. John S. Major, Sarah A. Queen, Andrew Seth Meyer, and Harold D. Roth (New York: Columbia University Press, 2010), 413–14 (11.12). It is curious that this work should link a *fangshi* like Wang Qiao with breath and *qi* cultivation. The original *qi* cultivation literature (for instance, the *Neiye*) was developed in opposition to *fangshi*, or ritual specialists, promising to empower practitioners of *qi* cultivation with powers that *fangshi* claimed to dispose of through knowledge of ritual formulas and mastery of divination and sacrifice. This alternation seems characteristic of the *Huainanzi*, which presents divine powers as obtained through self-cultivation rather than mantic formulas of control. See Michael J. Puett, *To Become a God: Cosmology, Sacrifice, and Self-Divinization in Early China* (Cambridge, Mass: Harvard University Asia Center, 2002), 243, 260.

25. Gil Raz, *The Emergence of Daoism: Creation of Tradition* (Milton Park: Routledge, 2012), 45, 99; Adeline Herrou, *A World of Their Own: Daoist Monks and Their Community in Contemporary China*, trans. Livia Kohn (St. Petersburg, Fla.: Three Pines Press, 2013), 220, 179–80.

26. Liu An, *Huainanzi*, 252. On *daoyin*, see Kristofer Schipper, *The Taoist Body*, trans. Karen C. Duval (Berkeley: University of California Press, 1993), 40–41,

137–38; and Livia Kohn, *Chinese Healing Exercises: The Tradition of Daoyin* (Honolulu: University of Hawai'i Press, 2008).

27. Louis Komjathy, *The Daoist Tradition: An Introduction* (London: Bloomsbury, 2013), 109, 192.

28. Harold D. Roth, "Bimodal Mystical Experience in the *Qiwulun* Chapter of the *Zhuangzi*," in *Hiding the World in the World: Uneven Discourses on the "Zhuangzi*," ed. Scott Cook (Albany: State University of New York Press, 2003), 16; Shahar, *Shaolin Monastery*, 149. The fanciful attribution of the *Yijinjing* to Bodhidharma was made plausible by an independent tradition among Daoists of attributing *daoyin* exercises to Bodhidharma, according to Shahar, *Shaolin Monastery*, 166, 172.

29. Robert W. Smith, *Chinese Boxing: Masters and Methods* (Berkeley, Calif.: North Atlantic Books, 1990), 31; Zheng Manqing, *Cheng Tzu's Thirteen Treatises on T'ai Chi Ch'uan*, trans. Benjamin Pang-Jeng Lo and Martin Inn (Berkeley, Calif.: Blue Snake Books, 1985), 55; Zheng Sanfeng, *Taijiquan Classic*, in *Essence of T'ai Chi Ch'uan*, ed. Lo et al., 21; Marnix Wells, *Scholar Boxer: Chang Naizhou's Theory of Internal Martial Arts* (Berkeley, Calif.: Blue Snake Books, 2005), 75–76.

30. Roel Sterckx, *Animal and the Daemon in Early China* (Albany: State University of New York Press, 2002), 128; Mark Edward Lewis, *Sanctioned Violence in Early China* (Albany: State University of New York Press, 1990), 112, 150–51, 166–67, 204–12; *The Classic of Changes*, trans. Richard John Lynn (New York: Columbia University Press, 1994), 77.

31. Dalun Gao, *A Study of the Han Bamboo Manuscript "The Stretching Book"* (Chengdu: Bashu shushe, 1995), 23–24, 167, 170; Puett, *To Become a God*, 115–16.

32. Livia Kohn, *Zhuangzi: Text and Context* (St. Petersburg, Fla.: Three Pines Press, 2014), 119; Hua Tuo, in *A Source Book in the Martial Arts*, vol. 1, *History, Philosophy, Systems, and Styles*, ed. James I. Wong (Stockton, Calif.: Koinonia, 1978), 13. The five-animal frolic (*wu qin zhi xi*) remained a theme of Daoist literature for centuries and still can be found in the Qigong movement. See Kohn, *Zhuangzi*, 119–20.

33. Brian Kennedy and Elizabeth Guo, *Chinese Martial Arts Training Manuals: A Historical Survey* (Berkeley, Calif.: Blue Snake Books, 2005), 4, 9–10, 12–13; Shahar, *Shaolin Monastery*, 147, 156. "Styles" in martial arts are subdivisions of systems. For example, taiji is a martial arts system, subdivided into the Yang style, Chen style, and so on.

34. *Secret Transmission of Acupuncture Point's Hand Combat Formulas*, in Shahar, *Shaolin Monastery*, 118.

35. Cao Huangdou, preface to *Hand Combat Classic*, in Shahar, *Shaolin Monastery*, 126.

36. Sun Bin, *The Art of War: Complete Texts and Commentaries*, trans. Thomas Cleary (Boston: Shambhala, 2003), chap. 30, 405; *Sunzi*, chap. 7, in *Art of War*, ed. Mair, 101. On Daoist–art-of-war interaction, see Christopher C. Rand, "Chinese Military Thought and Philosophical Taoism," *Monumenta Serica* 34 (1979–1980): 171–218.

37. Quoted in Douglas Wile, *Ta'i Chi's Ancestors: The Making of an Internal Martial Art* (New City, N.Y.: Sweet Ch'i Press, 1999), 119; Yu Dayou, *Sword Classic* (1565), in Wells, *Scholar Boxer*, 104; Chang Naizhou, in Wells, *Scholar Boxer*, 121. The oldest extant martial arts training manual, Qi Jiguang's *New Book on Effective Military Techniques*, which became the major source of later taiji techniques and internal boxing, reproduces the entire *Sword Classic* without attribution. The author, Yu Dayou, also says, "Using the staff is like reading the Four Books," that is, the basic works of Confucian philosophy (quoted in Lorge, *Chinese Martial Arts*, 182).

38. Munenori, *Book of Family Traditions*, 106–7, 114; Gichin Funakoshi, *The Essence of Karate*, trans. Richard Berger (Tokyo: Kodansha, 2010), 68.

39. Basil Henry Liddell Hart, *Strategy: The Indirect Approach*, 5th ed. (London: Faber & Faber, 1967), 328.

40. *Lieh-tzu*, trans. Eva Wong (Boston: Shambhala, 2001), 58. On archery, see also Lorge, *Chinese Martial Arts*, 52.

41. The *Daodejing* seems to have reached its final form by the late third century B.C.E. See William G. Boltz, "Lao tzu Tao te ching," in *Early Chinese Texts: A Bibliographical Guide*, ed. Michael Loewe (Berkeley, Calif.: Society for the Study of Early China, 1993), 269–92. My citations follow *The Daodejing of Laozi*, trans. Philip J. Ivanhoe (Indianapolis: Hackett, 2003), though I also consulted the bilingual *Dao De Jing: A Philosophical Translation*, trans. Roger T. Ames and David L. Hall (New York: Ballantine Books, 2003). Subsequent references are cited in the text, with the abbreviation DDJ.

42. A. C. Graham, "The Origins of the Legend of Lao Tan," in *Studies in Chinese Philosophy and Philosophical Literature* (Albany: State University of New York Press, 1990), 119. The story about Confucius and Laozi is recounted in Sima Qian, *Records of the Historian*, chap. 63. The Confucian *Record of Rites* (*Liji*, 7.33) has Lao Dan correct Confucius on funeral rites. See Michael David Kaulana Ing, *The Dysfunction of Ritual in Early Confucianism* (Oxford: Oxford University Press, 2012), 142–43.

43. Jigaro Kano [correctly Kanō Jigorō], "Jiujutsu [*sic*], the Old Samurai Art of Fighting Without Weapons, Part 1. Origins" (1888), trans. T. Lindsay, http:// www.fightingarts.com/reading/article.php?id=414 (accessed September 30, 2014).

44. Sunzi, *Art of War*, chaps. 3, 5, in *Seven Military Classics*, ed. Sawyer, 161, 165.

45. Kohn, *Zhuangzi*, 86–87; Kennedy and Guo, *Chinese Martial Arts Manuals*, 29.

46. Gao, The Stretching Book, 167.

47. The *Inward Training* (*Neiye*) is translated in Harold D. Roth, *Original Tao: Inward Training (Nei-yeh) and the Foundations of Taoist Mysticism* (New York: Columbia University Press, 1999), 86, 66, 92.

48. Zaou Shouzheng, *Guanzi* (Beijing, 1989), in Roth, *Original Tao*, 12.

49. On *wuwei*, see the authoritative study by Edward Slingerland, *Effortless Action: Wu-Wei as Conceptual Metaphor and Spiritual Ideal in Early China* (New York: Oxford University Press, 2003). Another valuable study is François Jullien,

A Treatise on Efficacy: Between Western and Chinese Thinking, trans. Janet Lloyd (Honolulu: University of Hawai'i Press, 2004). I elaborate on my understanding of *wuwei* in *Vanishing into Things*, chap. 2.

50. On *xü*, see Yi Wu, *Chinese Philosophical Terms* (Lanham, Md.: University Press of America, 1986), 82.

51. Guo Xiang, on *Zhuangzi* 3.2 (Z 166); Shi Deqing, on *Zhuangzi* 1.13 (Z 134).

52. Li I-ye, "Essentials of the Practice of Form and Push Hands," in *Essence of T'ai Chi Ch'uan*, ed. Lo et al., 81.

53. Robert W. Smith, *Martial Musings: A Portrayal of Martial Arts in the Twentieth Century* (Erie, Pa.: Via Media, 1999), 321, and *Hsing-I: Chinese Mind-Body Boxing* (Berkeley, Calif.: North Atlantic Books, 2003), 21.

54. "Yang Family Forty Chapters," 83; Wu Chengching, "Treatise on Boxing," in Wile, *Lost T'ai-chi Classics*, 83, 45. The idea of "really seeing the little things" is pervasive in Chinese tradition—for example, these words from *Guanzi* describing a sage: "From the inconspicuous he hits upon brightness" (*Guanzi*, trans. Zhai Jianyue [Guilin: Guangxi Normal University Press, 2005], chap. 51). I discuss this theme at length in *Vanishing into Things*.

55. "Yang Family Forty Chapters," 89, 81; Munenori, *Book of Family Traditions*, 144, 134–135.

56. Munenori, *Book of Family Traditions*, 105; Lawrence A. Kane and Kris Wilder, *The Little Black Book of Violence: What Every Young Man Needs to Know About Fighting* (Wolfeboro, N.H.: YMAA Publication Center, 2009), 114.

57. I draw from Komjathy, *Daoist Tradition*; Fabrizio Pregadio, *Great Clarity: Daoism and Alchemy in Early Medieval China* (Stanford, Calif.: Stanford University Press, 2006); and Isabelle Robinet, *The World Upside Down: Essays on Taoist Internal Alchemy*, ed. and trans. Fabrizio Pregadio (Mountain View, Calif.: Golden Elixir Press, 2011). Joseph Needham recounts the scientific and technical fabric of Chinese alchemy in prodigious detail in four book-length parts, "Spagyrical Discovery and Invention," of his magisterial *Science and Civilization in China*, vol. 5, *Chemistry and Chemical Technology* (Cambridge: Cambridge University Press, 1983).

58. Mu Changzhao, quoted in Robinet, *World Upside Down*, 94; Pregadio, *Great Clarity*, 132.

59. Robinet, *World Upside Down*, 36, 88.

60. Kennedy and Guo, *Chinese Martial Arts Manuals*, 80. On the martial arts and China's private security business, see Kennedy and Guo, *Chinese Martial Arts Manuals*, 143. On the usual understanding of "internal" and "external" martial arts, see Thomas A. Green, "External vs. Internal Chinese Martial Arts," in *Martial Arts of the World: An Encyclopedia*, ed. Thomas A. Green (Santa Barbara, Calif.: ABC-CLIO, 2001), 1:119–21.

61. "Yang Family Forty Chapters," 75, 89.

62. Chang Naizhou, quoted in Wile, *Ta'i Chi's Ancestors*, 95; *Romance of the Three Kingdoms*, in Wells, *Scholar Boxer*, 8.

63. Postscript to the "Yang Family Forty Chapters," in Wile, *Lost T'ai-chi Classics*, 45–46.

64. Stanley E. Henning, "Ge Hong: Famous Daoist Thinker and Practical Martial Artist," *Journal of the Asian Martial Arts* 16, no. 3 (2007): 22–25.

65. Komjathy, *Daoist Tradition*, 191, 192, 296; Pregadio, *Great Clarity*, 203.

66. I draw from Lorge, *Chinese Martial Arts*, 16; and Stanley E. Henning, "The Chinese Martial Arts in Historical Perspective," *Military Affairs* 45, no. 4 (1981): 173–79. Henning notes the record of a title, "Six Chapters on *shoubo*," in the *Hanshu yiwenzhi*, ca. 90 C.E. See Stanley E. Henning, "Review of Ma Mingda, *Discourses of the Sword*," *China Review International* 11 (2004): 141–45.

67. I draw from Michael Loewe, "The Western Han Army: Organization, Leadership, and Operation," 65–89; and Robin Yates, "Law and the Military in Early China," 23–44, both in *Military Culture in Imperial China*, ed. Nicola Di Cosmo (Cambridge, Mass.: Harvard University Press, 2009). Conscription was periodically suspended and the army demobilized. On village martial arts, see Kennedy and Guo, *Chinese Martial Arts Manuals*, 136, 144.

68. Boretz, *Gods, Ghosts, and Gangsters*, 53. I also drew from Lorge, *Chinese Martial Arts*, 8.

69. "The Significance of the Rite of Archery," in *The Book of Rites*, ed. Xu Chao, trans. Lao An (Jinan: Shandong Friendship Press, 2000), 409. I also draw from Lorge, *Chinese Martial Arts*, 199, 201.

70. Wang Yangming, quoted in Confucius, *Analects*, 66;."Significance of the Rite of Archery," 411.

71. Lorge, *Chinese Martial Arts*, 38, 52, 121, 71, 26, 31. The Han dictionary is cited in Lewis, *Sanctioned Violence*, 228. The five excellences of archery come from a Han ritual text cited by Slingerland, in Confucius, *Analects*, 19n.

72. Lorge, *Chinese Martial Arts*, 184, 33, 35. The *New Book on Effective Military Techniques* is cited in Kennedy and Guo, *Chinese Martial Arts Manuals*, 176.

73. The source of the story about Confucius is a Han musical text quoted in Confucius, *Analects*, 121.

74. *Mengzi, with Selections from Traditional Commentaries*, trans. Bryan W. Van Norden (Indianapolis: Hackett, 2008), 4A14, 2B1, 7B4.

75. *Xunzi*, trans. John Knoblock, Library of Chinese Classics (Changsha: Hunan People's Publishing House, 1999), chap. 15; *Record of Rites* and *Zuo Commentary*, in *Art of War*, ed. Mair, 48.

76. Quoted in Yu Kam-por, "Confucian Views on War," *Dao* 9, no. 1 (2010): 109.

77. Confucius, in the *Record of Rites*, in Yu, "Confucian Views on War," 100; I also draw from 109; and Mark E. Lewis, "The Just War in Early China," in *The Ethics of War in Ancient Asia: A Comparative Perspective*, ed. Torkel Brekke (London: Routledge, 2005), 185–200. On the European "just war" theory, see Gregory M. Reichberg, Henrik Syse, and Endre Begby, eds., *The Ethics of War: Classic and Contemporary Readings* (Malden, Mass.: Blackwell, 2006).

78. Philip J. Ivanhoe, "Mengzi's Conception of Courage," *Dao* 5, no. 2 (2006): 221–34. Aristotle says that a man "who faces and who fears the right things with the right aim, in the right way and at the right time, and who feels confident under the corresponding conditions, is brave; for the brave man feels and acts according

to the merits of the case and in whatever way reason directs" (*Nicomachean Ethics,* 1115a, in *The Basic Works of Aristotle,* ed. R. McKeon [New York: Random House, 1941]). All subsequent references to Aristotle are from this edition.

79. Lorge, *Chinese Martial Arts,* 72. On the limitations of the *wen/wu* dichotomy, see Barend J. Ter Haar, "Rethinking Violence in Chinese Culture," in *Meanings of Violence: A Cross Cultural Perspective,* ed. Göran Aijmer and Jon Abbink (Oxford: Berg, 2000); and Boretz, *Gods, Ghosts, and Gangsters,* 40–56.

80. *Jing Fa,* cited in Lewis, *Sanctified Violence,* 316n.140; *Zuo Zhuan Commentary,* cited in Anthony L. Schmieg, *Watching Your Back: Chinese Martial Arts and Traditional Medicine* (Honolulu: University of Hawai'i Press, 2005), 17.

81. I draw from Nicola Di Cosmo, "Introduction," 3–5, 8, 14–15; David A. Graff, "Narrative Maneuvers: The Representation of Battle in Tang Historical Writing," 148, 159, 161; and Jonathan Skaff, "Tang Military Culture and Its Inner Asian Influences," 175, all in *Military Culture in Imperial China,* ed. Di Cosmo.

82. I draw from Don J. Wyatt, "Unsung Men of War: Acculturated Embodiments of the Martial Ethos in the Song Dynasty," 192–218; and Kathleen Ryor, "*Wen* and *Wu* in Elite Cultural Practices During the Late Ming," 219–42, both in *Military Culture in Imperial China,* ed. Di Cosmo; Johnston, *Cultural Realism,* 213, 183, 216; Lorge, *Chinese Martial Arts,* 180.

83. Tan Lun, quoted in Ryor, "*Wen* and *Wu,*" 223; Song Maocheng, *Preface to Mr. Qian's Record of Swords,* "*Wen* and *Wu,*" 236.

84. I draw from Joanna Waley-Cohn, "Militarization of Culture in Eighteenth-Century China," 278–95; and S. R. Gilbert, "Mengzi's Art of War: The Kangxi Emperor Reforms the Qing Military Examinations," 243–56, both in *Military Culture in Imperial China,* ed. Di Cosmo.

85. I draw from Charles Holcombe, "Theater of Combat: A Critical Look at the Chinese Martial Arts," *The Historian* 52, no. 3 (1990): 411–31; Lorge, *Chinese Martial Arts,* 159, 162, 177; and Kennedy and Guo, *Chinese Martial Arts Manuals,* 100.

86. I draw from Sabrina Qiong Yu, *Jet Li: Chinese Masculinity and Transnational Film Stardom* (Edinburgh: Edinburgh University Press, 2012), 33–34, 50, 63; and Kennedy and Guo, *Chinese Martial Arts Manuals,* 74–77. See also Stephen Teo, *Chinese Martial Arts Cinema: The Wuxia Tradition* (Edinburgh: Edinburgh University Press, 2009).

87. *Spring and Autumn Annals of the Kingdoms of Wu and Yue,* in Stanley E. Henning, "The Maiden of Yue: Fount of Chinese Martial Arts Theory," *Journal of the Asian Martial Arts* 16, no. 3 (2007): 26–29. The interpolations are Henning's, though I have edited them. This passage is also cited by Wile, who says that it "contains all the elements of strategy, internal energetics, psychology, and *yin-yang* theory we associate with later *taiji* writings" (*Ta'i Chi's Ancestors,* 4).

88. Olivia Milburn, "The Weapons of Kings: A New Perspective on Southern Sword Legends in Early China," *Journal of the American Oriental Society* 128, no. 3 (2008): 423–37, and *The Glory of Yue: An Annotated Translation of the "Yuejue Shu"* (Leiden: Brill, 2010). The Maiden of Yue is also known as Nanlin Chu (South Forest Virgin) and supposedly lived around 500 B.C.E. Wells attributes

the *Spring and Autumn Annals of the Kingdoms of Wu and Yue* to Zhao Ye, ca. 150 C.E., of Zhejiang, in *Scholar Boxer*, 256n.44. Assuming that the attribution is credible, there is an earlier reference to Nanlin Chu and her school by the Han scholar Wang Chong (first century C.E.), who lauds the school's swordsmanship.

89. *Xunzi*, chap. 22; *Mengzi*, 5B1; Chang Naizhou, in Wells, *Scholar Boxer*, 114.

90. The "Epitaph for Wang Zhengnan," quoted in Wile, *Ta'i Chi's Ancestors*, 53. I also draw from Lorge, *Chinese Martial Arts*, 192.

91. Wells, *Scholar Boxer*, 3, 25–26, 42, 49–50. The *Change Muscles Classic* (*Yijinjing*), from which Chang quotes, was set down in 1624 by a Daoist author, Zi Ning, and apocryphally attributed to Bodhidharma. See Kennedy and Guo, *Chinese Martial Arts Manuals*, 95.

92. Wells, *Scholar Boxer*, 47, 54, 126, also 12, 16; *Mengzi* is 2A2.

93. Kennedy and Guo, *Martial Arts Manuals*, 108; Wile, "Taijiquan and Daoism," 21. On the *Jingwu* Association, see Brian Kennedy and Elizabeth Guo, *Jingwu: The School That Transformed Kung Fu* (Berkeley, Calif.: Blue Snake Books, 2010).

94. Quoted in Kennedy and Guo, *Martial Arts Manuals*, 106–7. When modern-day taiji practitioners say that their art is primarily for health and longevity rather than violence, they are paraphrasing Sun Lutang, whom these authors call "the most influential author in martial arts writing" (186).

95. Wile, *Lost T'ai-chi Classics*, 123; Zheng Manqing, *Thirteen Treatises*, 34–35, 59, 23, 35. As did Chang Naizhou in the eighteenth century, he alludes to the *Mengzi*, 2A2.

96. For the details of Xunzi's program, see Ori Tavor, "Xunzi's Theory of Ritual Revisited: Reading Ritual as Corporal Technology," *Dao* 12, no. 3 (2013): 313–30.

97. *Xunzi*, chap. 2, in Tavor, "Xunzi's Theory of Ritual Revisited," 318.

98. Schmieg, *Watching Your Back*, 1, 83; *Xunzi*, 469. Schmieg says that a "Daoist worldview shaped the Chinese martial disciplines" and that "the most dynamic developments of the Chinese martial arts were firmly established more than a thousand years before [the Buddha] was born," that is, circa 1500 B.C.E., or the late Shang dynasty (*Watching Your Back*, 142, 162). The hoary antiquity of Chinese martial arts—their systems and styles, creeds, oaths, and esoteric canons—is a staple of *wuxia* lore: "Chinese martial arts must be as old as Chinese written history, maybe even older, perhaps a lot older" (T. L. Tsim, foreword to Jin Yong [Louis Cha], *Fox Volant of the Snowy Mountain*, trans. Olivia Mok, 2nd ed. [Hong Kong: Chinese University Press, 1996], ix).

2. FROM DUALISM TO THE DARWINIAN BODY

1. Homer, *Odyssey*, book 8, lines 145–48, quoted in Michael B. Poliakoff, *Combat Sports in the Ancient World: Competition, Violence, and Culture* (New Haven, Conn.: Yale University Press, 1982), 105. I also draw from David Potter, *The*

Victor's Crown: Ancient Sport from Homer to Byzantium (Oxford: Oxford University Press, 2012), 20, 23; and Werner Jaeger, *Paideia: The Ideals of Greek Culture*, trans. Gilbert Highet (New York: Oxford University Press, 1945), 1:206–7.

2. Thomas F. Scanlon, *Eros and Greek Athletics* (New York: Oxford University Press, 2002), chap. 1; Jaeger, *Paideia*, 91; C. M. Bowra, "Xenophanes and the Olympic Games," in *Problems in Greek Poetry* (Oxford: Clarendon Press, 1953), 23–25.

3. Pausanius, in Debra Hawhee, *Bodily Arts: Rhetoric and Athletics in Ancient Greece* (Austin: University of Texas Press, 2004), 38. On Plato's wrestling, see Diogenes Laertius, *Lives of the Philosophers* 3.4; and Scanlon, *Eros and Greek Athletics*, 204–5.

4. Poliakoff, *Combat Sports*, 80–82; Pindar, quoted in Poliakoff, *Combat Sports*, 62. After the addition of *pankration*, some events were opened to boys, and races in armor and with mule carts were added but soon discontinued. See Potter, *Victor's Crown*, 41.

5. Sophocles, *Electra*, ll.75–76; Philostratus, *Peri Gymnastikes* (ca. 220 C.E.), 14.269, quoted in Hawhee, *Bodily Arts*, 84, also 72, 73, 76; Poliakoff, *Combat Sports*, 12.

6. Plato, *Protagoras*, 329e, in *Complete Works*, ed. John M. Cooper (Indianapolis: Hackett, 1997). All further citations from Plato's works are from this edition. I also draw from Hawhee, *Bodily Arts*, 76, 27, 28.

7. Potter, *Victor's Crown*, 77; Scanlon, *Eros and Athletics*, 207.

8. H. I. Marrou, *A History of Education in Antiquity*, trans. George Lamb (New York: Mentor Books, 1964), 25, 38, 4, 65, 69, 107, 165; Poliakoff, *Combat Sports*, 105–7.

9. Quoted in Steven G. Miller, *Arete: Ancient Writers, Papyri, and Inscriptions on the History and Ideals of Greek Athletics and Games* (Chicago: Ares, 1979), 44.

10. Quoted in Hawhee, *Bodily Arts*, 23; and Scanlon, *Eros and Athletics*, 18; Jaeger, *Paideia*, 206, also 208.

11. *The Odes of Pindar*, trans. Geoffrey Seymour Conway (London: Dent, 1975), 235.

12. Quoted in Jaeger, *Paideia*, 210; *Odes of Pindar*, 235.

13. Plato, *The Republic*, 410b, 411e. See also Plato, *Protagoras*, 326b; and Daniel A. Dombrowski, "Plato and Athletics," *Journal of the Philosophy of Sport* 6 (1979): 29–38.

14. Isocrates, *Panegyrikos*, 4.1, quoted in Poliakoff, *Combat Sports*, 142.

15. Quoted in Miller, *Arete*, 53; "Introduction," in *The Cynics: The Cynic Movement in Antiquity and Its Legacy*, ed. R. Bracht Branham and Marie-Odile Goulet-Cazé (Berkeley: University of California Press, 1996), 26.

16. Galen, *Exhortations for Medicine*, quoted in Scanlon, *Eros and Athletics*, 15; and Poliakoff, *Combat Sports*, 93–94. Earlier medical criticism of athletics in the Hippocratic *On Regimen in Health* says that an athlete's nature is unstable and "turns to extremes: in these types of bodies a good condition flourishes only for a short while" (Brooke Holmes, *The Symptom and the Subject: The Emergence of the Physical Body in Ancient Greece* [Princeton, N.J.: Princeton University Press, 2010], 186).

17. Euripides, *Autolykos*, fragment 282 (ca. 420 B.C.E.), quoted in Miller, *Arete*, 95, 96.

18. Jaeger, *Paideia*, 174. The *Autolykos* fragment is not the only instance of Euripides imitating Xenophanes, whose distinctive take on the gods he copies in his *Heracles:* "For the god, if he be truly god, lacks for nothing. [To say otherwise is] the wretched tales of singers" (quoted in W. K. C. Guthrie, *A History of Greek Philosophy* [Cambridge: Cambridge University Press, 1962], 1:373).

19. Xenophanes of Colophon, *Fragments*, ed. and trans. J. H. Lesher (Toronto: University of Toronto Press, 1992), fragments 34–35, 27; Lesher, in Xenophanes, *Fragments*, 179, 182–83. On rationalism and its inception in Greek medicine, see Michael Frede, "The Ancient Empiricists," in *Essays in Ancient Philosophy* (Minneapolis: University of Minnesota Press, 1987).

20. Xenophanes, *Fragments*, fragments 18, 11.

21. Xenophanes, fragment 2, in John Burnet, *Early Greek Philosophy* (London: Black, 1920); Bowra, "Xenophanes and the Olympic Games," in *Problems in Greek Poetry*, 18. According to Bowra, Xenophanes's lines were probably written around 550 to 520 B.C.E. (16). In Lesher's translation, the crucial line referring to *sophie* reads: "For our expertise [Diels: *unsere Weisheit*] is better than the strength of men and horses. But this practice [athletic competition] makes no sense nor is it right to prefer strength to this good expertise" (Xenophanes, *Fragments*, 15).

22. Lesher, in Xenophanes, *Fragments*, 61; Jaeger, *Paideia*, 173–74. "Though it is worthwhile to attain the good for an individual it is finer and more god-like to do it for the people and the city" (Aristotle, *Nichomachean Ethics*, 1094b; see also Plato, *Republic*, 465d).

23. Jaeger, *Paideia*, 207.

24. Quoted in Cicero, *Tusculan Disputations*, 5.3, cited in Andrea Wilson Nightingale, *Spectacles of Truth in Classical Greek Philosophy: Theoria in Its Cultural Context* (Cambridge: Cambridge University Press, 2004), 17.

25. Quoted in Nightingale, *Spectacles of Truth*, 85, also 40, 46, 52–53. For an account of these mysteries, including the crucial role of vision and initiation, see Walter Burkert, *Ancient Mystery Cults* (Cambridge, Mass.: Harvard University Press, 1987).

26. Nightingale, *Spectacles of Truth*, 77, 78, 49, 69, 70.

27. Plato, *Republic*, 495e, 590c; Aristotle, *Politics*, 1278a; Nightingale, *Spectacles of Truth*, 120.

28. Paul S. MacDonald, *History of the Concept of Mind: Speculations About Soul, Mind, and Spirit from Homer to Hume* (Aldershot: Ashgate, 2003), 147, 349–52; David B. Claus, *Toward the Soul: An Inquiry into the Meaning of Psyche Before Plato* (New Haven, Conn.: Yale University Press, 1981).

29. Walter Burkert, *Lore and Science of Ancient Pythagoreanism*, trans. E. L. Minar (Cambridge, Mass.: Harvard University Press, 1972), 163. Following E. R. Dodds, *The Greeks and the Irrational* (Berkeley: University of California Press, 1956), Burkert suggested a source for the new thinking about the soul in the shamanistic traditions of Central Asia. However, he apparently thinks that an Indian source is more likely, agreeing with Charles H. Kahn, *Pythagoras and the Pythago-*

reans (Indianapolis: Hackett, 2001), 19. He may have changed his mind too quickly, as Carlo Ginzberg has documented the Eurasian shamanistic influence on Pythagoreanism, in *Ecstasies: Deciphering the Witches' Sabbath*, trans. Raymond Rosenthal (New York: Pantheon, 1991).

30. Plato, *Charmides*, 156e; Claus, *Toward the Soul*, 179–80.

31. Plato, *Theaetetus*, 183c; Bowra, "The Proem of Parmenides," in *Problems in Greek Poetry*, 39–51.

32. Patricia Curd, "Thought and Body in Parmenides," in *Parmenides, Venerable and Awesome*, ed. Néstor-Luis Cordero (Las Vegas: Parmenides, 2011), 115–34.

33. Holmes, *Symptom and the Subject*, 190.

34. Plato, *Republic*, 405b; Holmes, *Symptom and the Subject*, 121, 190–91, 194, 275, 104. In *Phaedo*, Plato likens the *soma* to the strings and frame of the lyre; harmony is *asomatos*, incorporeal, also invisible, beautiful, and divine (86a).

35. Plato, *Phaedo*, 65b–c, 66b. Whether this is the voice of Socrates or Plato's ventriloquism is impossible to say. Xenophon, who also knew Socrates and was no Platonist, remembers him saying, "You may rest assured that there is no kind of contest, and no undertaking in which you will be the worse off by keeping your body in better shape" (Xenophon, *Memorabilia*, quoted in Potter, *Victor's Crown*, 119).

36. Plato, *Phaedo*, 82d–e, 66b, 64a.

37. Plato, *Alcibiades*, 128c.

38. Plato, *Alcibiades*, 131a, 131b, 129d–e, 130e, 133c.

39. Aristotle, *De Anima*, 412b; *Parts of Animals*, 645b; *De Anima* 407b; and *Politics*, 1258b, 1339a. After Aristotle, ethical philosophers usually spoke of three goods: body, soul, and externals. The core Aristotelian position was that happiness requires all three and began to change in a Stoic direction favoring rational activity only from the first century C.E. Cicero conceded bodily and external goods only on the condition that they "lie prostrate on the ground and are only called goods because they should be 'taken,' while those other divine goods [that is, of the soul] spread far and wide and right up to heaven" (quoted in Brad Inwood, *Ethics After Aristotle* [Cambridge, Mass.: Harvard University Press, 2014], 61).

40. Plotinus, *The Enneads*, trans. Stephen MacKenna, ed. John Dillon (Harmondsworth: Penguin, 1991), 1.1.3, 1.6.5, 1.6.8; Porphyry, *Porphyry's Letter to His Wife Marcella Concerning the Life of Philosophy and the Ascent to the Gods*, trans. Alice Zimmern (Grand Rapids, Mich.: Phanes Press, 1986), 44.

41. Plato, *Sophist* 245e. The propriety of describing these early Greek philosophers as "idealists" is explained in Jeremy Dunham, Iain Hamilton Grant, and Sean Watson, *Idealism: The History of a Philosophy* (Montreal: McGill–Queen's University Press, 2011).

42. *Empedocles: The Extant Fragments*, trans. M. R. Wright (New Haven, Conn.: Yale University Press, 1981), 167; Democritus, *Ancilla to the Pre-Socratic Philosophers*, trans. Kathleen Freeman (Cambridge, Mass.: Harvard University Press, 1948), fragment 156. Leucippus is usually named as a coinventor of atomism. We know nothing about him except that he has always been associated with Democritus. Already in antiquity, Epicurus doubted that Leucippus existed. Having

made the customary association, I proceed as if atomism were the invention of Democritus.

43. C. C. W. Taylor, "Pleasure, Knowledge, and Sensation in Democritus," 1–22, and "The Atomists," 181–203, in *Pleasure, Mind, and Soul: Selected Papers in Ancient Philosophy* (Oxford: Clarendon Press, 2008).

44. Aristotle, *Physics*, 252a–b.

45. Plato, *Laws*, 888b–e. Democritus's view of atheism is hard to make out. No extant fragment expresses doubt about the gods, only doubt about our knowledge of them. Yet the system of atomism forecloses immortality, which is the only quality distinguishing gods from mortals.

46. I draw from Samuel Sambursky, *Physics of the Stoics* (London: Routledge & Kegan Paul, 1959); and Jacques Brunschwig, "Stoic Metaphysics," in *The Cambridge Companion to the Stoics*, ed. Brad Inwood (Cambridge: Cambridge University Press, 2003), 206–32. Stoic ontology includes the paradoxical incorporeals, which are specifically said not to be bodies, indeed, not to be beings (*onta*), but nevertheless to be something (*to ti*). The usual list includes place, void, and time.

47. Stoic fragment, SVF 2.625, in Michael J. White, "Stoic Natural Philosophy (Physics and Cosmology)," in *Cambridge Companion to the Stoics*, ed. Inwood, 141. Eternal return was already a Pythagorean teaching before the Stoics: "Whatever happens will occur again according to certain cycles and nothing is absolutely new" (Porphyry, *Life of Pythagoras*, 19) and "If one believes the Pythagoreans, things recur numerically the same; and I, with this staff in my hand, will be speaking to you seated in this manner, and everything else will be the same" (Eudemus, fragment 88) (both quoted in Kahn, *Pythagoras and the Pythagoreans*, 11).

48. Aristotle, *Generation and Corruption*, 324a–325a.

49. Plato, *Laws*, book 10. The story about Plato and Democritus is recounted in a fragment from Aristoxenus (fragment 131, Diels-Kranz 54A2).

50. Catherine Wilson, *Epicureanism at the Origins of Modernity* (Oxford: Clarendon Press, 2008).

51. Although Abraham Trembley (1700–1784) is now the least known of the figures I mention, he was important in his time and to the history of modern materialism. He was an early microscopist, whose most famous observations concerned a freshwater polyp, *Chlorohydra viridissima*. Among his experiments, he cut off some of the creature's appendages, which then grew back. Many of his eighteenth-century readers, including La Mettrie, Diderot, and Pierre-Louis Maupertuis, thought that if so humble a machine as this polyp can regenerate living members, then we have hardly begun to understand what a body can do. Trembley's results thus became an important argument among materialists for extending new powers to matter.

52. For the new, nonreductive materialism, "inorganic matter is much more variable and creative than we ever imagined . . . a single matter-energy undergoing phase transitions of various kinds, with each new layer of accumulated stuff simply enriching the reservoir of nonlinear dynamics and nonlinear combinatorics

available for the generation of novel structures and processes" (Manuel De Landa, *A Thousand Years of Nonlinear History* [New York: Zone Books, 2000], 16, 22). See also Jane Bennett, *Vibrant Matter: A Political Ecology of Things* (Durham, N.C.: Duke University Press, 2010); and Diana Coole and Samantha Frost, eds., *New Materialisms: Ontology, Agency, and Politics* (Durham, N.C.: Duke University Press, 2010).

53. Baruch Spinoza, *Ethics*, in *A Spinoza Reader*, ed. and trans. Edwin Curley (Princeton, N.J.: Princeton University Press, 1994), part 2, prop. 16 (corol. 2), 129; prop. 26, 134; prop. 23, 133; prop. 19 (dem.), 131.

54. Friedrich Nietzsche, *The Gay Science*, trans. Walter Kaufmann (New York: Vintage, 1974), sec. 57. Nietzsche quarreled with Darwin about the value of adaptation, which, to Nietzsche, helps the weak. Strong individuals usually do not survive. See Friedrich Nietzsche, "Anti-Darwin," in *Twilight of the Idols, or How to Philosophize with a Hammer*, in *The Anti-Christ, Ecce Homo, Twilight of the Idols, and Other Writings*, ed. Aaron Ridley and Judith Norman (Cambridge: Cambridge University Press, 2005), 199. On Nietzsche's relation to Darwin, see Dirk R. Johnson, *Nietzsche's Anti-Darwinism* (Cambridge: Cambridge University Press, 2010).

55. William James, *Essays in Radical Empiricism*, ed. Ralph Barton Perry (New York: Dutton, 1971), 91n.; Maurice Merleau-Ponty, *The Phenomenology of Perception*, trans. Colin Smith (London: Routledge & Kegan Paul, 1962), 170; Bruno Latour, "How to Talk About the Body," *Body & Society* 10, nos. 2–3 (2004): 209, 206, 225; Spinoza, *Ethics*, part 3, prop. 2 (scholium), 155. I discuss this passage in chapter 4.

56. Gilles Deleuze, *Cinema 2: The Time-Image*, trans. Hugh Tomlinson and Robert Galeta (Minneapolis: University of Minnesota Press, 1989), 189.

57. Nietzsche, "Skirmishes of an Untimely Man," sec. 47, in *Twilight of the Idols*, 221. See also Alfred I. Tauber, "A Typology of Nietzsche's Biology," *Biology and Philosophy* 9 (1994): 25–44; and Scott H. Podolsky and Alfred I. Tauber, "Nietzsche's Conception of Health: The Idealization of Struggle," in *Nietzsche, Epistemology, and Philosophy of Science*, ed. Babette Babich (Dordrecht: Kluwer, 1999), 2:299–311.

58. Nancy Scheper-Hughes and Margaret M. Lock, "The Mindful Body: A Prolegomenon to Future Work in Medical Anthropology," *Medical Anthropology Quarterly*, n.s., 1, no. 1 (1987): 6–41. The expression "Darwinian body" is from Maxine Sheets-Johnstone, *The Roots of Thinking* (Philadelphia: Temple University Press, 1990).

59. Charles Darwin, *The Expression of the Emotions in Man and Animals*, 3rd ed. (Oxford: Oxford University Press, 1998), 61, fig. 10, and *The Formation of Vegetable Mould Through the Action of Worms, with Observations on Their Habits*, quoted in Maxine Sheets-Johnstone, *The Corporeal Turn: An Interdisciplinary Reader* (Charlottesville, Va.: Imprint Academic, 2009), 28; Martin Wells, *Lower Animals* (New York: McGraw-Hill, 1968), 80; Sheets-Johnstone, *Corporeal Turn*, 310.

60. Sheets-Johnstone, *Corporeal Turn*, 151, also 159, 164, 167; Maxine Sheets-Johnstone, *The Primacy of Movement*, 2nd ed. (Amsterdam: Benjamins, 2011), 463.

61. Sheets-Johnstone, *Primacy of Movement*, 128, and *Roots of Thinking*, 123, also 29, 32, 126, 308.

62. Mark Johnson, *The Meaning of the Body: Aesthetics of Human Understanding* (Chicago: University of Chicago Press, 2007), 21, 119; Andy Clark, *Supersizing the Mind: Embodiment, Action, and Cognitive Extension* (New York: Oxford University Press, 2008), 14, 30, 31, 42. See also George Lakoff and Mark Johnson, *Philosophy in the Flesh: The Embodied Mind and Its Challenge to Western Thought* (New York: Basic Books, 1999).

63. Michel Henry, *Philosophy and the Phenomenology of the Body*, trans. Girard Etzkorn (The Hague: Nijhoff, 1975), 60; Gabor Csepregi, *The Clever Body* (Calgary: University of Calgary Press, 2006), 18.

64. Richard Shusterman, *Body Consciousness: A Philosophy of Mindfulness and Somaesthetics* (Cambridge: Cambridge University Press, 2008), 19; F. M. Alexander, quoted in Michael T. Gelb, *Body Learning: An Introduction to the Alexander Technique* (New York: Holt, 1994), 53.

65. Shaun Gallagher, *How the Body Shapes the Mind* (Oxford: Clarendon Press, 2005), 152.

66. On mirror neurons, see Giacomo Rizzolatti, Leonardo Fogassi, and Vittorio Gallese, "Neurophysiological Mechanisms Underlying the Understanding and Imitation of Action," *Nature Neuroscience Review* 2 (2001): 661–70; and Marc Jeannerod, "The Representing Brain: Neural Correlates of Motor Intention and Imagery," *Behavioral and Brain Sciences* 17 (1994): 187–245.

67. Gallagher, *How the Body Shapes the Mind*, 159, also 76, 83.

68. Susan L. Hurley, *Consciousness in Action* (Cambridge, Mass.: Harvard University Press, 1998); James J. Gibson, *The Ecological Approach to Visual Perception* (Hillsdale, N.J.: Erlbaum, 1986); Gerald Edelman and Vernon B. Mountcastle, *The Mindful Brain: Cortical Organization and the Group-Selective Theory of Higher Brain Function* (Cambridge, Mass.: MIT Press, 1978), 9; Roger Sperry, "Neurology and the Mind-Brain Problem," *American Scientist* 40 (1952): 301. Well in advance of this clinical conclusion, the idea of perception as virtual action was an important thesis of Henri Bergson's *Matter and Memory* (1896).

69. *The Fragments of Parmenides*, ed. and trans. A. H. Coxon, rev. ed., ed. Richard McKirahan (Las Vegas: Parmenides Publishing, 2009), fragment 7.

70. John Dewey, *Human Nature and Conduct*, in *Middle Works*, ed. Jo Ann Boydston (Carbondale: Southern Illinois University Press, 1982), 14:51–52, 205; Csepregi, *Clever Body*, 51–54, 57; Gallagher, *How the Body Shapes the Mind*, 60–61; Paul Ricoeur, *Freedom and Nature: The Voluntary and the Involuntary*, trans. Erazim V. Kohák (Evanston, Ill.: Northwestern University Press, 1966), 289.

71. Pindar, Second Pythian Ode, line 72: *genoi, hoios essi mathon*.

72. Plato, *Sophist*, 246a–b, 247d–e. Body as a power to act (rather than a homogeneous stuff) was already the idea of Gorgias in the late fifth-century *Encomium to Helen*, in which he attributes a *soma* to *logos* in virtue of its *dunamis*.

73. Gilles Deleuze and Félix Guattari, *A Thousand Plateaus: Capitalism and Schizophrenia*, trans. Brian Massumi (Minneapolis: University of Minnesota Press, 1987), 400.

74. Chang Naizhou, in Marnix Wells, *Scholar Boxer: Chang Naizhou's Theory of Internal Martial Arts* (Berkeley, Calif.: Blue Snake Books, 2005), 74; Miyamoto Musashi, *The Book of Five Rings*, trans. Thomas Cleary (Boston: Shambhala, 2003), 84. See also Loren W. Christensen and Wim Demeere, *Timing in the Fighting Arts: Your Guide to Winning in the Ring and Surviving on the Street* (Santa Fe, N.M.: Turtle Press, 2004).

75. Deleuze and Guattari, "Treatise on Nomadology: The War Machine," in *Thousand Plateaus*, 351–423; Arthur Waldron, *The Great Wall of China: From History to Myth* (Cambridge: Cambridge University Press, 1990); John E. Wills Jr., *Mountain of Fame: Portraits in Chinese History* (Princeton, N.J.: Princeton University Press, 1994), 237. On the martial arts culture as a nomadic counterpoint to the authority of the civil bureaucratic state, see Peter A. Lorge, *Chinese Martial Arts: From Antiquity to the Twenty-First Century* (Cambridge: Cambridge University Press, 2011), 36, 49, 216.

76. Michael L. Raposa, *Meditation and the Martial Arts* (Charlottesville: University of Virginia Press, 2003), 59; Kenji Tokitsu, *Ki and the Way of the Martial Arts*, trans. Sherab Chödzin Kohn (Boston: Shambhala, 2003), 101.

77. Democritus, *Ancilla*, fragment 188.

78. Thomas Hobbes, *Leviathan*, ed. Michael Oakeshott (Oxford: Blackwell, 1946), part 1, chap. 11 (63–64).

79. *Zhuangzi*, chap. 25 (G 110); Wang Fuzhi, on *Zhuangzi* 6.38 (Z 200).

80. Joyce Carol Oates, *On Boxing* (New York: Doubleday, 1987), 93; Loïc Wacquant, *Body and Soul: Notebooks of an Apprentice Boxer* (New York: Oxford University Press, 2004), 34.

81. Wacquant, *Body and Soul*, 70, 95.

82. Wacquant, *Body and Soul*, 95; Norman Mailer, *The Fight* (Boston: Little, Brown, 1975), 5.

83. Wacquant, *Body and Soul*, 117, 69.

84. Wacquant, *Body and Soul*, 69, 97. Sociologist Pierre Bourdieu also discusses this corporeal understanding in "Programme for a Sociology of Sport," in *In Other Words: Essays Toward a Reflexive Sociology*, trans. Matthew Adamson (Stanford, Calif.: Stanford University Press, 1990), 166.

85. Phong Thong Dang and Lynn Seiser, *Advanced Aikido* (Tokyo: Tuttle, 2006), 190. On the toll that professional dance takes on the body, see Renée E. D'Aoust, *Body of a Dancer* (Wilkes-Barre, Pa.: Etruscan Press, 2011).

86. Wacquant, *Body and Soul*, 69.

87. Quoted in Douglas Wile, *Ta'i Chi's Ancestors: The Making of an Internal Martial Art* (New City, N.Y.: Sweet Ch'i Press, 1999), 111–12.

88. Marcel Mauss, "Body Techniques," in *Sociology and Psychology: Essays*, trans. Ben Brewster (London: Routledge & Kegan Paul, 1979), 95–123; Joseph S. Alter, *The Wrestler's Body: Identity and Ideology in Northern India* (Berkeley: University of California Press, 1992), 257. See also Frits Staal, "Indian Bodies," in *Self*

as Body in Asian Theory and Practice, ed. Thomas P. Kasulis (Albany: State University of New York Press, 1993), 59–102.

89. Alter, *Wrestler's Body*, 118–19, also 19, 24. On the "yogic," see Joseph S. Alter, *Yoga in Modern India: The Body Between Science and Philosophy* (Princeton, N.J.: Princeton University Press, 2004).

90. Alter, *Wrestler's Body*, 36.

91. Alter, *Wrestler's Body*, 66.

3. POWER AND GRACE

1. Paul Weiss, *Sport: A Philosophic Inquiry* (Carbondale: Southern Illinois University Press, 1969); Drew A. Hyland, *Philosophy of Sport* (New York: Paragon, 1990); William J. Morgan, *Leftist Theories of Sport: A Critique and Reconstruction* (Urbana: University of Illinois Press, 1994).

2. On constitutive rules, see John R. Searle, *The Construction of Social Reality* (New York: Free Press, 1995). A regulation is usually imposed by authority, while a rule is accepted as a standard and control, as defined in Weiss, *Sport*, 81–82.

3. Weiss, *Sport*, 3, 84–85, also 128.

4. Alasdair MacIntyre, *After Virtue: A Study in Moral Theory* (Notre Dame, Ind.: Notre Dame University Press, 1981), 187.

5. Morgan, *Leftist Theories of Sport*, 91, 92, 137.

6. Morgan, *Leftist Theories of Sport*, 229.

7. I explain the distinction between aesthetics and fine art at more length in *Artifice and Design: Art and Technology in Human Experience* (Ithaca, N.Y.: Cornell University Press, 2008).

8. Francis Sparshott, *Off the Ground: First Steps to a Philosophical Consideration of the Dance* (Princeton, N.J.: Princeton University Press, 1988), 109–10.

9. Yuriko Saito, *Everyday Aesthetics* (Oxford: Oxford University Press, 2007); Roger Scruton, *Beauty: A Very Short Introduction* (Oxford: Oxford University Press, 2011).

10. Immanuel Kant, *Critique of Judgment*, sec. 27, 59; Eckart Voland and Karl Grammar, eds., *Evolutionary Aesthetics* (Berlin: Springer, 2003).

11. I draw from Paul Souriau, *The Aesthetics of Movement*, trans. Manon Souriau (Amherst: University of Massachusetts Press, 1983). The example of a motorcycle wheel is from Laurence Gonzales, *Deep Survival: Who Lives, Who Dies, and Why* (New York: Norton, 2003), 91–92.

12. I draw from Mark Johnson, *The Meaning of the Body: Aesthetics of Human Understanding* (Chicago: University of Chicago Press, 2007), 22–24; Maxine Sheets-Johnstone, *The Primacy of Movement*, 2nd ed. (Amsterdam: Benjamins, 2011), 123, 126–27; Sandra Cerny Minton, *Body and Self: Partners in Movement* (Champaign, Ill.: Human Kinetics Books, 1998), 102–9; and Souriau, *Aesthetics of Movement*, 23–25.

13. Iris Marion Young, "Throwing Like a Girl," *Human Studies* 3 (1980): 146. On amplitude and gymnastics, see Benjamin Lowe, *The Beauty of Sport: A Cross-Disciplinary Inquiry* (Englewood Cliffs, N.J.: Prentice-Hall, 1977), 117, 119.

14. Charles Sherrington, *The Endeavour of Jean Fernel* (Cambridge: Cambridge University Press, 1946), 89; Chang Naizhou, in Marnix Wells, *Scholar Boxer: Chang Naizhou's Theory of Internal Martial Arts* (Berkeley, Calif.: Blue Snake Books, 2005), 76, 131.

15. I draw from Dennis H. Holding, *Human Skills* (Chichester: Wiley, 1981), 53; Karl M. Newell and Andrew B. Slifkin, "Nature of Movement Variability," in *Motor Behavior and Human Skill: A Multidisciplinary Approach*, ed. Jan P. Piek (Champaign, Ill.: Human Kinetics, 1998), 143; Andy Clark, *Being There: Putting Brain, Body, and World Together Again* (Cambridge, Mass.: MIT Press, 1997), 44; and Christine L. MacKenzie and Thea Iberall, *The Grasping Hand* (Amsterdam: North-Holland, 1994), 344. The experimental study of blacksmith movements is in Nicolai A. Bernstein, "On Dexterity and Its Development," in *Dexterity and Its Development*, ed. M. Latash and M. T. Turvey (Mahwah, N.J.: Erlbaum, 1996), 3–236. On the difficulty of a biomechanical analysis of martial arts movement, see Emeric Arus, *Biomechanics of Human Motion: Applications in the Martial Arts* (Boca Raton, Fla.: CRC Press, 2013), 206.

16. Herbert Spencer, "Gracefulness" (1852), in *The Works of Herbert Spencer*, vol. 14 (Osnabrück: Zeller, 1966); Souriau, *Aesthetics of Movement*, 82.

17. Souriau, *Aesthetics of Movement*, 34.

18. *The Daodejing of Laozi*, trans. Philip J. Ivanhoe (Indianapolis: Hackett, 2003), chap. 24.

19. Souriau, *Aesthetics of Movement*, 85, 86, 89, 91.

20. Souriau, *Aesthetics of Movement*, 90.

21. Hans Ulrich Gumbrecht, *In Praise of Athletic Beauty* (Cambridge, Mass.: Harvard University Press, 2006), 54; Lowe, *Beauty of Sport*, 20, 21, 180, 75. I also draw from R. Carlisle, "Physical Education and Aesthetics," 20–56; V. Hohler, "The Beauty of Motion," 49–56; and R. K. Elliot, "Aesthetics and Sport," 107–16, all in *Readings in the Aesthetics of Sport*, ed. H. T. A. Whiting and D. W. Masterson (London: Lepus Books, 1974).

22. E. F. Kaelin, "The Well-Played Game: Notes Toward an Aesthetic of Sport," *Quest* 10 (1968): 312; Gumbrecht, *In Praise of Athletic Beauty*, 195.

23. Geoffrey Green, *Soccer: The World Game* (London: Phoenix, 1953), 214–15; Lowe, *Beauty of Sport*, 31, 111, 114; Richard F. Galvin, "Aesthetic Incontinence in Sport," in *Sport Inside Out*, ed. David L. Vanderwirken and Spencer K. Wertz (Fort Worth: Texas Christian University Press, 1985), 520.

24. Loïc Wacquant, *Body and Soul: Notebooks of an Apprentice Boxer* (New York: Oxford University Press, 2004), 205; Carlo Rotella, *Cut Time: An Education at the Fights* (Chicago: University of Chicago Press, 2003), 56.

25. An example of the value in sport of the commitment to win occurred at the 2012 London Olympics when eight badminton players were disqualified from competition after they were accused of "not using one's best efforts to win" and thereby

"conducting oneself in a manner that is clearly abusive or detrimental to the sport." The players were attempting to manipulate their position in the elimination round through what might be called a "strategic loss." To do so, they made a series of egregious errors that elicited boos from the audience and the judges' disqualification. See "Olympics Badminton: Eight Women Disqualified from Doubles," August 1, 2012, BBC, http://www.bbc.co.uk/sport/o/olympics/19072677 (accessed February 15, 2014).

26. "Gymnastics," in *Sports Rule Encyclopedia*, ed. Jess R. White (Palo Alto, Calif.: National Press, 1966), 293294. That gymnastics is a sport rather than an art seems to be the view of the practice community, according to Sparshott, *Off the Ground*, 225–28.

27. Sparshott, *Off the Ground*, 253. The term "endotelic" comes from Curt John Ducasse, *The Philosophy of Art* (New York: Dial Press, 1929).

28. Hyland, *Philosophy of Sport*, 115.

29. Joseph Epstein, "Obsessed with Sport," in *Sport Inside Out*, ed. Vanderwirken and Wertz, 115.

30. Lowe, *Beauty of Sport*, 92; Randall Collins, *Violence: A Micro-Sociological Theory* (Princeton, N.J.: Princeton University Press, 2008), 308.

31. Gumbrecht, *In Praise of Athletic Beauty*, 216, 231; also 205, 208, 218.

32. Collins, *Violence*, 283, 311, 327; and Randall Collins, *Interaction Ritual Chains* (Princeton, N.J.: Princeton University Press, 2004), 59. On relations between audiences and competitors in Roman games, see David Potter, *The Victor's Crown: Ancient Sport from Homer to Byzantium* (Oxford: Oxford University Press, 2012).

33. Qi Jiguang, *Classic of Boxing*, quoted in Douglas Wile, *Ta'i Chi's Ancestors: The Making of an Internal Martial Art* (New City, N.Y.: Sweet Ch'i Press, 1999), 12; Dave Lowry, *The Karate Way: Discovering the Spirit of Practice* (Boston: Shambhala, 2009), 128; Phong Thong Dang and Lynn Seiser, *Advanced Aikido* (Tokyo: Tuttle, 2006), 31, 21.

34. Anthony L. Schmieg, *Watching Your Back: Chinese Martial Arts and Traditional Medicine* (Honolulu: University of Hawai'i Press, 2005), 81, 94.

35. Eugen Herrigel, *Zen in the Art of Archery*, in *The Overlook Martial Arts Reader*, ed. Randy F. Nelson (Woodstock, N.Y.: Overlook Press, 1989), 136.

36. Rory Miller, *Facing Violence: Preparing for the Unexpected* (Wolfeboro, N.H.: YMAA Publication Center, 2011), 180. On the history and theory of *kata*, see Nathan J. Johnson, *Barefoot Zen: The Shaolin Roots of Kung Fu and Karate* (York Beach, Minn.: Weiser, 2000); and Lawrence A. Kane, *Martial Arts Instruction: Applying Educational Theory and Communication Techniques in the Dojo* (Boston: YMAA Publication Center, 2004). Eric Mullis confirms the connection I posit between qualitative aesthetic intensity and martial effectiveness, in what he calls "a reciprocal relationship between the aesthetic appreciation of true martial encounters and the appreciation of the exercise and drills that make effective martial movement possible" ("Martial Somaesthetics," *Journal of Aesthetic Education* 47, no. 3 [2013]: 98).

37. Francis Sparshott, *A Measured Pace: Toward a Philosophical Understanding of the Arts of Dance* (Toronto: University of Toronto Press, 1995), 62. See also Mullis, "Martial Somaesthetics," 99.

38. On gender in dance, see Sparshott, *Off the Ground*, 134. The *xiannü*, a woman who excels in martial arts skill and exists in her own right rather than as a love interest for a male character, is a stock figure of the *wuxia* literature. See Sabrina Qiong Yu, *Jet Li: Chinese Masculinity and Transnational Film Stardom* (Edinburgh: Edinburgh University Press, 2012), 65. On gender and martial arts, see Patricia Petersen, "Grrrl in a Gi," in *Martial Arts and Philosophy: Beating and Nothingness*, ed. Graham Priest and Damon Young (Chicago: Open Court, 2010), 93–104. Also, "Technique may annul the muscular inequality of man and woman" (Simone de Beauvoir, *The Second Sex*, trans. H. M. Parshley [New York: Vintage Books, 1989], 53).

39. Allan Bäck, "The Way to Virtue in Sport," *Journal of the Philosophy of Sport* 36 (2009): 217–37.

40. I delve into these points more in *Artifice and Design*.

41. Allan Bäck and Daeshik Kim, "Towards a Western Philosophy of Eastern Martial Arts," *Journal of the Philosophy of Sport* 6 (1979): 24; Rory Miller, *Meditations on Violence: A Comparison of Martial Arts Training and Real World Violence* (Boston: YMAA Publication, 2008), 113; Bäck and Kim, "Towards a Western Philosophy of Eastern Martial Arts," 25. Elsewhere Miller writes, "The essence of an assault is the unpredictability and the extreme position of disadvantage. . . . An experienced, violent criminal, unarmed, will likely hit you four times before your brain can switch from whatever you were thinking about before to your fighting mode" (Rory Miller and Lawrence A. Kane, *Scaling Force: Dynamic Decision-Making Under Threat of Violence* [Wolfeboro, N.H.: YMAA Publication Center, 2012], 260, 194).

42. Sparshott, *Measured Pace*, 108.

43. Loren W. Christensen and Wim Demeere, *Timing in the Fighting Arts: Your Guide to Winning in the Ring and Surviving on the Street* (Santa Fe, N.M.: Turtle Press, 2004), 260–61.

44. Sparshott, *Measured Pace*, 134.

45. Schmieg, *Watching Your Back*, 87, 96.

46. Robert W. Smith, *Martial Musings: A Portrayal of Martial Arts in the Twentieth Century* (Erie, Pa.: Via Media, 1999), 306.

47. Merce Cunningham, *The Dancer and the Dance* (New York: Marion Boyars, 1985), 68; Eric Hawkins, "Pure Poetry," in *The Modern Dance: Seven Statements of Belief*, ed. Selma Jeanne Cohen (Middletown, Conn.: Wesleyan University Press, 1969), 41; Judy D. Salzman, "The Eye of the Beholder," in *Martial Arts and Philosophy*, ed. Priest and Young, 171–72.

48. Geoffrey Dyson, *The Mechanics of Athletics* (London: University of London Press, 1964), 196; Souriau, *Aesthetics of Movement*, 139; Smith, *Martial Musings*, 26–27; Phong and Seiser, *Advanced Aikido*, 47.

49. Mullis, "Martial Somaesthetics," 98.

50. Sparshott, *Off the Ground*, 302–3; on dance and martial arts, 314; Smith, *Martial Musings*, 225.

51. Brian Kennedy and Elizabeth Guo, *Chinese Martial Arts Training Manuals: A Historical Survey* (Berkeley, Calif.: Blue Snake Books, 2005), 144; Peter A.

Lorge, *Chinese Martial Arts: From Antiquity to the Twenty-First Century* (Cambridge: Cambridge University Press, 2011), 134. The most convincing performance I have seen of martial arts by a man who had no previous training (but was a quick study and received high-quality martial arts training in preparation for the role) is that of Chiwetel Ejiofor in David Mamet's *Red Belt* (2008).

52. José Saporta, "Juan Moreno's Olympic-Style Training for Taekwondo Athletes," *Journal of Asian Martial Arts* 15, no. 3 (2006): 41; Yu, *Jet Li*, 57–60. For an example of a *wuxia* martial arts novel by a contemporary master, see Louis Cha (Jin Yong), *The Deer and the Cauldron: A Martial Arts Novel*, trans. John Minford (Hong Kong: Oxford University Press, 1997).

53. Johnson, *Barefoot Zen*, 179. Another scholar of Japanese martial arts describes the translation of Okinawan *kata* into blocks and punches on transmission to Japan as "deskilled karate" (Gary J. Krug, "At the Feet of the Master: Three Stages in the Appropriation of Okinawan Karate," *Critical Studies: Critical Methodologies* 1, no. 4 [2001]: 397).

54. On Shaolin transmission to Okinawa and the origin of karate, see Richard M. Mooney, "Boxing, Chinese Shaolin Styles," in *Martial Arts of the World: An Encyclopedia*, ed. Thomas A. Green (Santa Barbara, Calif.: ABC-CLIO, 2001), 1:32–44. On fighting monks, see Albert E. Dien, *Six Dynasties Civilization* (New Haven, Conn.: Yale University Press, 2007), 15–45; Lorge, *Chinese Martial Arts*, 75, 107; and David Graff, *Medieval Chinese Warfare, 300–900* (London: Routledge, 2002), 161.

55. Johnson, *Barefoot Zen*, 182, 117, 121, also 37, 91.

56. Stanley E. Henning, "The Chinese Martial Arts in Historical Perspective," *Military Affairs* 45, no. 4 (1981): 174. There was full Han rule over the Korean Peninsula starting in 108 B.C.E. See John E. Wills Jr., *Mountain of Fame: Portraits in Chinese History* (Princeton, N.J.: Princeton University Press, 1994), 58. Taekwondo, also a Korean art, practices forms, though that is probably because it is deliberately modeled on Japanese karate.

57. Chang Naizhou, in Wells, *Scholar Boxer*, 132. On the mystery of practice, see Frank R. Wilson, *The Hand: How Its Use Shapes the Brain, Language, and Human Culture* (New York: Vintage Books, 1998), chap. 5; and Raymond Tallis, *The Hand: A Philosophical Inquiry into Human Being* (Edinburgh: University of Edinburgh Press, 2003), 187.

58. Henri Bergson, *Matter and Memory*, trans. Nancy Margaret Paul and W. Scott Palmer (Mineola, N.Y.: Dover, 2004), 137–38.

59. Good descriptions of repetition and the acquisition of skill can be found in Richard Sennett, *The Craftsman* (New Haven, Conn.: Yale University Press, 2008), 38, 175–77.

60. Phong and Seiser, *Advanced Aikido*, 175.

61. Yagyu Munenori, *The Book of Family Traditions on the Art of War*, in Miyamoto Musashi, *The Book of Five Rings*, trans. Thomas Cleary (Boston: Shambhala, 2003), 122.

62. Munenori, *Book of Family Traditions*, 101, 102.

63. Aleksandr Romanovich Luria, *The Working Brain: An Introduction to Neuropsychology*, trans. Basil Haigh (Harmondsworth: Penguin, 1973), 176, 253.

64. Phong and Seiser, *Advanced Aikido,* 48; Smith, *Martial Musings,* 27–28; Chang Naizhou, in Wells, *Scholar Boxer,* 126.

65. Henri Bergson, *Time and Free Will: An Essay on the Immediate Data of Consciousness*, trans. F. L. Pogson (Mineola, N.Y.: Dover, 2001), 12.

4. WHAT A BODY CAN DO

1. The World Health Organization defines violence as "the intentional use of physical force or power, threatened or actual, against oneself, another person, or against a group or community, that either results in or has a high likelihood of resulting in injury, death, psychological harm, maldevelopment, or deprivation" (Etienne G. Krug, James A. Mercy, Linda L. Dahlberg, and Anthony B. Zwi, "The World Report on Violence and Health," *Lancet* 360 [2002]: 1084).

2. Someone who thinks that "subjective" violence is merely half of a larger whole, which includes objective and symbolic violence is Slavoj Žižek, *Violence: Six Sideways Reflections* (New York: Picador, 2008).

3. Quoted in Thomas F. Scanlon, *Eros and Greek Athletics* (New York: Oxford University Press, 2002), 19.

4. Demosthenes and Isocrates, quoted in Michael B. Poliakoff, *Combat Sports in the Ancient World: Competition, Violence, and Culture* (New Haven, Conn.: Yale University Press, 1982), 92.

5. Pierre Bourdieu, *Outline of the Theory of Practice* (New York: Cambridge University Press, 1977), 195, and *In Other Words: Essays Toward a Reflexive Sociology*, trans. Matthew Adamson (Stanford, Calif.: Stanford University Press, 1990), 85.

6. Sigmund Freud, *Civilization and Its Discontents*, Pelican Freud Library (Harmondsworth: Penguin, 1985), 12:278, 302, 336. For evolutionary and psychological evidence against original violence, see Dennis L. Krebs, *The Origin of Morality: An Evolutionary Account* (New York: Oxford University Press, 2011), chap. 3.

7. On the evolutionary psychology of violence, see Jerome H. Barkow, Leda Cosmides, and John Tooby, eds., *The Adapted Mind: Evolutionary Psychology and the Generation of Culture* (Oxford: Oxford University Press, 1992). On the violence of children, see Randall Collins, *Violence: A Micro-Sociological Theory* (Princeton, N.J.: Princeton University Press, 2008), 25–26. Fighting among children is the most common form of violence in the family, more common than spousal violence or child abuse. Eighty percent of small children attack siblings, their violence peaking at age thirty months. They seldom cause serious injury, partly due to incapacity and partly because the fights are staged for adults, who break them up. See Collins, *Violence*, 17–18. See also Steven Pinker, *The Better Angels of Our Nature: Why Violence Has Declined* (New York: Penguin, 2011), 441–42, 483; and Laurence Brockliss and Heather Montgomery, eds., *Childhood and Violence in the Western Tradition* (Oxford: Oxbow Books, 2010).

8. On the futility of background in predicting violence, see Collins, *Violence*, 1–2. On the comparable futility of background for explaining or predicting crime, see Jack Katz, *Seductions of Crime: Moral and Sensual Attractions in Doing Evil* (New York: Basic Books, 1988), chap. 9.

9. Michael Tomasello and Josep Call, *Primate Cognition* (Oxford: Oxford University Press, 1997). On pointing and other forms of shared attention, see George Butterworth, "Pointing Is the Royal Road to Language for Babies," in *Pointing: Where Language, Culture, and Cognition Meet,* ed. Sataro Kita (Mahwah, N.J.: Erlbaum, 2003), 9–33; and Michael Tomasello, *The Cultural Origins of Human Cognition* (Cambridge, Mass.: Harvard University Press, 1999), 62–70. Randall Collins discusses the relevance of Tomasello's work on joint attention to the social psychology of ritual in *Interaction Ritual Chains* (Princeton, N.J.: Princeton University Press, 2004), 79–81.

10. Gabor Csepregi, *The Clever Body* (Calgary: University of Calgary Press, 2006), 81.

11. Elijah Anderson, *Streetwise: Race, Class, and Change in an Urban Community* (Chicago: University of Chicago Press, 1990), 173. On the exploitation of common civil requests as a first stage of robbery or assault, see Katz, *Seductions of Crime,* 172–75.

12. Collins, *Violence*, 339, 69; Pinker, *Better Angels*, 32.

13. Collins, *Violence*, 93, 155, 175, 184, 188–89; on professional killers, see 430–40.

14. Rory Miller, *Meditations on Violence: A Comparison of Martial Arts Training and Real World Violence* (Boston: YMAA Publication Center, 2008), 43. I also draw from 41, 52–53, 83, 97.

15. Dave Grossman, *On Killing: The Psychological Cost of Learning to Kill in War and Society* (New York: Back Bay Books, 1996), 259. On violence in prehistory, see Ian Tattersall, *Masters of the Planet: The Search for Our Human Origins* (New York: Palgrave Macmillan, 2012), 152–53, 172–73, 203; and Lawrence H. Keeley, *War Before Civilization: The Myth of the Peaceful Savage* (New York: Oxford University Press, 1996), 37–39.

16. Dave Grossman, with Loren W. Christensen, *On Combat: The Psychology and Physiology of Deadly Conflict in War and Peace*, 3rd ed. (Millstadt, N.J.: Warrior Science, 2008), 203; Grossman, *On Killing*, 31, 54.

17. Grossman, *On Killing*, 81, also 4–5.

18. Grossman, *On Killing*, 160. A fatal eye gouge was supposedly used in at least two murders by Mafia contract killer Joseph "Mad Dog" Sullivan, who, incidentally, is the only man to have escaped from Attica prison.

19. Grossman, *On Killing*, 304, 259.

20. Grossman, *On Killing*, 12.

21. Pinker, *Better Angels*, 485; Grossman, *On Combat*, 246; David Hansen-Miller, *Civilized Violence: Subjectivity, Gender, and Popular Cinema* (Farnham: Ashgate, 2011).

22. Grossman, *On Killing*, 88; Collins, *Violence*, 10, also 17–19.

23. Miller, *Meditations on Violence*, 29. I do not mean to say that it is impossible for cinema to represent violence realistically. The best example I have seen is Krzysztof Kieslowski's *A Short Film About Killing* (1988). However, it may be impossible for films to offer such representations and attract the commercial success necessary to make them viable productions. Audiences respond not with excitement but dread, just as they do to real-world violence.

24. Consider the entirely negative impression that Bruce Lee's cinematic debut made on the first American master of Chinese martial arts, in Robert W. Smith, *Martial Musings: A Portrayal of Martial Arts in the Twentieth Century* (Erie, Pa.: Via Media, 1999), 349. On Lee's all too cinematic Jeet Kune Do and its critics, see Paul Bowman, *Beyond Bruce Lee: Chasing the Dragon Through Film, Philosophy and Popular Culture* (London: Wallflower Press, 2013), 15–22.

25. Hannah Arendt, *On Violence* (New York: Harcourt, Brace & World, 1970); Demosthenes, quoted in Poliakoff, *Combat Sports*, 92. That violence depends on a mechanical advantage is also the view of Friedrich Engels: "The triumph of force is based on the production of arms" (*Anti-Dühring*, in *The Ethics of War: Classic and Contemporary Readings*, ed. Gregory M. Reichberg, Henrik Syse, and Endre Begby [Malden, Mass.: Blackwell, 2006], 590); and General Carl von Clausewitz: "War is an act of violence intended to compel our opponent to fulfil our will. Violence arms itself with the inventions of Art and Science in order to contend against violence" (*On War*, trans. Colonel J. J. Graham [London, 1874], book 1, chap. 1, sec. 2).

26. Michel Foucault, *The History of Sexuality*, vol. 1, *An Introduction*, trans. Robert Hurley (New York: Vintage Books, 1980), 89.

27. Michel Foucault, "The Ethics of Care for the Self as a Practice of Freedom," in *The Final Foucault*, ed. James Bernauer and David Rasmussen (Cambridge, Mass.: MIT Press, 1988), 18. For more details on these issues, see Johanna Oksala, *Foucault, Politics, and Violence* (Evanston, Ill.: Northwestern University Press, 2012).

28. Michel Foucault, "The Subject and Power," in Herbert Dreyfus and Paul Rabinow, *Michel Foucault: Beyond Structuralism and Hermeneutics* (Chicago: University of Chicago Press, 1983), 220, 221.

29. Auguste Comte, "Plan of the Scientific Operations Necessary for Reorganizing Society" (1822), in *Auguste Comte and Positivism: The Essential Writings*, ed. Gertrud Lenzer (New York: Harper & Row, 1975), 45.

30. On the political anatomy of the body, see Michel Foucault, *Discipline and Punish: The Birth of the Prison*, trans. Alan Sheridan (New York: Vintage Books, 1979).

31. Shigehisa Kuriyama, *The Expressiveness of the Body and the Divergence of Greek and Chinese Medicine* (New York: Zone Books, 1999), 199–200, 266. According to John Hay, "It is as a system of energy flow and transformation that Chinese medical theory was most distinctive in its achievement and most fundamentally integrated with the Chinese universe as a whole" ("The Human Body As a Microcosmic Source of Macrocosmic Values in Calligraphy," in *Self as Body in Asian Theory and Practice*, ed. Thomas P. Kasulis [Albany: State University of New York

Press, 1993], 191). On the difficulty of establishing biomechanical parameters for the analysis of martial arts techniques, see Emeric Arus, *Biomechanics of Human Motion: Applications in the Martial Arts* (Boca Raton, Fla.: CRC Press, 2013), 206.

32. Anthony L. Schmieg, *Watching Your Back: Chinese Martial Arts and Traditional Medicine* (Honolulu: University of Hawai'i Press, 2005), 151.

33. Innocent IV, "On the Restitution of Spoils," 151; Hugo Grotius, *On the Law of War and Peace*, 398, 401; and Clausewitz, *On War*, 554, all in *Ethics of War*, ed. Reichberg et al. Martial arts tradition tends to agree with Grotius and Clausewitz: "The way to do battle is the same whether it is a battle between one individual and another or a battle between one army and another" (Miyamoto Musashi, *The Book of Five Rings*, trans. Thomas Cleary [Boston: Shambhala, 2003], 12–13).

34. Saint Ambrose, "On the Duties of the Clergy," 67; Saint Thomas Aquinas, *Summa Theologica*, 177; and Thucydides, *Peloponnesian War*, 6, 13, all in *Ethics of War*, ed. Reichberg et al.

35. Alberico Gentili, *On the Law of War*, 374; Christian von Wolff, *The Law of Nations Treated According to a Scientific Method*, 474; Thomas Hobbes, *Elements of Law*, 450; Samuel von Puffendorf, *The Law of Nature and Nations*, 461; and Clausewitz, *On War*, 555, all in *Ethics of War*, ed. Reichberg et al.

36. Gratian, *Decretum*, 110; Gentili, *On the Law of War*, 376; and Saint Augustine, *On Free Choice of the Will*, 75, all in *Ethics of War*, ed. Reichberg et al.

37. Saint Thomas Aquinas, *Summa Theologica*, 190; and Daniel Webster, Letter to British Ambassador Henry Fox, April 24, 1841, 564, both in *Ethics of War*, ed. Reichberg et al.

38. Bartolus of Saxoferrato, *Commentary on Ulpian's Digest*, 207; Francisco de Vitoria, *On the Law of War*, 311; and Grotius, *On the Law of War and Peace*, 402, all in *Ethics of War*, ed. Reichberg et al.

39. Gilles Deleuze and Félix Guattari, "Treatise on Nomadology: The War Machine," in *A Thousand Plateaus: Capitalism and Schizophrenia*, trans. Brian Massumi (Minneapolis: University of Minnesota Press, 1987), 351–423.

40. J. Glenn Gray, *The Warriors: Reflections on Men in Battle* (New York: Harper & Row, 1970), 33, 31; Colonel David Hackworth, quoted in Grossman, *On Combat*, 153; Grossman, *On Combat*, 52–53.

41. Göran Aijmer and Jon Abbink, introduction to *Meanings of Violence: A Cross Cultural Perspective*, ed. Göran Aijmer and Jon Abbink (Oxford: Berg, 2000), 1; Simone de Beauvoir, *The Second Sex*, trans. H. M. Parshley (New York: Vintage Books, 1989), 330.

42. Susan Sontag, *Regarding the Pain of Others* (New York: Farrar, Straus and Giroux, 2003), 99; Piotr Hoffman, *Violence in Modern Philosophy* (Chicago: University of Chicago Press, 1989), 144, 145. Compare Theodor Adorno: "The true basis of morality is to be found in bodily feeling, in identification with unbearable pain" (*Metaphysics: Concepts and Problems*, ed. Rolf Tiedemann, trans. Edmund Jephcott [Cambridge: Polity Press, 2001], 116).

43. W. B. Yeats, "Easter, 1916," in *The Collected Poems of W. B. Yeats*, 2nd ed. (London: Macmillan, 1950); Robert Buch, *The Pathos of the Real: On the Aesthetics of Violence in the Twentieth Century* (Baltimore: Johns Hopkins University

Press, 2010), 147. See also Leon Whiteson, *A Terrible Beauty: An Exploration of the Positive Role of Violence* (Oakville, Ont.: Mosaic Press, 2000).

44. René Girard, *The Scapegoat*, trans. Yvonne Freccero (Baltimore: Johns Hopkins University Press, 1986), 234–35 (italics added); Chris Fleming, *René Girard: Violence and Mimesis* (Cambridge: Polity, 2004), 140, 143. See also René Girard, *Violence and the Sacred*, trans. Patrick Gregory (Baltimore: Johns Hopkins University Press, 1977); and Russell Jacoby, *Bloodlust: On the Roots of Violence from Cain and Abel to the Present* (New York: Free Press, 2011).

45. Katz, *Seductions of Crime*, 314, 315, 8, 9.

46. Katz, *Seductions of Crime*, 16, 18, 20; Anne Campbell, "The Streets and Violence," in *Violent Transactions: The Limits of Personality*, ed. Anne Campbell and John J. Gibbs (Oxford: Blackwell, 1986), 122–23, 154. On the length to which "badass" criminals will go to create the appearance of rule violation as a prelude to violence, see Katz, *Seductions of Crime*, 106–12.

47. Katz, *Seductions of Crime*, 73, 138, 169, 187.

48. J. H. Moore, *The Cheyenne* (Oxford: Blackwell, 1999), 107–8; Bryan Turner, "Warrior Charisma and the Spiritualization of Violence," *Body & Society* 9, no. 4 (2003): 102.

49. *The Daodejing of Laozi*, trans. Philip J. Ivanhoe (Indianapolis: Hackett, 2003), chap. 31.

50. Elijah Anderson, *Code of the Street: Decency, Violence, and the Moral Life of the Inner City* (New York: Norton, 1999), 126, 129; Grossman, *On Combat*, 183.

51. Marc MacYoung, *A Professional's Guide to Ending Violence Quickly: How Bouncers, Bodyguards, and Other Security Professionals Handle Ugly Situations* (Boulder, Colo.: Paladin Press, 1996), 30–31; Grossman, *On Combat*, 150.

52. Rory Miller and Lawrence A. Kane, *Scaling Force: Dynamic Decision-Making Under Threat of Violence* (Wolfeboro, N.H.: YMAA Publication Center, 2012), 65, 57, 164.

53. Miller and Kane, *Scaling Force*, 248.

54. Lawrence A. Kane, *Martial Arts Instruction: Applying Educational Theory and Communication Techniques in the Dojo* (Boston: YMAA Publication Center, 2004), 132.

55. Rory Miller, *Force Decisions: A Citizen's Guide* (Wolfeboro, N.H.: YMAA Publication Center, 2012), 71–72. Some statutes have a "duty to retreat" clause that requires a person to prove that he or she exhausted all means of escape. Others have a "stand your ground" clause that eliminates the duty to retreat, provided that one has a legal right to do what one is doing where one is doing it. So-called Castle laws provide an unfettered right of self-defense in one's home (or, sometimes, business). All these provisions apply only to defending life, not property.

56. Saint Augustine, *On Free Choice of the Will*, 1.5, in *Ethics of War*, ed. Reichberg et al., 75. Allan Bäck and Daeshik Kim argue that "everyone has a prima facie moral duty to learn how to fight, at least in the way taught by the Eastern martial arts" ("Pacifism and the Eastern Martial Arts," *Philosophy East and West* 32, no. 2 [1982]: 185).

57. Baruch Spinoza, *Ethics*, part 5, prop. 39, in *A Spinoza Reader: The Ethics and Other Works*, ed. and trans. Edwin Curley (Princeton, N.J.: Princeton University Press, 1994), 262. What Spinoza says here is a traditional understanding in the Chinese martial arts and their congeners. In the words of a contemporary bagua master, "If our movements are coarse, then our mind will also be coarse; if our movements are fine, then our mind will be fine. *Bagua daoyin* uses fine movements to train the mind to be fine" (He Jinghan, *Bagua Daoyin*, trans. David Alexander [London: Singing Dragon, 2008], 29).

58. Spinoza, *Ethics*, part 3, prop. 2 (scholium), in *Spinoza Reader*, ed. Curley, 155–56 (italics added).

59. Gilles Deleuze, *Spinoza: Practical Philosophy*, trans. Robert Hurley (San Francisco: City Lights, 1988), 22–23. See also Gilles Deleuze, *Expressionism in Philosophy: Spinoza*, trans. Martin Joughin (New York: Zone Books, 1990), 269.

60. Amartya Sen, *The Idea of Justice* (Cambridge, Mass.: Harvard University Press, 2009), 231. On master and slave values, see Friedrich Nietzsche, *On the Genealogy of Morals*, trans. Walter Kaufmann (New York: Vintage Books, 1967), First Essay.

61. The evidence for a comprehensive decline in violence is agreeably presented and carefully analyzed in Pinker, *Better Angels*. An independent evaluation of the European evidence reaches the same conclusion, as reported in Robert Muchembled, *A History of Violence: From the End of the Middle Ages to the Present*, trans. Jean Birrell (Cambridge: Polity Press, 2012).

62. Herman Kauz, *The Martial Spirit: An Introduction to the Origin, Philosophy, and Psychology of the Martial Arts* (Woodstock, N.Y.: Overlook Press, 1972), 129–30.

63. Jean-Jacques Rousseau, *Émile*, trans. Alan Bloom (New York: Basic Books, 1979), 54.

64. On body image and fitness, see Shaun Gallagher, *How the Body Shapes the Mind* (Oxford: Clarendon Press, 2005), 144, and the clinical studies cited there. On the health benefits of martial arts training, see Tracey Wai Man Tsang, Michael Kohn, Chin Moi Chow, and Maria Fiatarone Singh, "Health Benefits of Kung Fu: A Systematic Review," *Journal of Sport Sciences* 26, no. 12 (2008): 1245–67.

65. Phong Thong Dang and Lynn Seiser, *Advanced Aikido* (Tokyo: Tuttle, 2006), 181; Grossman, *On Combat*, 160.

66. Miller, *Meditations on Violence*, 26, 59, 58. The research on handgun accuracy was carried out by the New York City Police Department between 1994 and 2000.

67. Smith, *Martial Musings*, 288; Patricia Petersen, "Grrrl in a Gi," in *Martial Arts and Philosophy*, ed. Graham Priest and Damon Young (Chicago: Open Court, 2010), 100, 103.

68. Smith, *Martial Musings*, 341.

69. Kevin Krein, "Sparring with Emptiness," in *Martial Arts and Philosophy*, ed. Priest and Young, 85; Tamara Kohn, "Bowing onto the Mat: Discourse of Change Through Martial Arts Practice," in *The Discipline of Leisure: Embodying Cultures of "Recreation,"* ed. Simon Coleman and Tamara Kohn (New York:

Berghahn, 2007), 184; Richard Shusterman, *Body Consciousness: A Philosophy of Mindfulness and Somaesthetics* (Cambridge: Cambridge University Press, 2008), 1–14; Eric C. Mullis, "Martial Somaesthetics," *Journal of Aesthetic Education* 47, no. 3 (2013): 100.

70. Stephen Chan, "The Construction and Export of Culture as Artefact: The Case of Japanese Martial Arts," *Body & Society* 6, no. 1 (2000): 71; Nathan J. Johnson, *Barefoot Zen: The Shaolin Roots of Kung Fu and Karate* (York Beach, Minn.: Weiser, 2000), 215, 27.

71. Order of Shaolin Ch'an, *The Shaolin Grandmasters' Text: History, Philosophy, and Gong Fu of Shaolin Ch'an* (Beaverton, Ore.: Order of Shaolin Ch'an, 2004), 16. Another work of this sort, asserting lineal descent from displaced Shaolin masters, is O. E. Simon, *The Law of the Fist*, 5th ed. (Grand Forks, B.C.: Golden Bell, 2001). I trained for three years under one of Grand Master Simon's masters. The suggestion that a generation of Shaolin fighting monks escaped to the West around 1949 is difficult to square with the sad history of the Shaolin monastery. Already by the late seventeenth century, numerous visitors who traveled to Shaolin looking for martial arts were sorely disappointed by a ruin, a few starving monks, and no martial arts practice. The monastery had no head abbot for the entire period between 1661 and 1999. The idea of rebuilding the temple came when the producers of a Hong Kong movie, *Shaolin Temple* (1982), starring Li Lianjie (Jet Li), visited the site and found it too dilapidated to use as a set. See Peter Lorge, *Chinese Martial Arts: From Antiquity to the Twentieth Century* (Cambridge: Cambridge University Press, 2012), 204–5, 230.

72. Shaolin Ch'an, *Shaolin Grandmasters' Text*, 12, 84. On the Buddhist concept of skillful means, see Michael Pye, *Skillful Means: A Concept in Mahayana Buddhism* (London: Routledge, 2003).

EPILOGUE

1. Michel Foucault, *The History of Sexuality*, vol. 2, *The Use of Pleasure*, trans. Robert Hurley (New York: Pantheon, 1985); *The History of Sexuality*, vol. 3, *The Care of the Self*, trans. Robert Hurley (New York: Pantheon, 1986); and "Technology of the Self," in *Technologies of the Self: A Seminar with Michel Foucault*, ed. Luther H. Martin, Patrick H. Hutton, and Huck Gutman (Amherst: University of Massachusetts Press, 1988).

2. I am alluding to an argument in my book *Knowledge and Civilization* (Boulder, Colo.: Westview Press, 2004).

3. Friedrich Nietzsche, *Thus Spoke Zarathustra*, trans. Adrian Del Caro (Cambridge: Cambridge University Press, 2006), 58.

4. *Zuo Commentary on the Spring and Summer Annals*, in Confucius, *Analects, with Selections from Traditional Commentaries*, trans. Edward Slingerland (Indianapolis: Hackett, 2003), 155; in the same source, see *Analects*, 13.23: "The perfected person harmonizes and does not merely agree. The petty person agrees, but he does not harmonize."

5. Guo Xiang, comment on the *Zhuangzi*, 6.27, in *Zhuangzi: The Essential Writings, with Selections from Traditional Commentaries*, trans. Brook Ziporyn (Indianapolis: Hackett, 2009), 195.

6. This is John Dewey's argument, as is the concept of imagination as the conscious adjustment of old and new, in *Art as Experience* (New York: Putnam, 1934), 267.

INDEX

actions, 144, 176, 195; basic, 155, 212; double effect of, 181; and passions, 194

aesthetics, 116–57; of existence, 207; of martial arts, 131–42, 145–51; and violence, 183–88. *See also* sport: aesthetics of

aikido, 133, 147, 196

Alexander, F. M., 94

animals, fighting of, 17–20

archery, 42, 49, 50; and Confucianism, 2, 43–45; and Daoism, 23–24; and Zen, 134

Arendt, Hannah, 174–75, 176

arete, 63, 66, 67, 69, 75, 103, 192

Aristotle, 73, 75, 86; on body, 94; on courage, 48; on dualism, 82; and knowledge, 87

art of war, Chinese, 6–12, 21, 27–28, 40, 191; and deception, 8–9, 11; no-fighting principle of, 7, 34, 202. *See also* strategy

artifact, 117, 126–27

arts, 6, 117, 208, 212; work of art, 126–27. See also *techne*

atheism, 85, 87

athlete, 61, 130, 148

athletics, 98, 112–15; and aesthetics, 114; and dance, 128; Greek, 62–67; and gymnasium, 65, 110. *See also* sport

attention, shared, 165–66, 167, 185

authority, 175, 176

Bäck, Allan, 138–39

beauty, 117–19, 122–23, 125, 127; of athletics, 146; terrible, 183–85, 188

Beauvoir, Simone de, 184, 237n.38

becoming, 15, 35, 38, 86, 104; and beauty, 118; and body, 98

being, 74, 78

Bergson, Henri, 88, 92, 107, 152, 156–57

Bodhidharma, 3, 4–5, 16

language, 38, 97, 113, 208; and violence, 162. *See also* body language
Latour, Bruno, 89–90
law, 101, 159, 160, 163, 164, 175; of
self-defense, 181–83; of war, 179–80
lawyers, 191, 192
learning, conditioned, 171, 190, 200
logos, 77, 80, 84, 86, 97
longevity, 14, 29–30, 55, 107, 109, 212
Lucian, 66
Lucretius, 87
Luria, Akeksandr, 155

machismo, 168
Mailer, Norman, 106
Mao Zedong, 49, 174
martial arts: aesthetic quality of,
146, 156; differences among, 133;
effectiveness of, 140; elegance of,
140; ethical value of, 178–79, 207;
expressive intentionality of, 135;
forms of, 135 (see also *kata*); hard
and soft, 31, 35–40; health benefits
of, 55, 198, 199; internal and external, 36–40, 54–56, 57; mixed, 134;
movements of, 135–36, 137; skill
in, 157; somaesthetic qualities of,
147–48; and sport, 134, 137, 138–39,
140; styles and systems of, 19, 42;
techniques of, 134, 137, 141, 142–43,
158, 178; training in, 133, 142, 158
masochism, 102, 103
materialism, 78, 83–90, 98–99, 103–4.
See also idealism
Mauss, Marcel, 109
medicine: Asian, 178; Greek, 69, 78–79,
210
meditation: Daoist, 14, 28–30; and
martial arts, 140, 203–4
Mencius, 45, 48, 49, 54, 56, 57
Merleau-Ponty, Maurice, 89
military, Chinese, 41–43, 44; and civilian, 48–51, 56, 179; and Confucianism, 45–46, 48–49

Miller, Rory, 9, 169, 200, 201
mind, 105; and body, 71, 98, 209, 210
mirror neurons, 95–96, 130
Miyamoto Musashi, 10, 100
monks, military, 4, 150
morality, 164, 181, 192–93
movement, 92–93, 94–96, 97, 104, 106,
107; aesthetic, 117, 119–24, 158;
athletic, 112–14; circular, 156–57;
efficient, 121, 122–23; eloquence of,
146, 155, 157; endotelic, 128; graceful, 114, 122–24; intentionality of,
123; rhythmic, 121
multiplicity, 84, 86
music, 45, 65, 67, 145

Neo-Confucianism, 48, 55
neurology, 96, 121, 155, 167, 208. *See
also* mirror neurons
Nietzsche, Friedrich W., 73, 98, 167,
184; on body and soul, 90; and
Darwin, 89; and Spinoza, 88, 90, 99,
195, 210
no mind, 155, 198, 204
nomad, 101–2, 103, 183
non-action, 31–32, 36, 38. *See also* effortless efficacy; *wuwei*
non-contention, 34, 203
nonviolence, 133, 184, 193

pain, 80, 103, 104, 142, 194, 199
pankration, 63–64, 162
Parmenides, 61, 77–78, 96, 97, 152
peace, 29, 46, 175, 180, 185, 198
perception, sensory, 78, 80, 94, 96, 99;
and action, 106; and art, 117; and
repetition, 151–52
philosophy, 104; and ancient medicine,
210; and athletics, 68–73, 81, 104,
209; comparative, x, xii; ethical,
207; global, 209; and knowledge,
208–10; and martial arts, 208–9;
and poetry, 71; and rationalism,
208; Western, 74